THE PRIN

AND OTHER S

ANTON CHEKHOV was born in 1860 in south Russia, the son of a poor grocer. At the age of nineteen he followed his family to Moscow, where he studied medicine and helped to support the household by writing comic sketches for popular magazines. By 1888 he was publishing in the prestigious literary monthlies of Moscow and St Petersburg: a sign that he had already attained maturity as a writer of serious fiction. During the next fifteen years he wrote the short stories—fifty or more of them—which form his chief claim to world pre-eminence in the genre and are his main achievement as a writer. His plays are almost equally important, especially during his last years. He was closely associated with the Moscow Art Theatre and married its leading lady, Olga Knipper. In 1898 he was forced to move to Yalta, where he wrote his two greatest plays, *Three Sisters* and *The Cherry Orchard*. The première of the latter took place on his forty-fourth birthday. Chekhov died six months later, on 2 July 1904

RONALD HINGLEY, Emeritus Fellow of St Antony's College, Oxford, edited and translated The Oxford Chekhov (9 volumes), and is the author of *A Life of Anton Chekhov* (also published by Oxford University Press). He is the translator of four other volumes of Chekhov stories in Oxford World's Classics: *The Russian Master and Other Stories*, *Ward Number Six and Other Stories*, *A Woman's Kingdom and Other Stories*, and *The Steppe and Other Stories*. His translations of all Chekhov's drama will be found in two Oxford World's Classics volumes, *Five Plays* and *Twelve Plays*.

OXFORD WORLD'S CLASSICS

ANTON CHEKHOV

The Princess

and Other Stories

Translated with an Introduction and Notes by
RONALD HINGLEY

OXFORD
UNIVERSITY PRESS

OXFORD
UNIVERSITY PRESS

Great Clarendon Street, Oxford OX2 6DP

Oxford University Press is a department of the University of Oxford.
It furthers the University's objective of excellence in research, scholarship,
and education by publishing worldwide in

Oxford New York

Athens Auckland Bangkok Bogotá Buenos Aires Calcutta
Cape Town Chennai Dar es Salaam Delhi Florence Hong Kong Istanbul
Karachi Kuala Lumpur Madrid Melbourne Mexico City Mumbai
Nairobi Paris São Paulo Singapore Taipei Tokyo Toronto Warsaw

with associated companies in Berlin Ibadan

Oxford is a registered trade mark of Oxford University Press
in the UK and in certain other countries

Published in the United States
by Oxford University Press Inc., New York

Translations and editorial material © Ronald Hingley 1965, 1970, 1971, 1975, 1978, 1980
Introduction © Ronald Hingley 1990
Chronology © Oxford University Press 1984
Select Bibliography © Patrick Miles 1998

The moral rights of the author have been asserted

Database right Oxford University Press (maker)

This selection first issued as a World's Classics paperback 1990
Reissued as an Oxford World's Classics paperback 1999

British Library Cataloguing in Publication Data

Data available

Library of Congress Cataloging in Publication Data

Chekhov, Anton Pavlovich, 1860–1904.
[Short stories. English. Selections]
The princess and other stories / Anton Chekhov ; translated with an introduction and
notes by Ronald Hingley.
p. cm.—(Oxford world's classics)
"Text . . . taken from . . . The Oxford Chekhov, translated and edited by
Ronald Hingley"—T.p. verso.
Bibliography: p.
Contents: The party—Lights—The princess—After the theatre—Three years—
The artist's story—Home—A case history—All friends together—The bishop—
A marriageable girl.
1. Chekhov, Anton Pavlovich, 1860–1904—Translations, English.
I. Hingley, Ronald. II. Title. III. Series.
PG3456.A15H56 1990 891.73'3—dc20 89-35637

ISBN 0-19-283788-5

The text of the eleven stories in this volume is taken from volumes 4, 5, 6, 7, 8, 9
of The Oxford Chekhov, translated and edited by Ronald Hingley

3 5 7 9 10 8 6 4 2

Printed in Great Britain by
Cox & Wyman Ltd.
Reading, Berkshire

CONTENTS

INTRODUCTION

A romantically run-down estate and feckless owners facing the auctioneer's hammer; a potential rescuer who fails to come to their aid by marrying one of the doomed family—these features of the story *All Friends Together* (1898) are shared by a later and better-known work of Chekhov's, his play *The Cherry Orchard* (1903–4). To some extent, then, the story may be considered a preliminary study for the play, with the four characters Podgorin, Nadya, Tatyana, and Sergey respectively figuring as distant prototypes of *The Cherry Orchard*'s Lopakhin, Varya, Lyuba, and Gayev. But there is more than this to *All Friends Together*. It does not deserve the critical neglect which has befallen it, besides which it was also slighted by its author when he failed to include it (perhaps inadvertently) in his *Collected Works* of 1899–1902.[1]

Here is a brilliant example of Chekhov's art, and one of his many studies of love unfulfilled. As such it is also one among several items in the present volume which reflect aspects of his life.

Why, one finds oneself asking again and again, was Chekhov so dedicated to demonstrating in his fiction that the love of man and woman is inevitably frustrating, low-key, traumatic, and desultory? Can he have been using his own stories and plays to reply to the many unsuccessful attempts to propel him into wedlock made by members of his family, friends, well-wishers, and sundry other officious persons during his twenties and thirties?

Nadya, the heroine of *All Friends Together*, has reached the precise make-or-break age for Chekhov's spinsters, being twenty-three years old, while Podgorin (whom her family want her to marry) is a young lawyer much irked

---

[1] See further *The Oxford Chekhov* (London, 1964–1980), vol. 9, pp. ix–x.

by the role of husband-designate. Far from succumbing to Nadya's feminine charms, he finds them most embarrassing. When she appears in a white, open-necked dress the sight of her long, white, bare neck is 'not altogether nice'. Distasteful too is the spectacle of her legs in flesh-coloured stockings as revealed when her skirt billows up. The inverted Romeo is so disconcerted by these sinful glimpses that he hurriedly flees by train and resumes his bachelor life in Moscow. How lucky an escape Chekhov thought this may be inferred from the story itself, and the same point is repeated in the many recorded comments on marriage which he made in his own person.

Home is another potent variant on the anti-marriage theme. Its lively and attractive heroine is gradually demoralized by the relentless triviality of life on a provincial estate. She capitulates in the end by agreeing to wed the lugubrious Dr. Neshchapov, who lacks spiritual resonance and is one of the few unsympathetic doctors in the medically qualified Chekhov's work.

However many stories Chekhov might write in seeming disparagement of wedlock, he succumbed in the end by marrying the actress Olga Knipper when he was in his early forties. The marriage did not realize the gloomiest implications of his fiction, for all its ups and downs. But Chekhov was now a sick man, the victim of long-standing tuberculosis, and he was only to write two more stories after facing the ordeal of the altar. One of these, *The Bishop,* is the only item in the present volume in which his characteristic blend of love/non-love is not at least a minor theme. And in his last story of all, *A Marriageable Girl,* that same preoccupation surfaces yet again.

Here is another Nadya, one who lives an unfulfilled life in a dreary Russian provincial town, where she has become engaged to a worthy, lazy, complacent, dim young man. Depressed by an inspection of her future marital home, where the mere sight of the new bath-taps disconcerts her, she suddenly decides to run away from her town, from her fiancé and from her no less dreary mother and grandmother. Nadya proves more determined than any of the Three Sisters in Chekhov's play, and she actually does succeed in escaping: not to the Moscow which they dream of, but to St. Petersburg, where she pursues an unspecified course of studies. In this she is abetted by Sasha, an old friend of her family. He dispenses advice much in tune with the author's own thinking, while also dying of consumption, and he comes as near as anyone in Chekhov's work to being a fictional portrait of his ailing self.

Since *A Marriageable Girl* has an ardent young woman erupting from the stuffy provinces to pursue a course of studies in the capital, it has been interpreted by Kremlin-instructed Russian literary processors as a work of revolutionary significance. This is true to the extent that Nadya, under the censorship conditions of the time, was recognizable as an embryonic revolutionary by those who could read between the lines; as what Russian reader could not? To leave home, to reject a conventional marriage, to embark on university studies on one's own: there was, in the Russia of the early 1900s, the merest hair's breadth between these activities and conspiracy against the state. But Chekhov unfortunately tells us nothing of Nadya's new activities beyond indicating that they are vaguely exciting and satisfying, whereas the stifling atmosphere of the provinces—that vintage Chekhov theme—is skilfully evoked.

The Party provides yet another impressive variation on the theme of marital disharmony. It is a study of late pregnancy as experienced by a hostess compelled to smile hypocritically at guests whom she finds irksome. She is provoked into a pointless quarrel with her husband, himself also an exponent of social hypocrisy, after which she gives birth to a stillborn child. Here is a Tolstoyan topic: the vanity of upper-class social conventions in collision with such basic human realities as birth and death. Tolstoy's influence is also evident at the sophisticated heroine's first encounter with her maid, whom Chekhov began to portray as the embodiment of innate rustic wisdom—but only to modify this approach, perhaps to the discriminating reader's relief, in the childbirth scene at the end.

In *Lights* romance *à la* Chekhov is again a major concern, and again the context is Tolstoy's exegesis of the Christian ethic: man should love his neighbour; abstain from swearing oaths and from extra-marital (or all) sexual intercourse; repent his sins; not resist evil by force; and so on. The story's hero is a jolly but repentant engineer who ruefully recalls how he had once seduced a pathetic, waif-like young woman (hardly the sort of 'loving one's neighbour' which Tolstoy had in mind); he then callously abandoned her after a night of sin and sneaked out of town by train—only to slink back soon afterwards, much ashamed, to beg her forgiveness and turn over a new leaf.

Engineer Ananyev did well to apologize and reform, but virtuous conduct does not automatically lead to good art—rather the reverse, often enough. Chekhov himself must have thought the story weak, marred as it is by too obtrusive a moralizing urge, and he asserted as much by excluding it from his first *Collected Works*. It is an extreme example of the moral earnestness of some of his work of the late eighties, as written under Tolstoy's influence, and it is best regarded as part of an experiment which failed. Still, even the failures of genius may be instructive. It was through writing such stories, and the play *The Wood Demon,* that Chekhov learnt to abandon overt attempts to improve the human race.

Trying to teach his readers how thay should behave soon proved counter-productive. However, Chekhov did persevere successfully with fictional attempts to show, tactfully and obliquely, how they should *not* behave. By the early 1890s he was eloquently attacking the Tolstoyan do-goodery and simple-lifery which he had earlier advocated.

A foretaste of this more mature attitude may be traced as early as *The Princess* (1889), which makes a powerful onslaught on the benefactress of the title. Princess Vera is principally discredited through the mouth of the doctor with whom she converses—one of those honest, decent, hard-working physicians who often figure in Chekhov's pages as the targets for ill-usage by persons less sensitive. It is not surprising that Chekhov showed such relish in lambasting the odious Vera; as passages in his letters show, he himself was sometimes exposed to the insolence of such as she when resident and medically active in the village of Melikhovo in the mid-nineties.

Another unmasked philanthropist is the Lydia of *An Artist's Story*. She educates the local peasants and gives them medical treatment, thus mirroring the activities of her creator, whose work for the villagers of the Melikhovo area was persistently beneficial and practical, while also done with minimal fuss. It might therefore seem surprising that Lydia is so much the villainess of the story: a complacent, priggish, beautiful busybody who destroys her young sister's happiness by officiously ending the girl's romance with the visiting artist. A philanthropist *à la* Chekhov the non-approved Lydia might be, but Chekhov clearly gives his preference to her enemy the artist, a lazy, moony individual who tells Lydia that to dose and teach her villagers only means adding to their existing burdens. Nothing could illustrate more vividly how unsentimental Chekhov was towards the peasants than this fictional rejection of a woman who took them so seriously in favour of a man who would not lift a finger to help them. May Chekhov have been mocking or criticizing himself, subconsciously or consciously, in his portrait of the unsympathetic Lydia? Not only was she a teacher and healer, like her creator, but she also succeeded in preventing a sister's marriage. Now, that was the very operation which Chekhov himself was unkindly performing, at about the time when the story was written, at the expense of his devoted sister Mariya.[2]

Two stories in this volume show Chekhov studying the Russian industrial and commercial world. *A Case History* is the shorter, and here again a sympathetic doctor is the hero. Chekhov well knew that Russian workers of the intensely industrializing 1890s were often miserable and exploited. But he did not draw the too obvious conclusion that all factory owners and bosses must be deliberate and heartless oppressors. Rather does he suggest that his very capitalists may be as much victims of a hopeless situation as their employees. In *A Case History* Mrs. Lyalikov and her heiress-daughter are no happier than the thousand or so dimly-discerned workers who toil so gloomily on their behalf. It is only the family governess—the ludicrous Miss Christine, a vulgar, silly old maid in a pince-nez—who derives any benefits from the Russian industrial revolution, being one of those disapproved Chekhov characters whose lives centre on eating and drinking. 'What are those five mills working for? Just so that Miss Christine can eat her sturgeon and drink her Madeira.'

Three Years is the longer of the two stories in this volume to be set in the commercial and industrial world. It is unusual in Chekhov's work in being so circumstantially placed in a specific locality and social milieu. Here, if anywhere in his mature fiction, he emerges as a documentarist. For instance, he concentrates heavily on the topography of Moscow, his own home between 1880 and 1892, so that the Baedeker guide for that period enables the reader to trace the story's various comings and goings in great detail. He also draws on his father's experience as a clerk in a Moscow wholesale haberdashers,

---

[2] For further details see Ronald Hingley, *A New Life of Anton Chekhov* (London, 1975; reissued in paperback as *A Life of Chekhov*, Oxford, 1989), p. 164.

Gavrilov's, which was the model for the Laptev establishment in the story.

All this detail brings Chekhov closer to Balzac or Dickens than usual, but it does not stand in the way of yet another grand anticlimax in the familiar territory of unrequited love. The heroine of *Three Years* marries a man whom she does not love and who loves her, after which the story shows her coming to love him, while he is cooling off. Thus Chekhov, in effect, stands Pushkin's *Eugene Onegin* on its head. However, the frustrations of *Three Years* are muted by Chekhov's standards. By the end of the story he is suggesting that if things are not so very good, neither are they so very bad: the household will go on living or partly living for the next thirteen or thirty years. The common pattern is also varied in that neither of the partners is portrayed as the victim of the other, for Chekhov seems to sympathize with them in turn. This even balance within a single relationship by no means represents his norm. Elsewhere he has a tendency to indicate, when portraying man–woman confrontations, that one party is the predator or persecutor, whether through indifference or malice, while the other is the innocent victim, whether through feebleness or bad luck.

Alone among the stories in this volume, *The Bishop* is not about love, or lack of it. This study of a dying prelate was Chekhov's penultimate story, it was based on the conflated lives of no less than three actual clerics, and it was at least fifteen years in the gestation. The work is a tribute to his objectivity as a writer, for so gentle and respectful is his treatment of the Orthodox Church that no uninstructed reader could suspect what was in fact the case: Chekhov himself had long been a convinced (though far from militant) unbeliever. *The Bishop* is also a moving study of death by one who must have been well aware, even as he laboured on a text of which the birth-pangs were unusually painful, that his own end could not be far away.

SELECT BIBLIOGRAPHY

Biography and Autobiography

Heim, Michael Henry (trans.), and Karlinsky, Simon (ed.), *Letters of Anton Chekhov* (New York, 1973).

Hingley, Ronald, *A Life of Chekhov* (Oxford, 1989).

Rayfield, Donald, *Anton Chekhov: A Life* (London, 1997).

Bibliography

Lantz, Kenneth, *Anton Chekhov: A Reference Guide to Literature* (Boston, 1985).

Background

Bruford, W. H., *Chekhov and His Russia* (London, 1948).

Tulloch, John, *Chekhov: A Structuralist Study* (London, 1980).

Criticism

Bitsilli, Peter M., *Chekhov's Art: A Stylistic Analysis* (Ann Arbor, 1983).

Clyman, Toby W. (ed.), *A Chekhov Companion* (Westport, Conn., 1985).

Gerhardi, William, *Anton Chekhov: A Critical Study* (London, 1923).

Hahn, Beverly, *Chekhov: A Study of the Major Stories and Plays* (Cambridge, 1977).

Jackson, Robert Louis (ed.), *Reading Chekhov's Texts* (Evanston, 1993).

Kramer, Karl D., *The Chameleon and the Dream: The Image of Reality in Čexov's Stories* (The Hague, 1970).

Llewellyn Smith, Virginia, *Anton Chekhov and the Lady with the Dog* (Oxford, 1973).

Turner, C. J. G., *Time and Temporal Structure in Chekhov* (Birmingham, 1994).

Winner, Thomas, *Chekhov and His Prose* (New York, 1966).

Further Reading in Oxford World's Classics

Twelve Plays, translated and edited by Ronald Hingley (*On the High Road; Swan Song; The Bear; The Proposal; Tatyana Repin; A Tragic Role; The Wedding; The Anniversary; Smoking is Bad for You; The Night Before the Trial; The Wood-Demon; Platonov*).

Early Stories, translated and edited by Patrick Miles and Harvey Pitcher.

The Steppe and Other Stories, translated and edited by Ronald Hingley.

Ward Number Six and Other Stories, translated and edited by Ronald Hingley.

The Russian Master and Other Stories, translated and edited by Ronald Hingley.

A CHRONOLOGY OF ANTON CHEKHOV

All dates are given old style.

1860   16 or 17 January. Born in Taganrog, a port in the Sea of Azov in south Russia.

1876   His father goes bankrupt. The family moves to Moscow, leaving Anton to finish his schooling.

1879   Joins family and enrols in the Medical Faculty of Moscow University.

1880   Begins to contribute to *Strekoza* ('Dragonfly'), a St. Petersburg comic weekly.

1882   Starts to write short stories and a gossip column for *Oskolki* ('Splinters') and to depend on writing for an income.

1884   Graduates in medicine. Shows early symptoms of tuberculosis.

1885–6   Contributes to *Peterburgskaya gazeta* ('St. Petersburg Gazette') and *Novoye vremya* ('New Time').

1886   March. Letter from D. V. Grigorovich encourages him to take writing seriously.
       First collection of stories: *Motley Stories*.

1887   Literary reputation grows fast. Second collection of stories: *In the Twilight*.
       19 November. First Moscow performance of *Ivanov*: mixed reception.

1888   First publication (*The Steppe*) in a serious literary journal, *Severny vestnik* ('The Northern Herald').

1889   31 January. First St. Petersburg performance of *Ivanov*: widely and favourably reviewed.

June. Death of brother Nicholas from tuberculosis.

1890   April–December. Crosses Siberia to visit the penal settlement on Sakhalin Island. Returns via Hong Kong, Singapore and Ceylon.

1891   First trip to western Europe: Italy and France.

1892   March. Moves with family to small country estate at Melikhovo, fifty miles south of Moscow.

1895   First meeting with Tolstoy.

1896   17 October. First—disastrous—performance of *The Seagull* in St. Petersburg.

1897   Suffers severe haemorrhage.

1897–8   Winters in France. Champions Zola's defence of Dreyfus.

1898   Beginning of collaboration with the newly founded Moscow Art Theatre. Meets Olga Knipper. Spends the winter in Yalta, where he meets Gorky.
    17 December. First Moscow Art Theatre performance of *The Seagull*: successful.

1899   Completes the building of a house in Yalta, where he settles with mother and sister.
    26 October. First performance of *Uncle Vanya* (written ?1896).

1899–1901   First complete edition of his works (10 volumes).

1901   31 January. *Three Sisters* first performed.
    25 May. Marries Olga Knipper.

1904   17 January. First performance of *The Cherry Orchard*.
    2 July. Dies in Badenweiler, Germany.

THE PRINCESS
AND OTHER STORIES

THE PARTY

AFTER the eight-course banquet and the interminable conversation Olga Mikhaylovna went out into the garden. It was her husband's name-day party, and she was utterly exhausted by the obligation to smile and talk incessantly, by the clatter of dishes, by the servants' stupidity, by the long intervals between courses, and by the corset that she had put on to hide her pregnancy from the guests. She wanted to get away from the house, sit in the shade, and relax by thinking of the child that she was to bear in about two months' time. Such thoughts habitually occurred to her whenever she turned left from the main avenue into a narrow path. Here, in the dense shade of plum and cherry trees, dry branches caught her neck and shoulders, and cobwebs brushed her face, while she would find herself imagining a small, vague-featured person of indefinite sex, and feeling as if it was not the cobwebs but this small person that was affectionately tickling her face and neck. When, at the path's end, a flimsy wattle fence appeared, and beyond it the pot-bellied hives with their earthenware roofs, and when the scent of hay and honey, accompanied by the brief buzz of bees, infused the still and stagnant air, this small person would take complete control of her. She would sit brooding on the bench near the hut of plaited osiers.

This time too she went as far as the bench, sat down, and began thinking. But instead of the small person it was the big persons she had just left that came to mind. She was greatly distressed that she, the hostess, had abandoned her guests, and she remembered her husband Peter and her Uncle Nicholas arguing about trial by jury, the press and women's education at luncheon. As usual her husband had argued to parade his conservative views to his guests, and above all so that he could disagree with her uncle, whom he disliked. But her uncle contradicted him and quibbled over every word to show the company that he, the uncle, still retained a young man's alertness and mental flexibility despite his fifty-nine years. By the end of the meal Olga herself could not resist embarking on a clumsy defence of higher education for women. It was not that it needed defending—simply that she wanted to annoy her husband, whom she believed to have been unfair. The guests were bored by the argument, but they all thought fit to make verbose interventions, though none of them cared a fig for trial by jury or women's education.

Olga was sitting on the near side of the fence by the hut. The sun was hidden behind clouds, the trees and the air were sombre, rain seemed likely—and yet it was hot and sultry. Hay had been cut under the trees on St. Peter's Eve, and still lay ungathered. Sad, with its wilting flowers in a variety of hues, it gave off an irksome, cloying smell. All was quiet, and bees buzzed monotonously beyond the fence.

Then footsteps and voices were unexpectedly heard—someone was coming down the path towards the hives.

'How stuffy it is!' It was a woman's voice. 'Will it rain or won't it, what do you think?'

'It will, my precious, but not before dark—there will be a shower.' The voice was male, languid and only too familiar.

If she quickly hid in the hut they would pass on without noticing her, Olga calculated. Then she would not be compelled to talk and force herself to smile. She picked her skirts up, bent down and went inside, whereupon her face, neck and arms were plunged into an atmosphere as stifling as steam. Had it not been for the stuffiness and a choking smell, of rye bread, of dill and osiers, that took away her breath, this would have been the perfect place, with its thatched roof and dim light, to hide from her guests and think about the small person. It was snug and quiet.

'What a lovely spot! Let's sit down, Peter.' It was the woman's voice again.

Peeping through a crack between the reeds, Olga saw her husband Peter and a guest, Lyubochka Sheller, a girl of seventeen who had just left boarding-school. Peter—hat pushed to the back of his head, relaxed and slothful from drinking too much at dinner—was strolling near the fence and kicking the hay into a pile. Pink from the heat and pretty as always, Lyubochka stood with her hands behind her back watching the indolent motions of his big, handsome frame.

Knowing how attractive her husband was to women, Olga disliked seeing him with them. There was nothing remarkable in his idly kicking some hay into a pile so as to sit on it with Lyubochka and gossip. Nor was there anything remarkable in pretty Lyubochka gazing at him so tenderly. Yet Olga felt annoyed with her husband, and both frightened and pleased at the prospect of eavesdropping.

'Sit down, enchantress.' Peter sank on to the hay and stretched. 'That's right. Now, talk to me.'

'Oh yes! And as soon as I start talking you'll fall asleep.'

'Fall asleep? Allah forbid! Can one sleep with those pretty little eyes gazing at one?'

Her husband's words, his lolling about in a lady's presence with his hat on the back of his head—these things too were wholly unremarkable. He had been spoilt by women. Knowing that he attracted them, he would address them in the special tone generally thought to become him. He was treating Lyubochka just like any other woman, but that did not stop Olga feeling jealous.

'Tell me something,' said Lyubochka after a short pause. 'Do you really face prosecution?'

'Me? Yes, indeed. I've joined the criminal classes, my precious.'

'But what for?'

'No reason at all. It just happened—largely a matter of politics.' Peter yawned. 'It's Left versus Right. I'm a reactionary fuddy-duddy who dared to employ, in an official document, expressions derogatory to such Gladstonian paragons as our local Justice of the Peace Mr. Kuzma Vostryakov, not to mention Vladimir Vladimirov Esquire.

'In our society,' he continued with another yawn, 'you may disparage the sun, the moon and anything you please, but God help you and heaven preserve you if you lay a hand on a liberal! Your liberal's just like that foul puff-ball toadstool which covers you with clouds of dust if you accidentally touch it.'

'But what happened to you?'

'Nothing really—just a case of much ado about nothing. Some miserable little schoolmaster of clerical origin brought suit in Vostryakov's court against an innkeeper for slander and assault in a public place. Both teacher and innkeeper were drunk as lords by all accounts, and both behaved equally badly. Even if an offence was committed there were certainly faults on both sides. Vostryakov should have fined both for disturbing the peace and thrown the case out of court—and that would have been that. But such is not our way, oh dear me no! What counts with us is never the individual, never the facts, but the pigeonhole they go into. However scoundrelly a schoolmaster may be, he's automatically right just because he's a schoolmaster. And a publican is always wrong just because he's a money-grubbing publican. Vostryakov gave the publican a gaol sentence, and the man appealed to Sessions, which solemnly confirmed Vostryakov's findings.

Well, I expressed a dissenting judgement—got a bit heated, that's all.'

Peter spoke calmly, with casual irony, though he was in fact seriously worried about his impending trial. Olga remembered him returning from that ill-fated hearing and doing his utmost to hide his dejection and feeling of inadequacy from the household. As an intelligent man he could not help feeling that he had overstepped the mark in expressing dissent, and what a lot of dissemblance had been necessary to hide this feeling from himself and others! How many unnecessary discussions there had been, how much muttering and false laughter at things that were not funny at all! On learning that he was to stand trial he had suddenly felt fatigued and depressed, had begun sleeping badly, and had taken to standing by a window and drumming his fingers on the panes more often than was his wont. He was ashamed to confess his distress to his wife, and that riled her.

'I'm told you've been down Poltava way,' said Lyubochka.

'Yes, I got back the day before yesterday,' Peter answered.

'It must be awfully nice there.'

'Very nice indeed. I happened to arrive just in time for haymaking, and that's the most romantic season in the South, I can tell you. Now, this house and garden here are large, with no end of servants and commotion, and so you never see the mowing, it all goes unnoticed. But my place down south has forty acres of meadowland, all open to the view, and you can see the mowers from any window. They mow the meadows, they mow the garden. There are no visitors or ructions, so you can't help seeing, hearing and feeling haymaking. There's the scent of hay outdoors and indoors, and the clang of scythes from dawn to dusk. It's charming country, is the good old South. Drinking the water at the wells with their sweeps, and the ghastly vodka in those Jewish taverns, with the sound of the local fiddles and tambourines wafted on the calm evening air—do you know, I was taken by the enchanting thought of settling down on my southern farm and living out my life far from these appeal sessions, intellectual conversations, philosophizing women and interminable dinners.'

Peter was not lying. He had been dispirited and longed for a holiday, and had only gone to Poltava to escape his study, his servants, his friends and all reminders of his wounded vanity and blundering.

Lyubochka suddenly jumped up with a horrified gesture. 'Oo, a bee, a bee—it'll sting me!' she shrieked.

'Nonsense, it won't. What a little coward you are!'

'No, no, I can't bear it!' cried Lyubochka, looking back at the bee as she beat a hasty retreat.

Peter followed her, gazing at her with melancholy appreciation. As he looked he must have been thinking of his southern farm, of solitude, and—who knows—he may even have thought how warm and snug life on his farm would be if this child—young, pure, fresh, unspoilt by higher education, not pregnant—had been his wife.

When their voices and footsteps had died away Olga emerged from the hut and set off for the house. She was on the verge of tears, and by now she was terribly jealous. She understood Peter's fatigue, his sense of inadequacy, his embarrassment. And embarrassed people always do shun their intimates above all, unburdening themselves only to strangers. She also realized that Lyubochka was no danger to her—nor were any of the other women now having coffee in the house. But it was all so puzzling and frightening, and Olga felt that Peter only half belonged to her.

'He has no right, none whatever,' she muttered, trying to analyse her jealousy and her annoyance with her husband. 'I'm going to give him a piece of my mind this instant.'

She decided to find her husband at once and have it out with him. It was downright disgusting, the way he attracted strange women, seeking their admiration as if it were the elixir of life. It was unfair and dishonourable of him to bestow on others what rightly belonged to her, his wife, and to hide his heart and conscience from her only to reveal them to the first pretty face. What harm had she done him? What had she done wrong? And, finally, she was sick and tired of his subterfuges. He was always posturing, flirting, saying things he didn't mean, trying to seem other than what he was and should be. Why all the dissimulation? How ill it became any decent man! His affectations insulted both herself and those at whom they were directed, also showing disrespect for the material of his prevarications. Posing and giving himself airs on the bench, holding forth on the prerogatives of power at mealtimes just to annoy her uncle—well, really! Couldn't he see that it all showed he didn't give a rap for the court, for himself, or for anyone listening to him and watching him?

Emerging into the avenue, Olga tried to look as if she had been engaged on some domestic errand. There were gentlemen drinking liqueurs and eating soft fruit on the veranda. One of them, the examining magistrate—a stout, elderly man, a great clown and wit—must have been telling a *risqué* story because he suddenly clapped his hand over his fat lips when he saw his hostess and sat down goggle-eyed.

Olga did not care for the local officials. She disliked their clumsy, self-important wives, their tittle-tattle, their constant visiting and their flattery of her husband, whom they all hated. But now, as they sat drinking—having had plenty to eat and making no move to leave—she found their presence excruciatingly irksome, yet greeted the examining magistrate with a smile, wagging a threatening finger at him to avoid any suggestion of ungraciousness. She crossed the ballroom and drawing-room, smiling and looking as if she was off to issue some order and make some arrangements.

'I hope to God no one stops me,' she thought, but forced herself to pause in the drawing-room and listen for appearance' sake to a young man playing the piano. She stood for a minute, shouted 'Bravo, bravo, Monsieur Georges!', clapped her hands twice and went on.

She found her husband sitting at the desk in his study deep in thought and looking stern, preoccupied and guilty. This was not the Peter who had argued at dinner, and whom his guests knew, but a different man —exhausted, guilty, inadequate-feeling—whom only his wife knew. He must have come to the study for some cigarettes. Before him lay a full case, open, and one hand was still in the desk drawer—he had suddenly become immobile in the act of taking out the cigarettes.

Olga felt sorry for him. He was tired, out of sorts, and probably at odds with himself—that was as clear as daylight. She approached the desk without a word, shut the cigarette case and put it in his side pocket, trying to pretend that she had forgotten the argument at dinner and was not angry with him any more.

'What can I tell him?' she wondered. 'I'll say that dissimulation is a morass—the farther you get in the harder it is to get out. I'll tell him he's been carried away by the false role he's been playing and has gone too far. "You've insulted people who were devoted to you and never did you any harm. So go and tell them you're sorry, laugh at yourself, and you'll feel better. And if you want quiet and solitude let's go away together." '

Meeting his wife's eyes, Peter suddenly adopted the indifferent and mildly ironical expression that he had worn at dinner and in the garden. He yawned, stood up and looked at his watch.

'It's after five. Even if our guests take pity on us and leave at eleven we still have to get through another six hours. A cheerful prospect, I must say!'

Whistling some tune, he slowly left the room, his gait as magisterial as ever. His sedate tread was heard as he traversed the hall and drawing-room, uttered his proconsular laugh, and called a casual 'Bravo!' to the young pianist. His footsteps soon died away—he must have gone into the garden. It was no longer jealousy and annoyance, now, that obsessed Olga, but downright hatred of his walk, his hypocritical laugh, his voice. When she went to the window and looked into the garden Peter was strolling down the avenue. He had one hand in his pocket and was snapping the fingers of the other. With his head thrown slightly backwards he rolled portentously along, looking exceedingly satisfied with himself, his dinner, his digestion and his scenery.

Two little schoolboys appeared on the path—sons of a Mrs. Chizhev-sky, an estate owner. They had just arrived with their tutor, a student in a white tunic and very narrow trousers. Coming up to Peter, they stopped, probably to wish him a happy name-day. He patted the children's cheeks, twisted his shoulders elegantly, and casually pre-sented his hand to the student without looking at him. The student must have praised the weather, comparing it to St. Petersburg's, because Peter answered in a loud voice in the tone of one addressing a court bailiff or a witness rather than a guest.

'Eh? Cold in St. Petersburg, is it? Now, here, my dear fellow, we have a salubrious atmospheric mix, what? And fruits of the earth in abundance, eh?'

Placing one hand in his pocket and clicking the fingers of the other, he strode off. Olga continued to stare at the back of his neck in be-wilderment until he vanished behind the hazel bushes. Where did this man of thirty-four acquire his pompous, person of consequence's walk? Whence the ponderously elegant tread? And whence the authoritative resonance in his voice, and all this 'eh?', 'what!', 'my dear fellow!' stuff?

To escape being bored and lonely at home in the first months of her marriage, Olga had (she recalled) attended court hearings in town—at which her husband sometimes presided in place of her godfather Count Alexis. In his judge's seat, in his uniform, wearing the chain on his chest, Peter was a different man, what with all the majestic gestures, the thunderous voice, the 'What, sirs?' the 'H'm, very wells', the off-hand tone. Ordinary human qualities, everything individual that Olga was used to seeing in him at home—it was all swamped in grandeur, and the man in the judge's seat was not her Peter but someone else: a Your Honour, as everyone called him. Conscious of being a power in

the land, he found it impossible to sit still, but seized every opportunity
to ring his bell, glare at the public and shout. And what of his short-
sightedness and deafness? Suddenly myopic and hard of hearing,
frowning his proconsular frown, he would require people to speak
louder and approach the bench. Such difficulty did he have in dis-
tinguishing faces and sounds from so sublime an eminence that, if
Olga herself had come near him at such times, he would probably have
shouted: 'Your name, madam?' He condescended to peasant witnesses, and he bellowed at the public in a voice that could be heard out
in the street. As for his treatment of counsel, that was impossible. When
a barrister came to speak Peter would sit half turned away, squinting at
the ceiling and thereby indicating that the man was utterly superfluous
here, and that he would neither acknowledge him nor listen to him.
But if some poorly dressed local solicitor spoke, then Peter was all
ears, surveying him with a look of withering scorn that said: 'Is this
what the legal profession has come to?'

'Just what are you trying to say?' he would interpose.

If some rhetorically-minded barrister employed a word of foreign
origin—'factitious' instead of 'fictitious', say—Peter would suddenly
become agitated.

'Eh? What was that, sir? Factitious, eh? And just what is that
supposed to mean?'

Then he would tell the man sententiously not to 'use words you
don't understand'. His speech finished, the lawyer would retreat
from the bench red-faced and bathed in sweat, while Peter lolled back
in his seat, celebrating his triumph with a complacent grin. In his
handling of lawyers he tended to ape Count Alexis. But when, for
instance, the Count said, 'Will defence counsel kindly be silent?' the
effect was paternally good-humoured and natural, whereas Peter made
it sound forced and rather uncouth.

II

Applause broke out as the young pianist finished playing. Remembering her guests, Olga hurried to the drawing-room and
approached the piano.

'I did so much enjoy your playing. You do have a remarkable gift,
but don't you think our piano needs tuning?'

At that moment the two schoolboys and the student entered the
room.

'Heavens! Why, it's Mitya and Kolya!' Olga joyously drawled, going to meet them. 'How you *have* grown! I hardly recognized you! But where's your mother?'

'Many happy returns and all best wishes to our host,' said the student rather offhandedly. 'And Mrs. Chizhevsky also sends her best wishes, coupled with her apologies—she's not feeling very well.'

'Oh, how unkind of her! And I've been looking forward to seeing her all day! Now, when did you leave St. Petersburg? And how is the weather there?'

Not waiting for a reply, she looked fondly at the little boys. 'And aren't they big boys now! It's not so long since they used to visit us with their nanny, and now they're at high school! Old folk grow old and young folk grow up! Have you had dinner?'

'Oh, please don't trouble,' said the student.

'But you haven't, have you?'

'Please don't go to any trouble.'

'Well, you are hungry, aren't you?' Olga asked in a rude, harsh, impatient, irritated voice. The effect was unintended and immediately set her coughing, smiling and blushing. 'How they have grown!' she said softly.

'Please don't bother,' the student repeated.

He begged her not to bother, and the boys did not speak—obviously all three were hungry. Olga led them to the dining-room and told Vasily to set the table.

'How unkind of your mother!' She sat them down. 'She has quite forgotten me! It's downright cruel of her, and you must tell her so from me. And what are you studying?' she asked the student.

'Medicine.'

'Ah, I'm very partial to doctors, you know. I'm sorry my husband isn't one. What courage it must take to operate, say, or dissect corpses. Simply dreadful! Aren't you scared? I think I'd die of fright. You will take vodka of course?'

'Please don't bother.'

'But you must, must, must have a drink after your journey. I myself sometimes drink, even though I am a woman. And Mitya and Kolya can have some Malaga—it's not a strong wine, don't worry. What fine young men they are, honestly—it's high time they were married, ha, ha, ha.'

Olga spoke without pausing, knowing from experience how much easier it is to talk than to listen when entertaining. So long as you talk there is no need to tax your brain, think of answers to questions and vary your facial expression. But she inadvertently raised some serious question, and the student began to hold forth, so that she had no choice but to listen. Knowing that she had been to university, the student adopted an air of earnestness when addressing her.

'And what is your subject?' she asked, forgetting that she had already put the question.

'Medicine.'

She remembered that she had neglected the ladies for some time.

'Really? You're to be a doctor then?' She stood up. 'How nice—I wish I'd studied medicine myself. Now, you have your meal, gentlemen, and then come out into the garden and I'll introduce you to the young ladies.'

She looked at her watch as she went out—it was five minutes to six. She was amazed that time should pass so slowly, and horrified that there were still six hours till midnight, when her guests would leave. How could she get through those six hours? What words was she to utter? How should she treat her husband?

There was not a soul in the drawing-room or on the veranda, all the guests having wandered off into the garden.

'I'll have to suggest a walk to the birch wood before tea, or else boating,' thought Olga as she hurried to the croquet lawn, whence talking and laughter proceeded. 'And we must get the old people playing bridge.'

The footman Gregory came towards her from the croquet lawn carrying some empty bottles, and she asked him where the ladies were.

'In the raspberry patch. The master's there too.'

An exasperated shout came from the croquet lawn. 'Oh, for heaven's sake! If I've told you once I've told you a thousand times—to know your Bulgarians you have to visit them, you can't go by the newspapers!'

Either because of this outburst, or for some other reason, Olga suddenly felt utterly weak all over, especially in the legs and shoulders. She had a sudden urge to stop speaking, listening and moving.

'When you serve tea or anything, Gregory, please don't come to me,' she said languidly and with some effort. 'Don't ask me anything, don't bother me with anything. You do it all yourself. And don't, please don't, make all that noise with your feet. This is all beyond me, because——'

She continued towards the croquet lawn without finishing what she was saying, but remembered the ladies on the way and turned to the raspberry patch. The sky, air and trees were still sombre, still threatening rain. It was hot and stuffy. Huge flocks of crows sailed, cawing, over the garden in anticipation of bad weather. The closer the paths were to the kitchen garden the more neglected, dark and narrow they became. On one of them—hidden in a thicket of wild pears, wood-sorrel, young oaks and hops—clouds of tiny black midges enveloped her. She covered her face with her hands, making an effort to imagine the small person, but through her mind flitted Gregory, Mitya, Kolya and the faces of the peasants who had come to offer their best wishes that morning.

Hearing footsteps, she opened her eyes to find her Uncle Nicholas approaching at speed.

He was out of breath. 'That you, my dear? I'm so glad, I want a word with you.'

He mopped his red, clean-shaven chin with a handkerchief, took an abrupt backward step, threw up his arms and opened his eyes wide. 'My dear, how long will this go on?' he spluttered. 'Are there no limits, that's what I'd like to know? I ignore the demoralizing effect of his die-hard views on our set, and the fact that he is a living insult to me and to all that is best and most sublime in every honest, thinking man. These things I pass over, but let him at least observe the proprieties! Well, really! He shouts, he snarls, he gives himself airs, he struts about as if he was Lord God Almighty, he won't let anyone else get a word in edgeways, dash it! And what of his lordly gestures, his peremptory laugh, his patronizing tone? And just who does he think he is, may I ask? You tell me that! He's his wife's shadow, a nobody, a petty land-owner turned jack-in-office who had the luck to marry money. He's just one more bounder and popinjay! He's a sort of stage fuddy-duddy! I swear to God that he's either suffering from megalomania or else that demented old fogey Count Alexis is right in saying that children and young people mature very late nowadays, and go on playing cab-drivers and generals till they're forty.'

Olga agreed. 'All very true. And now do you mind if I go?'

'And where's it all going to end, eh?' he continued, blocking her path. 'Where will this hidebound, dyed-in-the-wool act lead? He's already being prosecuted, oh yes he is. And I'm delighted! That's where all the tumult and shouting have got him, into the dock! And not just locally either—in the High Court! Could anything be worse?

And then again, he has quarrelled with everyone. Today's his name-day, but just look who's missing! Neither Vostryakov, nor Yakhontov, nor Vladimirov, nor Shevud, nor the Count has come. Who could be more conservative than Count Alexis—but even he hasn't shown up. And he'll never come here again, you mark my words.'

'Oh dear, what has all this to do with me?' Olga asked.

'What has it to do with you? You're his wife, aren't you? You're intelligent, you've been to college, and it's in your power to make an honest citizen of him.'

'They don't teach you how to influence difficult people at college. I suppose I shall have to apologize to all of you for going to the university.' She spoke sharply. 'Look here, Uncle, if someone kept practising scales right in your ear over and over again all day, you wouldn't stay put, but run off. Well, I've been hearing the same thing day in day out all year long, and it really is time you all took pity on me.'

Her uncle looked very grave, glanced at her quizzically and curled his lip in an ironical smile. 'So that's how it is,' he crooned like an old crone. 'My apologies, madam.' He gave a ceremonious bow. 'If you have fallen under his influence yourself and changed your convictions, then you should have told me so before. I'm very sorry, madam!'

'Yes, I have changed my convictions,' she shouted. 'And you can put that in your pipe and smoke it!'

'I beg your pardon, madam.' Her uncle made a last formal bow from a rather sideways-on position, cringed low, clicked his heels and went his way.

'Imbecile,' thought Olga. 'I hope he's going home.'

She found the ladies and the young people among the raspberries in the kitchen garden. Some were eating the fruit, while others had had enough of it and were strolling through the strawberry beds or ferreting in the sugar peas. A little to one side of the raspberries, near a spreading apple tree comprehensively propped up with poles pulled out of an old fence, Peter was scything grass. His hair hung over his forehead, his tie had untied itself, his watch chain dangled from his fob. Each step that he took, each sweep of his scythe, showed skill and great resources of strength. Near him stood Lyubochka and the daughters of a neighbour, Colonel Bukreyev—Natalya and Valentina, or 'Nata and Vata', as everyone called them. These were anaemic, unhealthy, plump, fair-haired girls of sixteen or seventeen, wearing white dresses and strikingly similar in looks. Peter was teaching them to mow.

'It's all very simple,' said he. 'You only need to know how to hold the scythe. And you mustn't get excited and use too much force. This is the way. Now, how about having a go?'

He offered Lyubochka the scythe. 'Come on.'

Lyubochka clumsily picked up the scythe, suddenly blushed and burst out laughing.

'Don't be afraid, Lyubochka, don't be afraid,' Olga shouted loudly enough for all the ladies to hear her and know that she was among them. 'You must learn. If you marry a Tolstoyan he'll make you mow.'

Lyubochka picked up the scythe but burst out laughing again, which so enfeebled her that she dropped it. She felt embarrassed, but pleased to be treated as a grown-up. Then Nata—unsmiling, with no sign of nervousness, looking cool and solemn—picked the scythe up, swung it and got it tangled in the grass. Vata, also unsmiling, also cool and solemn like her sister, silently took the scythe and got it stuck in the ground. After this exploit the two sisters linked arms and went off to the raspberry patch without a word.

Playful as a schoolboy, Peter laughed at them, and this childlike, frolicsome, exceedingly good-natured mood suited him far better than any other. Olga loved him like that. But his boyishness did not usually last, and so it proved on this occasion. After fooling with the scythe he thought fit to introduce a serious note.

'You know, I feel healthier and more normal when I'm mowing,' said he. 'I think I'd go out of my mind if I was limited to a purely intellectual life. I don't think I was born for the cultivated life—I need to mow, plough, sow, break in horses.'

Peter and the ladies discussed the advantages of physical labour, culture, and the evils of money and property. Listening to her husband, Olga remembered her dowry for some reason, and thought that a time would surely come when he would blame her for being richer than he was. 'He's proud and conceited, and perhaps he'll hate me because I've done so much for him.'

She stopped by Colonel Bukreyev, who was eating raspberries while also taking part in the conversation.

'Do join us.' He made room for Olga and Peter. 'The ripest ones are here. And so, in Proudhon's view,' he went on, raising his voice, 'property is theft. But, frankly, I don't recognize Proudhon or consider him a philosopher. For me the French are no authority, confound them.'

'Now, I'm a bit weak on the Proudhons and the Buckles,' said Peter.

'For philosophy you must apply to my lady wife here. She has been to college, and Schopenhauer, Proudhon and Company she has thoroughly——'

Olga again felt dispirited. Again she set off through the garden, down the narrow path by the apple and pear trees, and again she had the air of one engaged on some vital errand. She came to the gardener's cottage. In the doorway sat his wife Barbara and her four small children, all with big, close-cropped heads. Barbara was pregnant too, and reckoned that her baby was due by Elijah's Day. After greeting her, Olga silently examined her and the children.

'Well, how do you feel?' she asked.

'Oh, all right.'

Silence followed, both women seeming to understand each other without words.

Olga thought for a moment. 'It's frightening, having a first baby. I keep thinking I won't get through it, that I'll die.'

'That's how I felt. But I'm alive, ain't I? There's worse worries.'

Pregnant for the fifth time and a woman of experience, Barbara treated her mistress somewhat condescendingly, addressing her in a lecturing tone, and Olga could not but recognize her authority. She would have liked to speak of the child, and of her fears and sensations, but was afraid to seem trivial and naïve. And so she said nothing, waiting for Barbara to speak.

'We're going indoors, dear,' called Peter from the raspberry patch.

Olga liked silently waiting and watching Barbara. She would have been willing to stand there without speaking till nightfall, pointless though it would be. But she had to go. Just as she left the cottage Lyubochka, Vata and Nata ran to meet her. The two sisters stopped a couple of yards short, as if rooted to the spot, but Lyubochka ran and flung herself on Olga's neck.

'Darling! Dearest! Treasure!' She kissed Olga's face and neck. 'Do let's have tea on the island.'

'Yes, yes, yes, the island!' chorused the unsmiling doubles Vata and Nata.

'But it's going to rain, dears.'

'It isn't, it isn't,' shouted Lyubochka with a tearful pout. 'Everyone wants to go, my dearest darling.'

Peter joined them. 'They've all decided to have tea on the island,' he said. 'You arrange it. We'll all go in the boats, and the samovars and other stuff can go by carriage with the servants.'

He fell in beside his wife and took her arm. Olga wanted to say something unpleasant and wounding, and even to mention her dowry perhaps—the more brusquely the better, she felt. But she thought for a moment and said:

'Why hasn't Count Alexis come? What a pity!'

'I'm only too glad he hasn't,' Peter lied. 'I'm sick of that pious freak. He gets on my nerves.'

'And yet before lunch you were dying to see him!'

III

Half an hour later the guests were all thronging on the bank near the stakes to which the boats were moored. There was a lot of talk and laughing, and so much unnecessary commotion that the seating arrangements went sadly awry, three boats being jam-packed while two stood empty. The keys for these boats were nowhere to be found, and there was a lot of rushing to and fro between river and house by people sent to look for them. Some said that Gregory had them, others that the steward had them, while a third faction was for fetching the blacksmith to break the padlocks. All spoke at once, interrupting and shouting each other down.

'In hell's name!' yelled Peter, impatiently pacing the bank. 'Those keys are supposed to be left on the window-sill in the hall. Who dared take them? The steward can get himself a boat of his own if he wants.'

In the end the keys were found. Then two oars turned out to be missing and chaos broke loose again. Bored with striding up and down, Peter jumped into a long, narrow skiff hollowed out of a poplar trunk, and pushed off with a lurch that nearly tumbled him into the water, whereupon the other boats followed one after the other amid loud laughter and shrieks from the young ladies.

The white, cloudy sky, the trees on the banks, the reeds and the boats with their passengers and oars—all were mirrored in the water. Under the boats, in that bottomless abyss far down below, was another sky with birds flying about. The bank belonging to the estate was high, steep and wooded, while the other sloped gently, with broad green water-meadows and gleaming inlets. When the boats had gone a hundred yards some cottages and a herd of cows came into sight from behind the melancholy weeping willows on the low bank. Songs, drunken cries and the strains of a concertina were heard.

Here and there on the river scurried the craft of fishermen who had come to place their nets for the night. In one boat tipsy amateur musicians played on home-made fiddles and a cello.

Olga sat at the tiller, smiling affably and chattering away to entertain her guests, while shooting sideways glances at her husband. He was standing up and sculling away in his skiff ahead of everyone else. The light, sharp-prowed vessel moved swiftly. To all the guests it was 'the old crock', but Peter for some reason called it *Penderakliya*. It had an air of lively cunning, seeming to resent the heavy Peter while awaiting a convenient moment to slip from under him. Looking at her husband, Olga was repelled by his good looks and attractiveness, by the back of his neck, by his posturing, by his familiar manner with the women. She hated all the women in the boat, feeling jealous of them, while constantly trembling with fear of Peter's wobbly craft capsizing and causing further disasters.

'Not so fast, Peter,' she shouted, her heart sinking with fear. 'Sit down, can't you? There's no need to prove how brave you are.'

She was also disconcerted by those in the boat with her. They were all ordinary folk—not bad sorts, fairly average—but now each seemed abnormal and evil. She saw nothing but falseness in any of them.

'Take that young man rowing over there,' she thought, '—the one with the auburn hair, the gold-rimmed spectacles and the handsome beard. He's a rich, smug, invariably lucky mother's darling universally regarded as an honest, independent-minded, progressive person. It's less than a year since he graduated and moved to the country, yet he's already talking of "us social workers". But in a year he'll be bored, too, and off he'll go to St. Petersburg like so many others, and he'll justify his flight by telling everyone how useless the local government organizations are, and how disappointed he has been. Meanwhile his young wife, who's in that other boat, can't take her eyes off him, believing him to be a pillar of the local council, though she'll be equally convinced, one year from now, that the whole thing is pointless. And take that stout, meticulously shaved gentleman in the straw hat with the broad ribbon—the one with the expensive cigar in his mouth. He's always on about it being "time we gave up pipe dreams and tackled a real job of work". He has Yorkshire pigs, Butlerov hives, a crop of rapeseed, pineapples, two dairies—one for butter, one for cheese—and Italian double-entry bookkeeping. But every summer he sells some of his woods for timber, and mortgages part of his land, so that he can spend the autumn with his mistress in the Crimea. And there's Uncle Nicholas, who's furious with Peter, yet won't go home for some reason.'

Glancing at the other boats, Olga could see nothing but cranks, bores, humbugs and morons. She remembered everyone she knew in the county, but couldn't recall a single person of whom she could say or think anything good. She found them all so crass—so insipid, dim, narrow, bogus and callous. They neither said what they meant nor did what they wanted. Suffocated by *ennui*, desperate, she wanted to wipe the smile off her face, spring up, shout 'I'm fed up with you all', and then jump out of the boat and swim ashore.

'I say, everyone, let's give Peter a tow,' someone shouted.

The others picked up the cry. 'Tow him, tow him! Take your husband in tow, Olga!'

Sitting at the tiller, Olga had to seize the right moment, nimbly grasping *Penderakliya* by the chain at its prow. As she leant over to reach for it Peter frowned and looked at her in alarm. 'I do hope you won't catch cold.'

'If you're so worried about me and the baby then why torment me?' Olga wondered.

Acknowledging defeat, but not wanting to be towed, Peter jumped from *Penderakliya* into the already overcrowded boat—jumped so clumsily that it keeled hard over and everyone screamed in terror.

'He did that jump to please the ladies,' thought Olga. 'He knows how dashing it looks.'

Her arms and legs began to shake—the result, she supposed, of dejection, vexation, forced smiling and the discomfort that she felt all over her body. To conceal her trembling from the guests she tried to talk louder, to laugh, and to keep moving. 'If I suddenly burst into tears I'll say I have toothache,' she thought.

Well, they finally beached the boats at the 'Isle of Good Hope', this being a peninsula formed by a sharp bend in the river and overgrown with a coppice of old birch trees, willows and poplars. Under the trees stood tables with steaming samovars on them. Vasily and Gregory, in tail-coats and white knitted gloves, were busy with the tea things. On the far bank, opposite 'Good Hope', were the carriages that had brought the provisions, and from them baskets and bundles of food were being ferried to the Isle in a skiff much like *Penderakliya*. The footmen, the coachmen, and even the peasant manning the skiff—all had the solemn, festive air seen only in children and servants.

While Olga made tea and poured the first glasses, the guests were busy with cordials and sweetmeats. There ensued the kind of tea-drinking chaos usual at picnics and so tiresome and exhausting for hostesses. Hardly had Gregory and Vasily had time to take the tea round when empty glasses were already being held out to Olga. One asked for it without sugar, another wanted it strong, a third wanted it weak, and a fourth was saying no more thank you. Olga had to remember all this and then shout, 'Were you the one without sugar, Ivan Petrovich?' or, 'I say, all of you, who wanted it weak?' But the person who had asked for it weak or without sugar had now forgotten which, being engrossed in agreeable conversation, and took the first glass that came to hand. A little way from the table drifted disconsolate ghostlike figures pretending to look for mushrooms in the grass or read the labels on boxes. These were the ones for whom there were not enough glasses.

'Have you had tea?' Olga would ask, and the person in question would tell her not to worry, adding that he would have some later, though it would have suited her better if the guests didn't have some later, but got a move on.

Some of them were absorbed in conversation and drank their tea slowly, holding on to their glasses for half an hour, while others—especially those who had drunk a great deal at dinner—stayed close to the table drinking glass after glass, so that Olga hardly had time to fill them. One young wag sipped his tea through a lump of sugar, and kept saying: 'I love to pamper myself, sinner that I am, with the Chinese herb.' From time to time he sighed deeply, asking for 'the favour of another tiny dish'. He drank a lot and crunched the sugar aloud, thinking this all very funny and original—and a superb take-off of a typical Russian merchant. That these trivialities were all agony to the hostess no one realized, and it would have been hard for them to do so because Olga was all affable smiles and idle chit-chat.

She was not feeling well. She was irritated by the crowd, by the laughter, by the questions, by the funny young man, by the footmen—at their wits' end and run off their feet—by the children hanging round near the table. She was irked by Vata looking like Nata, and Kolya like Mitya, so that you couldn't tell which had had tea and which hadn't. She sensed her strained smile of welcome turning sour, and she felt ready to burst into tears at any moment.

'I say, it's raining,' someone shouted.

Everyone looked at the sky.

'Yes, it's rain all right,' Peter affirmed, wiping his cheek.

The sky let fall only a few drops and it was not really raining, but the guests forsook their tea and made haste to leave. At first they all wanted to go back in the carriages, but then they changed their minds and made for the boats. On the pretext that she was behindhand with her supper arrangements Olga asked to be excused for leaving the company and going home by carriage.

The first thing she did in the carriage was to give her face a holiday from smiling, and she drove grim-visaged through the village, responding ungraciously to the bows of the peasants that she passed. Arriving home, she went to her bedroom by the back entrance and lay on her husband's bed.

'Merciful God, why this hellish drudgery?' she whispered. 'Why do they all mill around pretending to enjoy themselves? Why my hypocritical smiles? I don't understand at all.'

She heard footsteps and voices. Her guests had returned. 'I don't care,' she thought. 'I'll lie down a bit longer.'

But the maid came into the bedroom. 'Marya Grigoryevna's leaving, mum.'

Olga jumped up, tidied her hair and rushed out of the room. 'My dear, but this is unheard of!' she began in an insulted voice, going up to her guest. 'Why all the hurry?'

'I can't stay, darling, I really can't. I've been here too long already—my children are expecting me at home.'

'Well, I think you're most unkind! Why didn't you bring your children with you?'

'I'll bring them on an ordinary day, my dear, if you'll allow me, but today——'

'But of course!' Olga broke in. 'I'll be delighted! You have such nice children—do give them all a kiss from me. But I'm seriously offended! Where's the hurry, that's what I don't understand.'

'I can't stay, really. Good-bye, dearest, and do look after yourself. In your, er, condition, you know——'

They kissed. After seeing her to her carriage, Olga joined the ladies in the drawing-room where the lamps had been lit and the gentlemen were sitting down to cards.

IV

After supper, at a quarter past twelve, the guests began to leave while Olga stood in the porch and saw them off. 'Now, you really should take a shawl,' she said. 'It's getting rather cool. I do hope you won't catch cold.'

'Don't worry,' the guests answered, getting into their carriages. 'Well, good-bye. And remember we're expecting you. Don't disappoint us.'

'Whoa there!' The coachman held back the horses.

'Off we go, Denis! Good-bye, Olga.'

'Kiss the children for me.'

The carriage moved off and instantly vanished in the darkness. In the red circle cast on the drive by the lamp a new pair or trio of impatient horses would appear, their driver silhouetted with his arms thrust out in front of him. There were more kisses, more reproaches, and more requests to come again or take a shawl. Peter kept running out of the hall and helping the ladies into their carriages.

'Make straight for Yefremovshchina, my man,' he instructed a coachman. 'The Mankino route's shorter, but that road is worse—you could overturn as easily as anything. Good-bye, my precious. *Mille compliments* to your artistic friend.'

'Good-bye, Olga darling. Go inside or you'll catch cold—it's damp.'

'Whoa there! Play me up, would you?'

'Now, where did you get those horses?' Peter asked, and the coachman told him that they had 'bought them from Khaydarov in Lent'.

'Fine horses.' Peter slapped the trace-horse on the crupper. 'All right, off with you! Godspeed!'

Finally the last guest left. The red circle on the drive wavered, drifted off to one side, shrank, and vanished as Vasily took the lamp from the porch. After seeing their guests off on previous occasions Peter and Olga had usually danced up and down in the ballroom, face to face and clapping hands as they sang: 'They've gone, gone, gone!' But Olga did not feel like that now. She went to the bedroom, undressed and got into bed.

She felt that she would doze off at once and sleep soundly. There was a nagging ache in her legs and shoulders, and her head was clogged with talk. Once again she felt vaguely uncomfortable all over. Covering her head, she lay there for a few minutes, then peeped out from the blanket at the icon-lamp, listened to the silence and smiled.

'Good, good,' she whispered, curling her legs, which seemed to have been stretched by so much walking about. 'Sleep, sleep——'

Her legs would not stay still, her whole body felt uncomfortable and she turned over on her other side. A large fly flew about the room, buzzing and banging restlessly against the ceiling. She could also hear the careful tread of Gregory and Vasily as they cleared the tables in the ballroom. She sensed that she would never feel at ease or fall asleep until these noises stopped. Once more she turned over impatiently.

She heard her husband's voice in the drawing-room. A guest must be staying for the night because Peter was addressing someone in a loud voice. 'I'm not saying Count Alexis is a hypocrite, but he can't help seeming so because you people all try to see him as different from what he really is. People think he's original because he's a crank, kind-hearted because he's over-familiar, and conservative because he has no views at all. Let us even grant that he really is a hundred per cent copper-bottomed Tory. But what, actually, is conservatism?'

Enraged with Count Alexis, with his guests and with himself, Peter was really letting himself go. He abused the Count, he abused his guests, and he was so vexed with himself that he was ready to hold forth and blurt out absolutely anything. Having seen the guest to his room, he stalked up and down the drawing-room, then paced the dining-room, the corridor and his study, and then the drawing-room again before entering the bedroom. Olga lay on her back with the blanket only up to her waist—by now she was hot—and she was looking peevishly at the fly thumping into the ceiling.

'Is someone staying the night?' she asked.

'Yegorov.'

Peter undressed and lay on his bed. He lit a cigarette in silence, and he too started watching the fly. His gaze was grim and troubled. Olga examined his handsome profile for five minutes without speaking, somehow feeling that if he suddenly turned to her and said: 'I'm so miserable, darling,' she would burst into tears or laugh, and would feel better. The ache in her legs and the discomfort of her whole body were due to nervous tension, she thought.

'What are you thinking about, Peter?' she asked.

'Oh, nothing,' replied her husband.

'You've started having secrets from me lately. That's wrong.'

'What's wrong about it?' Peter answered drily, after a pause. 'We all have our own personal lives, so we're bound to have our own secrets.'

'Personal lives, own secrets—that's just words. Can't you see how much you're hurting me?' She sat up in bed. 'If you're worried, why hide it from me? And why do you think fit to confide in strange women rather than your own wife? Oh yes, I heard you by the bee-hives this afternoon, pouring your heart out to Lyubochka.'

'My congratulations, I'm glad you did hear it.' This meant: 'Leave me alone, and don't bother me when I'm thinking.'

Olga was outraged. The irritation, hatred and anger that had accumulated inside her during the day—it all seemed to boil over suddenly. She felt like speaking her mind to her husband at once, without waiting for the morning, she wanted to insult him and have her own back.

'It's all so odious, loathsome and vile, I tell you.' She was trying not to shout. 'I've hated you all day—now look what you've done!'

Peter sat up in bed.

'Oh, how utterly, utterly vile!' Olga added, shaking all over. 'And don't you congratulate me—better congratulate yourself! It's a down-right disgrace! You've become such a fraud that you're ashamed to be in the same room as your own wife. You're so bogus! I can see right through you, and I understand every single step you take.'

'Perhaps you could warn me when you're in a bad mood, Olga, so I can go and sleep in the study.'

With these words Peter took his pillow and left the room. This Olga had not foreseen. For a few minutes she gazed—silent, open-mouthed and quivering all over—at the door through which her husband had disappeared, and tried to understand what this meant. Was it one of those procedures employed during quarrels by deceitful persons when they are in the wrong? Or was it a deliberate insult to her self-respect? How should she take it? She remembered her cousin the army officer—a cheerful sort, who had often laughingly told her that, 'when my lady wife nags me of a night', he usually took a pillow and went whistling off to his study, leaving her looking very foolish. She was a rich, neurotic, silly woman whom he did not respect and barely tolerated.

Olga jumped out of bed feeling that she had only one recourse—to dress as fast as she could and leave home for ever. The house belonged to her, but so much the worse for Peter. Without thinking whether it was necessary or not, she rushed to the study to inform her husband of her decision—the thought 'how like a woman' flashed through her mind—and add some sarcastic parting shot.

Peter lay on the sofa, pretending to read a newspaper. There was a lighted candle on a chair near him, and his face was hidden behind the paper.

'Be so good as to tell me the meaning of this! I await your explanation.'

'Be so good as—.' Peter mimicked her voice, not showing his face. 'I've had enough of this, Olga, honestly. I'm tired and I'm not in the mood. We can have our quarrel tomorrow.'

'Oh, I see through your little game,' she went on. 'You hate me—oh yes, you do—because I'm better off than you. For that you will never forgive me, and you'll never be straightforward with me.' (The thought 'how like a woman' flashed through her mind again.) 'At this very moment you're laughing at me, I know. I'm quite certain you only married me for my money and those horrid horses. Oh, I'm so unhappy!'

Peter dropped his paper and sat up, dumbfounded by the un-expected insult. He smiled as helplessly as a baby, looked perplexedly at his wife, held out his hands to her, as if to ward off blows, and called her name as if pleading with her.

Expecting her to make some further outrageous remark, he shrank against the back of the sofa, his large frame looking as childishly helpless as his smile.

'My dear, how can you say such things?' he whispered.

Coming to her senses and suddenly realizing that she loved this man passionately, Olga remembered that he was her husband Peter, that she couldn't live one day without him, and that he loved her madly too. Bursting into loud sobs, not recognizable as hers, she clutched her head and ran back into the bedroom.

She collapsed on the bed, and the room echoed to curt, hysterical sobs that choked her and cramped her arms and legs. Remembering that they had a guest sleeping three or four rooms away, she buried her head under the pillow to stifle her sobs, but the pillow slipped to the floor and she almost fell off the bed herself as she bent down for it. She made to pull the blanket up to her face, but her hands would not obey her, tearing convulsively at everything they clutched.

She felt that all was lost, and that the lie she had told to wound her husband had shattered her life into fragments. Never would he forgive her, for the insult was not such as any vows or embraces could gainsay. How to convince her husband that she did not mean what she had said?

'It's all over—finished,' she shouted, not noticing that the pillow had slipped to the floor again. 'Oh, for heaven's sake——'

No doubt her cries had roused the guest and the servants by now, and tomorrow the whole county would know that she had had hysterics, and everyone would blame Peter. She strove to restrain herself, but her sobs grew louder every minute.

'For God's sake, for God's sake!' she shouted in a voice not her own and without knowing why.

She felt as if the bed had collapsed under her and her legs were tangled in the blanket. Peter came in wearing his dressing-gown and carrying a candle.

'Hush,' he said.

She raised herself on to her knees in bed, squinting in the candle-light. 'You must, must understand—', she said between sobs.

She wanted to tell him that she had been plagued by their visitors, by his lies and by her own lies, till everything was seething inside her, but all she could bring out was that he 'must, must understand'.

'Here, drink this.' He gave her some water. She obediently took the glass and began drinking, but the water splashed and spilt over her hands, breast and knees.

'I must look hideous,' she thought.

Silently Peter put her back in bed, covered her with the blanket, took his candle and went out.

'For God's sake!' she shouted again. 'Try to understand, Peter.'

Then, suddenly, something took a grip beneath her stomach and back so violently that it cut short her tears, and made her bite the pillow in agony, but the pain relented at once and she began sobbing again.

In came the maid and rearranged the blanket. 'Mistress—what's the matter, my dear?' she asked anxiously, but Peter, who was coming towards the bed, told the girl to clear out.

'You must, must understand,' kept on Olga.

'Please calm yourself, dear,' said he. 'I didn't want to hurt you. I wouldn't have left the room if I'd known it would affect you like that. I simply felt miserable. I tell you quite honestly——'

'But you must understand! You behaved so falsely, and so did I——'

'I do understand. There, there, that'll do. I understand,' he said tenderly as he sat down on the bed.

'You spoke in anger, it's understandable. I swear to God I love you more than anything on earth, and when I married you I never once thought about your being rich. I loved you infinitely, that's all. Believe me, I've never been short of money or known the value of it, and so I can't appreciate the difference between your means and mine. I've always felt as if we were equally well off. As for my dissembling over trifles—well, that's true of course. Till now the pattern of my life has been so frivolous that it's somehow been impossible to avoid prevarication. I'm pretty depressed myself at the moment. Let's not go on like this, for heaven's sake.'

Once more Olga felt a sharp pain and clutched her husband's sleeve. 'It hurts, oh how it does hurt!' she said rapidly.

'Damn and blast those guests!' Peter muttered, standing up. 'You shouldn't have gone to the island this afternoon,' he shouted. 'Why didn't I have the sense to stop you, God help me?'

He scratched his head irritably and left the room with a gesture that dismissed the subject.

After that he kept coming back, sitting on her bed and talking at length, now most tenderly, now angrily, but she barely heard. Her sobs alternated with atrocious pangs, each more violent and prolonged than the last. At first she held her breath when the pain came, biting her pillow, but later she uttered hideous, piercing screams. Once, seeing her husband near her, she remembered insulting him, and, without stopping to think whether it was a hallucination or the real Peter, she seized his hand in both hers and began kissing it.

'We've both been dishonest,' she pleaded. 'You must, must understand. They've tortured me, driven me out of my mind——'

'We're not alone, dear,' Peter told her.

She raised her head and saw Barbara kneeling by the chest of drawers and pulling out the lowest drawer. The top drawers were already out. Having done this, she stood up, flushed by her exertions, and began opening a small chest, looking cool and solemn.

'I can't unlock it, Marya,' she whispered. 'You do it, can't you?'

The maid Marya, who was digging a candle stub out of the candlestick with a pair of scissors so that she could fit a fresh one, went over to Barbara and helped her open the chest.

'Nothing must be left shut,' whispered Barbara. 'Open this little box too, my dear.' She turned to Peter. 'You should send to Father Michael, sir, to open the gates in front of the altar—you must.'

'Do whatever you like.' Peter breathed unevenly. 'Only get the doctor or midwife quickly, for God's sake. Has Vasily gone? Send someone else as well. Send your husband.'

'I'm in labour,' Olga realized. 'But it won't be born alive, Barbara,' she groaned.

'Now, 'twill be all right, mum,' whispered Barbara—to say 'it will' was beyond her, it seemed. ' 'Twill live, God willing. 'Twill live.'

When Olga came to after the next pain she was no longer sobbing or tossing about, but just moaning. She just could not help moaning even in the intervals between the pangs. The candles were still burning, but daylight was already thrusting through the shutters—it must be about five o'clock. A modest-looking woman in a white apron, whom Olga did not know, sat at a round table in the bedroom, her posture indicating that she had been there for some time. Olga guessed that she was the midwife.

'Will it be over soon?' she asked, detecting an odd, unfamiliar ring, never heard before, in her own voice. 'I must be dying in childbirth,' she thought.

Peter came cautiously into the bedroom wearing his day clothes, and stood by the window with his back to his wife. He raised the blind and looked out.

'What rain!' he said.

'What's the time?' Olga asked in order to hear the unfamiliar ring of her voice again.

'A quarter to six,' the midwife answered.

'But what if I really am dying?' wondered Olga, watching her husband's head and the window panes on which the rain was beating. 'How will he live without me? Who will he drink tea and have his meals with, talk to in the evenings, sleep with?'

He seemed like a little orphan child to her, and she felt sorry for him, wanting to say something nice, kind and soothing to him. She remembered his intending to buy some hounds in the spring, but she had stopped him because she thought hunting a cruel, dangerous sport.

'Peter, do buy those hounds,' she groaned.

He lowered the blind, went to the bed and made to say something, but just then Olga felt a pang and gave a hideous, piercing shriek.

She was numb with the pain and all the screaming and groaning. She could hear, see and occasionally speak, but she understood little, conscious only of being, or of being about to be, in pain. It was as if Peter's name-day had ended long, long ago—not yesterday, but something like a year earlier, as if her new life of agony had lasted longer than her childhood, boarding-school days, university course and married life combined, seeming likely to go on for ever and ever without end. She saw them bring the midwife her tea, and call her for lunch at midday, and later for dinner. She saw Peter acquire the habit of coming in, standing for some time by the window, and going out, and she saw that certain strange men, the maid and Barbara had also taken to coming in. All Barbara could do was to say ''twill this' and ''twill that', and she was annoyed when anyone closed the drawers in the chest of drawers. Olga watched the light change in the room and at the windows. Sometimes it was twilight, sometimes it was dim and misty, sometimes it was bright daylight, as at dinner time on the previous day, and then twilight again. Each of these changes seemed to last as long as her childhood, her schooldays, her university course.

In the evening two doctors—one bony, bald, with a broad red beard, another swarthy and Jewish-looking, wearing cheap spectacles —performed an operation on her. She was wholly indifferent to strange men touching her body, having lost all shame and will-power. Anyone could do what he liked to her. If, at this time, someone had attacked her with a knife, insulted Peter or deprived her of the right to the small person, she would not have said a word.

She was given chloroform for the operation. Later, when she came to, the pains were still there, still unbearable. It was night, and Olga remembered another such night—the stillness, the icon-lamp, the midwife sitting motionless by the bed, the drawers of the chest of drawers pulled out and Peter standing by the window. But that had been long, long ago.

V

'I'm not dead,' Olga reflected when the pain was over and she was once more aware of her surroundings.

A fine summer day peeped in through the two wide open bedroom windows. Outside in the garden sparrows and magpies kept up their incessant din.

The drawers of the chest of drawers were now shut, and her husband's bed had been made. There was no midwife, no Barbara, no maid in the bedroom, but only Peter standing stock-still by the window as before, and looking into the garden.

There was no baby's crying to be heard, there were no congratulations or rejoicing, and it was clear that the small person had not been born alive.

She called Peter's name and he looked round. Much time must have passed since the last guest's departure and her insults to her husband, for he had become noticeably thin and haggard.

'What is it?' He came over to the bed.

He looked away, his lips twitched and he smiled his helpless childlike smile.

'Is it all over?' she asked.

Peter wanted to answer, but his lips trembled and his mouth twisted like an old man's—like toothless Uncle Nicholas's.

'My darling.' He was wringing his hands, and great tears suddenly fell from his eyes. 'I don't need your property, dear, I don't need any court hearings, or'—he gulped—'dissenting judgements, or those guests, or your dowry. I don't need anything at all. Why did we have to lose our baby? Oh, what's the point of talking?'

With a gesture of despair he left the room.

But nothing mattered to Olga any more. Her head was hazy from the chloroform, she felt spiritually drained, and still numb with the apathy that had come over her while the two doctors had been performing the operation.

LIGHTS

Outside the hut a dog was barking nervously. The engineer, who was called Ananyev, his student assistant (a Baron Von Stenberg) and I went out to see who had caused it to bark. As a visitor I could have stayed inside, but I confess my head was somewhat fuddled with wine, and I was glad of a breath of fresh air.

'No one about,' said Ananyev, when we were outside. 'So why pretend, Azorka? Stupid dog!'

There was not a soul to be seen. Timidly, wagging his tail, the stupid black watchdog Azorka came towards us, probably wanting to apologize for his pointless barking. The engineer bent down and touched him between the ears.

'Why bark for nothing, you silly creature?' he asked in the tone that easygoing people employ with children and dogs. 'Had a bad dream, eh? I commend him to your attention, Doctor,' he went on, addressing me. 'A remarkably neurotic specimen. He can't stand being on his own, believe it or not. He has terrible dreams—excruciating nightmares—and if you shout at him he goes into hysterics or something.'

'Yes, he's a delicate hound,' the student confirmed.

Azorka must have known that we were discussing him, for he lifted his muzzle and whimpered piteously. 'Yes,' he seemed to say. 'My sufferings are sometimes past endurance, so pray excuse me.'

It was an August night, with stars, but dark. Never having been in surroundings as peculiar as those I had now stumbled upon, I found the starry night dull, inhospitable and gloomier than it actually was. I was on a railway line under construction. The high, half-completed embankment, the heaps of sand, clay and rubble, the huts, the pits, the wheelbarrows dotted here and there, the low mounds above the dugouts where the navvies lived—rendered monochrome by the darkness, all this clutter somehow gave the earth a weird, bizarre configuration redolent of primeval chaos. So little order was there in what met my eyes, and so hideously rutted was the monstrous scene, that human silhouettes and graceful telegraph poles looked rather out of place. These things spoilt the general impression, seeming to belong to another world. It was quiet, except for the telegraph wires droning their mournful chant high above our heads.

We climbed the embankment and looked down. A hundred yards

away, where ruts, pits and heaps merged with nocturnal gloom, a dim light flickered. Beyond that shone a second light, and then a third, after which two red eyes glowed side by side about another hundred yards on—the windows of some hut, probably—and a long row of such lights, growing ever dimmer and closer to each other, followed the line to the very horizon, before wheeling left in a crescent and vanishing in the distant gloom. The lights were motionless. There seemed to be something in common between them, the night's stillness and the telegraph wires' disconsolate chant. Under the embankment, it seemed, lay buried some vital secret known only to the lights, the night and the wires.

'God, how marvellous!' Ananyev sighed. 'That great expanse, all that splendour—it's almost too much! And what of our embankment? That's no embankment, man, it's a regular Mont Blanc. It's costing millions.'

Exulting in the lights and the embankment that was costing millions, a little tipsy from the wine that he had drunk, and in sentimental mood, the engineer clapped young Von Stenberg on the shoulder.

'Found food for thought, have you, Michael?' he continued whimsically. 'I bet you're glad to see the work of your own hands, aren't you? Last year it was all bare steppe just here, there wasn't even a whiff of humanity. But see now—the place has come alive, it's being civilized. And, ye Gods, how wonderful it all is! We're building a railway, you and I, and after us—in a century or two, say—good people will be building factories, schools and hospitals here, and things will start moving, eh?'

The student stood quite still, his hands in his pockets, his eyes fixed on the lights. He did not hear Ananyev, for his mind was elsewhere, and he was obviously in no mood for talking or listening. After a long silence he turned to me.

'Know what those endless lights remind me of?' he asked quietly. 'They suggest something long extinct that lived thousands of years ago—an Amalekite or Philistine encampment, that kind of thing. It's as if some Old Testament tribe had pitched camp, and was waiting for dawn to do battle with a Saul or a David. All we need to complete the illusion is trumpets blaring and sentries calling to each other in Ethiopian or something.'

'Perhaps,' the engineer agreed.

As if on cue, a gust of wind blew down the line with a noise like the clash of weapons. Silence followed. What the engineer and the student were thinking I don't know, but I felt I really could see a long departed scene before me. I even heard sentries talking in an unknown tongue. My imagination hastened to picture tents, outlandish folk, their raiment, their martial gear.

'Yes,' muttered the student pensively. 'Philistines and Amalekites did once live on this earth. They waged their wars, they played their part, but now they're gone without trace. It will be the same with us too. We're building our railway now, we stand here, we air our thoughts. But in a couple of thousand years this embankment, and all those men asleep after a hard day's work—they'll have vanished into thin air. It's truly appalling.'

'You mustn't think such things,' the engineer solemnly insisted.

'Why not?'

'Because—. Those are thoughts for life's end, not for its beginning. You're too young for them.'

'But why?' the young man asked him again.

'These ideas about transience and futility, about life being pointless and death inevitable, about the shadows of the grave and all that—take it from me, old chap, all these lofty notions are perfectly acceptable and natural in old age, when they're the outcome of prolonged spiritual travail, have been earned by suffering, and represent a genuine intellectual asset. But for a young brain, scarcely launched on independent life, they're sheer disaster!

'Sheer disaster!' repeated Ananyev with a dismissive gesture. 'At your age it's a sight better to have no head on your shoulders at all than to think along those lines. Or so I think. I'm perfectly serious, Baron, and I've meant to discuss it with you for some time because I spotted your addiction to these pernicious notions the very first day we met.'

'But, good God, why pernicious?' The young man smiled, his voice and face showing that he replied only out of ordinary courtesy, and that the engineer's argument interested him not at all.

I could hardly keep my eyes open, longing for us to say good night and go to bed as soon as our walk was over, but it was some time before my wish was granted. When we had returned to the hut the engineer put the empty bottles under the bed, took two full ones out of a wicker hamper, opened them, and sat down at his desk with the obvious intention of going on drinking, talking and working. Taking an occasional sip from his glass, he pencilled jottings on some plans while continuing to impress upon the young man that his attitude was mistaken. Von Stenberg sat beside him checking accounts and saying nothing. Like me, he did not feel like talking or listening. To avoid interrupting their work, I sat away from the table on the engineer's crooked-legged camp bed. I expected them to suggest that I went to bed at any moment, and I was bored. It was past midnight.

Having nothing to do, I watched my new friends. I had never seen Ananyev or the young man before, for the night that I am describing was the occasion of our first meeting. Late that evening I had been riding back from a fair to the house of a landowner where I was staying, had taken the wrong turning in the dark and lost my way. Wandering around near the railway line, and seeing the dark night grow darker, I had recalled the tales of those 'barefoot navvies' who waylay passers-by on foot and on horseback. Feeling scared, I had knocked at the first hut I came to, where Ananyev and the student had made me welcome. As happens when strangers meet by accident, we had quickly hit it off together, and struck up a friendship. Over tea followed by wine we had come to feel as if we had known each other for years. Within an hour or so I knew who they were, and how their destiny had brought them from the capital into the distant steppe, while they knew who I was, what my job was, and how my mind worked.

Nicholas Ananyev, the engineer, was thickset and broad-shouldered, looking as if, like Othello, he was already 'declined into the vale of years', and was putting on weight. He was of exactly the age known as 'the prime of life' to marriage-brokers—neither young nor old, in other words, fond of a square meal, a drink, a talk about the good old days, given to puffing slightly when he walked, to snoring loudly when he slept, and to displaying in his manner towards those around him the calm, imperturbable benevolence acquired by decent men when they stumble into senior rank and start putting on weight. Though his head and beard were still far from grey, he was already— without meaning to, somehow, and all unconsciously—patronizing young men as 'my dear chap', and feeling entitled to lecture them good-humouredly about their general attitude. His movements and voice were calm, level, confident—those of one well aware of being a successful self-made man, of possessing a definite job, a secure livelihood and a fixed outlook.

'I'm well-fed, healthy and content,' his sunburnt face, stubby nose and muscular neck seemed to say. 'And in good time you young fellows will also be well-fed, healthy and content.'

He wore a cotton shirt with the collar cut slantwise, and wide linen trousers stuck into large riding boots. From certain details—his coloured worsted belt, for instance, his embroidered collar, the patch on his elbow—I could tell that he was married and, in all probability, dearly loved by his wife.

Baron Michael Von Stenberg, a student at the Transport Institute, was a young man of twenty-three or twenty-four. Only his fair hair and sparse beard, and perhaps a certain crudity and leanness of the facial features, hinted at a Baltic baronial ancestry. Everything else— his Christian name, his religion, his ideas, his manner, his facial expression—were purely Russian. Sunburnt, dressed—like Ananyev—in an open-necked cotton shirt and high boots, somewhat stooping, and much in need of a hair-cut, he resembled neither a student nor a baron, but an ordinary Russian apprentice. His words and gestures were few, he drank his wine reluctantly, without gusto, and he checked his accounts automatically, seeming to have his mind on something else. His movements and voice were calm and smooth too, but with a calm entirely different from the engineer's. His sunburnt, slightly ironical, pensive face, a somewhat distrustful look in his eyes, and his whole figure expressed spiritual sloth and mental sluggishness. He looked as if he did not in the least care whether or not he had a light burning in front of him, whether his wine was palatable or not, whether the accounts that he was checking did or did not balance.

The message conveyed by his calm, intelligent face was this. 'So far I see no merit in a definite job, a secure livelihood or a fixed outlook. That's all rubbish. I used to live in St. Petersburg. Now I'm stuck in this hut. In autumn I shall go back to St. Petersburg. I shall return here in the spring. What good will come of it I don't know. Nor does anyone else, and so there's no point in discussing it.'

He listened to the engineer without interest, condescendingly in-different like senior cadets when their kindly old corporal sounds off about something. None of the engineer's remarks were new to the young man, apparently, and he would have said something cleverer and more original himself, if he could have been bothered to speak. Meanwhile Ananyev had the bit between his teeth. Having dropped his relaxed, jocular tone, he was speaking earnestly, and with a passion wholly incompatible with his calm expression. He was obviously keen on abstract problems. But, fond of them though he was, he lacked aptitude and practice in handling them. So strongly was this

unfamiliarity reflected in his words that I could not catch his drift
at first.

'I wholeheartedly loathe those ideas,' he said. 'I was infected by
them myself in youth, I'm still not entirely rid of them. And I tell you
this—they did me nothing but harm, perhaps because I'm stupid and
they were the wrong nourishment for my brain. Now, there's no
mystery about this. The pointlessness of life, the futility and transience
of the visible world, Solomon's vanity of vanities—these concepts have
constituted, they still do constitute, the ultimate zenith, in the realm
of thought. When the thinker reaches that stage the machine stops.
There's nowhere else to go. The culminating point of a normal
brain's activity has been reached, and that's all very right and proper.
But it's at this apogee that we begin our thinking, worse luck. Our
starting point is what ordinary people end with. In the first flush of
our brain's independent activity we climb to the ultimate, the very
topmost rung, ignoring the lower stages.'

'And what's wrong with that?' the young man asked.

'Can't you see it's unnatural?' shouted Ananyev, looking at him with
something like anger. 'If we've found a way to climb to the top rung
without using the lower ones, then the whole long ladder—the whole
of life with its colours, sounds and thoughts, in other words—loses all
meaning for us. How evil and absurd such thinking is at your age you
can see from every stage of your rational independent life. Let's say
you sit down this minute to read Darwin, Shakespeare or someone.
Hardly have you finished one page before the poison begins to work.
Your own long life, with Shakespeare and Darwin thrown in, seems
just so much fatuous tomfoolery because you know you're going to
die. You know Shakespeare and Darwin have died too, and without
their ideas saving either themselves or the world or you. You also
know that, if life is so utterly pointless, then all your knowledge,
poetry and fine thoughts are just idle playthings, the futile toys of
grown-up children. And so you stop reading at the second page. Now,
suppose someone comes to you and asks what you, as an intelligent
man, think about war, say. Is it desirable, is it morally justified, or
isn't it? In reply to this awesome question you'll only shrug your
shoulders and limit yourself to some truism, because you, with your
slant on things, don't care a rap whether hundreds of thousands of
people die a violent or a natural death. In either event the outcome's
exactly the same—ashes and oblivion. We're building this railway, you
and I. But why, one wonders, should we rack our brains, tax our

ingenuity, rise above routine, take care of our men, steal or not steal, when we know the railway will be dust and ashes in a couple of thousand years? And so on and so forth.

'This lamentable frame of mind rules out all progress, you must agree, together with all science, all art and even thought itself. We think ourselves cleverer than the rabble, and cleverer than Shakespeare, but in fact our reasoning is nullified because we don't feel like descending to the lower rungs, because we have nowhere higher to climb, and so our brain just sticks at freezing point without going up or down.

'I was in bondage to such notions for about six years, and all that time I swear to God I never read a single decent book. I neither grew one whit more intelligent nor raised my moral stature by an iota. What a calamity! Furthermore, not content with being poisoned ourselves, we also poison the lives of those around us. If we turned our backs on life in our pessimism and withdrew to the catacombs, or hurried up and died, it would be all right, but we submit to the universal law, don't we? We live, we feel, we love women, we bring up children, we build railways.'

'Our ideas are neither one thing nor the other,' said the young man reluctantly.

'Oh, honestly. Do chuck it, for heaven's sake! You haven't even smelt life yet. When you've lived as long as I have, young fellow, you'll know what's what. That way of thinking isn't as harmless as you think. In practice, when you come up against other people, it leads to horror and folly. I've found myself in predicaments I wouldn't wish on my worst enemy.'

'Such as?' I asked.

'Such as?' repeated Ananyev. He thought for a moment and smiled. 'Such as the following incident, for instance. Or, rather, it's not so much an incident as a regular drama complete with plot and dénouement. A most splendid lesson—a fine lesson indeed!'

He poured us wine, gave himself some, emptied his glass, stroked his broad chest and continued, addressing himself to me more than to the student.

This took place one summer in the late 1870s, soon after the War, when I had just completed my studies. I was going to the Caucasus, and on my way there I put up in the seaside town of N. for five days. It's the town where I was born and grew up, I must explain. And so there's nothing odd in my thinking it exceedingly comfortable, congenial and attractive, though people from St. Petersburg or Moscow find life as boring and uncomfortable there as in Chukhloma, Kashira or anywhere like that. I walked miserably past the high school where I had been a pupil, and took a melancholy stroll in the town park that I knew so well, sadly trying to take a closer look at people whom I still remembered, though I hadn't seen them for years.

It was all rather depressing.

Amongst other things I drove out to the so-called Quarantine one evening—a small, scraggy bit of copse that had once been a real quarantine station during some long-forgotten plague outbreak, but was now the site of holiday cottages. It was about three miles' drive from town on a good, soft surface. As you drove along you could see the blue sea on your left and the unending, melancholy steppe on your right. A man can breathe there and look about him freely. The copse itself is right above the sea. Dismissing my cab, I passed through the familiar gate, and at once turned down the avenue leading to a small stone summer-house, a favourite haunt of my childhood. Resting on clumsy columns, and combining the picturesque atmosphere of an old tomb with an uncouth, rough-hewn air, this cumbrous circular build-ing was to me the town's most romantic spot. It stood on the very cliff edge with a good view of the sea.

I sat on a bench, leant over the railing and looked down. From the summer-house a path ran down the steep, almost sheer cliff, past lumps of clay and burdock clumps. Far below, where it ended at the sandy beach, low waves lazily foamed, purring gently. The sea was as majestic, as vast and as forbidding as it had been seven years earlier when I had left the high school and my home town for St. Petersburg. There was a dark plume of smoke in the distance—a passing steamer—but apart from this barely visible and unmoving streak, and terns flitting over the water, nothing animated the monotonous vista of sea and sky. To right and left of the summer-house stretched irregular clay cliffs.

You know, when a man of melancholy disposition is on his own by the sea, or contemplates any scenery that impresses him with its grandeur, his sadness is always combined with a conviction that he'll live and die in obscurity, and his automatic reaction is to reach for a pencil and hasten to write his name in the first place that comes handy. That's probably why all lonely, secluded spots like my summer-house are always covered with pencil scrawls and knife carvings. I remember, as if it were today, looking at the railings and reading: 'Ivan Korolkov was here, 16 May 1876.' Alongside Korolkov some local philosopher had signed his name, and added:

'He stood on that deserted strand,
  His mind obsessed with concepts grand.'

The handwriting was dreamlike, and limp as wet silk. A certain Kross—a trivial little man, probably—had felt his own insignificance so acutely that he had let fly with his penknife, inscribing his name in deep letters nearly two inches high. Mechanically taking a pencil from my pocket, I too signed my name on a column. But all this is beside the point, actually. I'm sorry, I don't know how to keep a story short.

I felt sad and a little bored. The boredom, the quiet, the waves' purring, gradually brought on that very train of thought of which we were just speaking. At that time, the end of the seventies, it was coming into vogue with the public, after which, at the beginning of the eighties, it gradually spread from the public into literature, science and politics. Though no more than twenty-six years old at the time, I was already well aware that existence lacked all meaning and purpose, that every-thing was a sham and an illusion, that the life of convicts in Sakhalin was essentially and ultimately no different from life in Nice, that the difference between the brain of a Kant and that of a fly had no real significance, that no one in this world was either right or wrong, that everything was stuff and nonsense, and could go to hell. I lived as if I was conferring a favour on the unknown force that forced me to live. It was as if I was telling it: 'Look, you, I don't care a damn about life, but I go on living all the same.' My thoughts all followed a single definite pattern, but with every possible variation, in which I resembled the artful gourmet who could make a hundred tasty dishes from nothing but potatoes. I was one-sided, no doubt, and even rather narrow, but at the time I felt that my intellectual horizon had neither beginning nor end, and that my thinking was as boundless as the sea. Well, judging from my own case, the line of thought under discussion has an addictive, narcotic element, like tobacco or morphia, at its core. It becomes a habit, a craving. You exploit every moment of solitude, seize every chance to gloat over the pointlessness of existence and the darkness of the grave. While I sat in the summer-house, some long-nosed Greek children proceeded decorously down the avenue, and I took the opportunity to reflect along the following lines as I looked round at them.

'Why are these children born, I wonder, what do they live for? Is there any sense in their existence? They'll grow up not knowing why, they'll live in this God-forsaken dump for no good reason, and they'll die.'

I actually felt annoyed with those children for walking so decorously and conversing in their dignified fashion, as if they indeed did set a high value on their colourless little lives and knew what they were living for. Then I remember three female figures appearing far away at the end of the avenue, young ladies of some sort. One in a pink dress and two in white, they walked side by side and arm in arm, talking and laughing.

'It would be nice to distract oneself with a woman for a couple of days,' I thought as I watched them.

I incidentally remembered that it was three weeks since my last visit to my St. Petersburg lady friend, and I reflected that a brief romance would come in very handy at the moment. The girl in white in the middle seemed younger and better-looking than her friends. To judge from her manner and laughter she was in the top form of the girls' high school.

'She'll learn music and deportment,' I meditated, looking somewhat lecherously at her bosom. 'Then she'll marry some greasy little Greek, Lord love us! She'll lead a grey, stupid, futile life, she'll bear a litter of children without knowing why, and she'll die. An absurd life!'

As a rule I was pretty good, I may say, at combining flights of lofty fancy with the lowliest of prose. Thoughts of the darkness of the grave did not prevent me paying due tribute to bosoms and legs, just as our dear Baron's high-flown ideas don't in the least prevent him from driving over to conduct amorous forays in Vukolovka of a Saturday. To be perfectly honest with you, my relations with women have been highly invidious for as long as I can recall. Remembering that high-school girl at this moment, I blush to think of my attitude, but my conscience was completely clear at the time. The son of respectable parents, a Christian, a university man, not naturally vicious or stupid, I never felt the faintest compunction when I paid women what the Germans call *Blutgeld*, or when I pursued schoolgirls with offensive glances.

The trouble is, youth has its rights, and our philosophy has no objection in principle to those rights, be they good or be they ob-

jectionable. You can't know that life is pointless and death inevitable
without being highly indifferent to the struggle against your own
nature, and to the concept of sin. Struggle or not, you're going to die
and rot anyway. And in the second place, good sirs, our philosophy
induces even very young men to adopt the so-called 'rational approach'.
Our reason dominates our heart, overwhelmingly so. Spontaneous
feeling and inspiration are smothered in pernickety analysis. Now, to
adopt the rational approach is to be cold-blooded, and—let's face it—
cold-blooded people know nothing about chastity, a virtue that's
confined to the warm-hearted, to the impulsive, to those capable of
love. Thirdly, by denying life all meaning, our philosophy scouts the
validity of the individual personality. If I deny the individuality of
some Natalya or other, then I must obviously be entirely indifferent to
whether I give her offence or not. One day you insult her dignity as a
human being and pay her *Blutgeld*, and by the next day you've already
forgotten her.

So there I sat in the summer-house looking at the girls, when another
female figure appeared in the avenue. Her fair head was uncovered,
and she wore a white knitted shawl over her shoulders. After walking
along the avenue she entered the summer-house and gripped the
railings, looking listlessly down at the distant sea. She paid me no
attention when she came in—it was as if she had not noticed me. I
looked her over—not from top to toe, as one looks at a man, but the
other way round—and found her young, not more than twenty-five,
nice-looking, with a good figure, probably married, and a respectable
woman. She was dressed casually, but fashionably and tastefully, as
middle-class married women do dress in N. as a rule.

'That one would do,' I thought, looking at her shapely waist and
arms. 'Not bad at all. She must be the wife of some local medico or
schoolmaster.'

But to have an affair with her, to make her the heroine of a typical
tourist's lightning romance, in other words—that would not be easy,
it might barely be possible. Or so I felt as I gazed at her face. Her
look, her whole expression seemed to say that she was fed up with
the sea, the distant smoke and the sky, that she was sick and tired of
looking at them. Obviously weary, bored and a prey to cheerless
thoughts, she did not even have the air of preoccupation and affected
nonchalance that almost all women adopt on sensing the presence of
a strange man.

The fair girl gave me a bored glance, and sat on the bench deep in thought. I could tell from her face that she took no interest in me, that I and my metropolitan countenance did not arouse even ordinary curiosity in her. But I decided to talk to her all the same.

'Madam,' said I, 'may I ask at what time the public conveyances go to town from here?'

'At ten or eleven, I think.'

I thanked her. She glanced at me once or twice, and then a quizzical look suddenly flickered on her impassive face, followed by something like surprise. I hurriedly adopted an indifferent expression, and assumed the proper pose—she had taken the bait! But she suddenly shot to her feet as if stung, smiled gently and quickly looked me over.

'I say, your name isn't Ananyev by any chance?' she asked nervously.

I replied that it was.

'You don't recognize me then?'

Somewhat disconcerted, I stared at her, and did recognize her, not—would you believe it?—by her face or figure but by her gentle, weary smile. It was Natalya Stepanovna, also known as Kitty, the girl I had been head over heels in love with seven or eight years earlier when I was still wearing my schoolboy's uniform.

'But these are tales of ancient times
Long-buried myths, ancestral legends.'

I remember her as a thin little schoolgirl of fifteen or sixteen, when she was a sort of schoolboy's ideal created specially by nature for platonic love. And what a delightful little creature she had been! The pale, fragile, dainty little thing, she looked as if one breath would send her flying like thistledown to the very skies. Her face was gentle and puzzled, her hands were small, her long, soft hair reached down to her belt, she was wasp-waisted. Altogether she was a creature ethereal and transparent as moonlight—a boy's idea of perfection, in sum.

I loved her, ah, how I loved her! Couldn't sleep at night, wrote poetry. In the evenings she'd sit on a park bench and we boys would crowd around, gazing reverently. In response to all our compliments, posturings and sighs, she would nervously hunch her shoulders together in the damp of the evening, narrow her eyes and smile gently, looking terribly like a pretty little kitten. As we gazed at her, we each longed to fondle and stroke her like a cat, which is how she got the name of Kitty.

She had changed a great deal in the seven or eight years since our last meeting. She had matured and grown more buxom, she no longer bore the faintest resemblance to a soft, fluffy kitten. It was not so much that her features had faded and grown older as that they had somehow lost their sparkle and become more austere. Her hair seemed shorter, she was taller, her shoulders were almost twice as broad, and above all her face already wore the expression of motherliness and resignation characteristic of respectable women of her age, though I had never seen her look like that before, of course. All that remained of her former schoolgirlish sexless quality, in fact, was her gentle smile.

We started talking, and she was immensely pleased to learn that I was now a qualified engineer. 'How marvellous!' She gazed happily into my eyes. 'What a splendid thing! And what wonderful boys you all are! Not one failure in all your year, everyone's turned out well. One's an engineer, another's a doctor, a third's a teacher, and yet another's a famous singer in St. Petersburg, they say. Well done, all of you! Now, isn't it wonderful?'

Her eyes shone with unfeigned joy and good will as she took pride in me like an elder sister or former schoolmistress. Looking at her lovely face, I thought how nice it would be to become her lover that very day.

I asked whether she remembered my once bringing her a bunch of flowers and a note in the park. 'You read the note, and looked quite flabbergasted.'

'No, I'd forgotten.' She laughed. 'But I do remember you wanting to challenge Florens to a duel over me.'

'Now, that I'd forgotten, can you believe it?'

'Yes, it's all over and done with.' Kitty sighed. 'Once I was your idol, but now it's my turn to look up to all of you.'

From further discussion I learnt that she had married a couple of years after leaving school—a local man, half-Greek and half-Russian, who worked for a bank or an insurance company, and was also in the grain business. He had a rather elaborate surname—Popoulakis, Skarandopoulos or something. I've forgotten what, damn it. Of herself she spoke seldom and reluctantly, the sole topic of conversation being me. She asked about my institute, my colleagues, St. Petersburg, my plans. Everything I said afforded her the most active delight.

'Now, isn't that splendid!' she would exclaim.

We climbed down to the shore and strolled on the sands. Then, when the damp evening breeze blew off the sea, we went back up the cliff. The talk was all about me, and about the past. We continued strolling until the sunset's reflection began to fade from the cottage windows.

'Come in and have tea,' Kitty suggested. 'The samovar must have been on the table for ages.

'I'm all alone at home,' she added, as her cottage appeared through the leaves of the acacias. 'My husband's always in town. He only comes back at night, and not always then. I'm bored to death, I confess.'

I followed her, admiring her back and shoulders, and glad that she was married, since married women are better material for a brief affair than young girls. I was glad, too, that the husband was out. And yet my instincts also told me that there was no romance in the offing.

We went indoors. The rooms were small and low-ceilinged with the appointments typical of summer cottages, for your holiday-making Russian likes awkward, cumbrous, dingy furniture that he has no room for, but thinks too good to throw away. One or two small details showed that she and her husband lived pretty well, though, and must get through five or six thousand roubles a year. In what she called the dining-room there was, I remember, a round table which had six legs for some reason. On it were a samovar and cups, and on its edge lay an open book, a pencil and an exercise book. Glancing at the book, I recognized Malinin and Burenin's *Arithmetic Problems*. It was open, as I now remember, at 'The Rules of Proportion'.

'Who are you coaching?' I asked.

'No one. It's just something I've been doing. Being bored and at a loose end, I think of the old days and do the sums.'

'Have you any children?'

'I had a baby boy, but he only lived a week.'

We started drinking tea. Delighting in me, Kitty repeated how splendid it was for me to be an engineer, and how pleased she was by my success. The more she said, and the more sincerely she smiled, the stronger grew my conviction that there was nothing doing. Already a connoisseur of love affairs, I could gauge my chances of success or failure accurately. You can bank on succeeding if you're pursuing a foolish woman, one who craves adventure and excitement like yourself, or some insinuating creature with whom you have nothing in common. But if you meet a sensible, serious woman who looks fatigued, submissive and kind, who is genuinely pleased to see you, who above all respects you, then you can kiss your chances good-bye. To succeed in such cases requires more than one day.

Now, Kitty looked even more attractive in the evening light than by day. I was more and more drawn to her, and she seemed to like me. The situation, too, had eminently romantic possibilities—the husband out, no servants in evidence, and everything so quiet. Low as I rated my prospects, I nevertheless decided to launch the attack on the off chance. The first thing was to adopt a familiar tone, converting her exalted solemnity into something more light-hearted.

'Let's change the subject,' I began. 'Let's talk about something amusing. But first permit me to call you Kitty for old time's sake.'

She gave her permission.

'I'd like to ask you something,' I went on. 'What on earth has bitten the fair sex around here? What's going on, Kitty? They always used to be so moral and virtuous—but now! Upon my word! Whoever you ask about you're told things to make you simply despair of human nature. One young woman elopes with an officer. Another seduces a schoolboy and goes off with him. A third woman, married, leaves her husband for an actor, a fourth takes up with an officer. And so on and so forth, it's a positive epidemic! This way there soon won't be one girl or young wife left in town.'

I spoke in a vulgar, playful tone. Had her response been to laugh I would have gone on in the following style. 'Now, you mind some officer or actor doesn't carry you off, Kitty dear!'

She would have lowered her eyes. 'Who'd want to run away with someone like me. There are younger and prettier girls.'

'Oh, get away with you, my dear,' I'd have said. 'I for one would be delighted.'

And so it would have gone on, all in that style, and in the end I'd have pulled the thing off. But she gave no answering laugh. On the contrary, she looked grave.

'Those stories are all true.' She sighed. 'My cousin Sonya left her husband for an actor. It's quite wrong of course. Everyone must endure his lot in life, but I don't condemn them or blame them. Circumstances can be too strong for people.'

'Just so. But what circumstances could produce such a regular epidemic?'

She raised her eyebrows. 'It's easy enough to see. Our local middle-class girls and women have absolutely nothing to do. Not all of them can go away to college, become teachers—lead, in fact, purposeful intellectual lives like men. They can only marry. But where are they supposed to find husbands? You boys leave school, go away to university, and never return to your home town. You marry in St. Petersburg or Moscow, while the girls are left behind here. So who do you want them to marry? Now, since there are no decent educated men they marry any old husband—commission agents, Levantine gentlemen whose skills are limited to drinking and horseplay at the local club. The girls marry anyone, pretty well at random. What sort of life do you expect after that? A cultivated, well-bred woman living with a curmudgeonly oaf of a husband—you can see what happens. She meets a professional man—an officer, actor or doctor—and, well, she falls in love with him, the situation becomes intolerable, and she leaves her husband. You can't condemn her.'

'Then why marry at all?'

'Why indeed?' She sighed. 'But don't all girls think any husband better than none at all? It's a poor, a very poor sort of life here for the most part, Nicholas. Married or single, a woman feels she can't breathe round here. People laugh at Sonya for leaving home, and with an actor too, but if they could know her true feelings they wouldn't laugh.'

Once again Azorka barked outside the door. He snarled viciously at someone, then gave an anguished howl and crashed heavily into the hut wall. Frowning sympathetically, Ananyev broke off his tale, went out and could be heard comforting the dog outside the door for a couple of minutes.

'Good dog! Poor old fellow!'

'Friend Nicholas does like his little chat,' laughed Von Stenberg. 'He's a good sort,' he added after a pause.

Returning to the hut, the engineer filled our glasses, smiled, stroked his chest and continued.

So my assault failed. But since there was nothing I could do about it I put impure thoughts aside for a more favourable occasion, resigned myself to my failure, and 'wrote the thing off', as the phrase goes. Indeed, I too gradually succumbed to a calm, sentimental mood, lulled by Kitty's voice, by the evening air and the quiet. I remember sitting in an armchair by the wide-open window, looking at the trees and the darkening sky. The outlines of the acacias and limes were just as they had been eight years ago. There was the tinkling of a cheap piano in the far distance, as in my boyhood, and the locals had kept their habit of strolling up and down the avenues. But they were different people. It was no longer I and my friends and the objects of my adoration who promenaded the avenues, but schoolboys and young ladies whom I did not know, and I felt sad. When my questions about acquaintances had received the answer 'dead' five times from Kitty, my melancholy turned into the sensation that one has at some worthy's funeral service. Sitting by the window, watching people promenading, and listening to the tinkling piano, I witnessed with my own eyes, for the first time in my life, the eagerness with which one generation hastens to supplant another and the momentous significance that even seven or eight years have in a man's life.

Kitty put a bottle of Santorin wine on the table. I had a drink, felt a bit sentimental, and embarked on some long story. She listened, still admiring me and my cleverness. Time passed. By now the sky was so dark that the silhouettes of the acacias and limes had merged, the locals had stopped promenading, the piano-playing had stopped too, and the only sound was the sea's even murmur.

Young men are all the same. Show one of them some affection, make a fuss of him, give him wine, let him feel he's attractive, and he'll put his legs under the table, forget it's time to leave, and talk, talk, talk. His hosts can't keep their eyes open, and it's already past their bedtime, but still he sits and talks. I was just the same. At one point I chanced to glance at the clock. It was half past ten, and I began to say good-bye.

'Have one for the road,' said Kitty.

I had one, embarked on another long rigmarole, forgot it was time to leave and sat down. But then came the sound of men's voices, footsteps and the clink of spurs as some people passed beneath the windows and stopped by the door.

Kitty listened. 'My husband must be back.'

The door clicked, voices were heard in the hall, and I saw two men go past the door to the dining-room. One was a stout, thick-set, dark-haired man with a hooked nose, wearing a straw hat, and the other a young officer in a white tunic. Both cast a casual glance at Kitty and me as they passed the door, and I fancied that both were drunk.

A minute later a loud voice, with a marked nasal twang, was heard. 'She must have been lying then. And you believed her! Now, in the first place it didn't happen at the big club but at the little one——'

'Thou art angry, Jupiter. Therefore thou art wrong.' It was another voice, obviously that of the officer, who was laughing and coughing. 'I say, can I stay the night? Be honest with me, would I be a nuisance?'

'What a question! You not only can, you must. Will you have beer or wine?'

They were sitting two rooms away from us, talking loudly and

evidently taking no interest in either Kitty or her visitor. But a per-
ceptible change came over her on her husband's return. First she
blushed, then her face took on a timid, guilty expression. She was
rather ill at ease, and I fancied she was ashamed to let me see her
husband and wanted me to leave.

I began saying good-bye, and she saw me to the front door. I well
remember her sad, gentle smile and the meek, tender look in her eyes
as she shook my hand.

'We'll probably never meet again,' she said. 'Ah well, may God
grant you every happiness. And thank you.'

There were no sighs, no fine phrases. As she said good-bye she was
holding a candle, and bright patches danced over her face and neck as
if chasing her sad smile. I imagined the former Kitty, the one you felt
you wanted to stroke like a cat, while I stared intently at her as she now
was, for some reason recalling what she had said—'Everyone must
endure his lot in life'—and I felt deeply disturbed. Happy and uninvolved though I was, I instinctively guessed, and my conscience
whispered, that I was face to face with a good, well-meaning and loving
but tortured human creature.

I bowed and made for the gate. It was now dark. In the south night
falls early and rapidly in July, and by ten o'clock you can't see an inch
before your nose. I lit a couple of dozen matches while groping my
way to the gate.

'Cab!' I shouted once I was clear of the gate, but not a peep nor a
whisper did I hear.

'Cab!' I repeated. 'Hey, any cabs about?'

But there were no cabs or other vehicles for hire, there was only the
silence of the tomb. All I could hear was the murmur of the drowsy
sea, and my heart beating from the Santorin wine. I raised my eyes
to the sky, but not a star could be seen. It was dark and gloomy—
obviously the sky was overcast. For some reason I shrugged my
shoulders, smiled stupidly and again called, rather more hesitantly, for
a cab, only to be answered by a muffled echo of my own voice.

A three-mile walk across country in darkness was a disagreeable
prospect, and before making up my mind to it I spent some time
pondering and shouting for a cab. Then I shrugged my shoulders and
strolled languidly back to the copse with no definite aim. It was fearfully dark. Here and there between the trees glowed dull red cottage
windows. Roused by my footsteps, and frightened by the matches with
which I was lighting my way to the summer-house, a crow was flying

from tree to tree, making the foliage rustle. I was annoyed and ashamed, and the crow seemed to sense this, for there was a jeering note in its cawing. I was annoyed at having to walk, and ashamed to have gossiped so childishly to Kitty.

I made my way to the summer-house, felt for the seat and sat down. Far below me, beyond the dense blackness, the sea softly and angrily grumbled. I remember feeling like a blind man, for I could see neither sea nor sky, nor even the summer-house in which I sat. The thoughts fermenting in my wine-befuddled head, the unseen power murmuring so monotonously somewhere down below—these were the only things left in the whole wide world, I felt. Later, when I dozed off, I felt as if it was not the sea but my own thoughts that were murmuring. It was as if the entire world consisted of me alone. Having thus reduced the universe to the dimensions of myself, I forgot the cabs, the town and Kitty, and yielded to my favourite mood—one of terrible isolation, when it seems as if, in the whole of creation, dark and formless, only you exist. This proud, satanic sensation is something that only a Russian can feel—he whose thoughts and emotions are as broad, as boundless and as austere as his plains, forests and snows. Were I a painter I would make a point of portraying the facial expression of a Russian sitting motionless with his legs tucked under him and his head in his hands as he yields to this emotion. It is accompanied by thoughts about the pointlessness of life, about death and the darkness of the grave. The thoughts aren't worth a brass farthing, but the facial expression must be fine.

While I sat dozing, not venturing to stand up—I was warm and at peace—certain sounds suddenly detached themselves from the background of the sea's monotonous murmur, and distracted my attention from myself. Someone was rapidly approaching along the path. Reaching the summer-house, the unknown stopped, and there was a sound like a little girl sobbing.

'God, God, when will it all end?' asked a voice like a weeping child's.

To judge by the voice and the weeping it was a girl of between ten and twelve. She came hesitantly into the summer-house, sat down and began half-praying, half-lamenting.

'Merciful heavens!' she said tearfully, drawling out the words. 'This is past all endurance. It would try anyone's patience. I suffer in silence, but I do need something to live for, you must see that. Oh, my God, my God!'

There was more in the same style. I wanted to see the child and speak to her. So as not to frighten her I gave a loud sigh, coughed, and then cautiously struck a match. The bright light flashed in the darkness and illuminated the weeper. It was Kitty.

'Wonders will never cease,' sighed Von Stenberg. 'Black night, murmuring sea, weeping heroine, hero with feeling of cosmic isolation! Good grief, man! All that's lacking is Circassians with daggers.'

'This isn't a tale I'm telling you, it really happened.'

'What if it did? It's all pointless, and as old as the hills.'

'Don't be so quick to find fault. Let me finish.' Ananyev made a gesture of annoyance. 'Don't interrupt, I beg you. I'm talking to the doctor, not you.

'Well then.' He addressed himself to me, casting sidelong glances at the young man, who had bent over his abacus and seemed delighted to have baited him a little.

Well then (he went on), Kitty was not surprised or frightened to see me. It was as if she had known beforehand that she would find me in the summer-house. She was gasping and trembling all over, as if in fever. From what I could see, lighting match after match, her tear-stained face had lost its former intelligent, submissive, weary expression and changed into something that I still utterly fail to interpret. It conveyed nothing—neither pain, alarm nor anguish—of what was expressed in the words and tears. And it was probably because I failed to interpret it that, as I have to admit, I took her expression to be meaningless and the result of intoxication.

'I can't go on,' she muttered in her weeping little girl's voice. 'I can't cope, Nicholas, I'm sorry, I can't live like this. I'll go to my mother's in town. Take me there, for God's sake.'

When confronted by tears I could neither speak nor remain silent. I was flustered, and muttered some nonsense to console her.

'Yes, yes, I'll go to my mother's,' said Kitty resolutely, standing up and convulsively clutching my arm, her hands and sleeves being wet with tears. 'I'm sorry, Nicholas, but I'm going. I just can't bear any more.'

'But there are no cabs. How will you get there?'

'Don't worry, I'll walk. It's not far. It's just that I can't——'

I was disconcerted, but not profoundly moved. Her tears, her trembling, the blank look in her eyes—all suggested some trivial

French or Ukrainian melodrama where every cheap and empty dram of woe is drenched in gallons of tears. I didn't understand her, was aware of not doing so, and I should have said nothing. Yet, for some reason—probably to prevent my silence being interpreted as stupidity —I thought fit to urge her not to go to her mother's, but to stay at home. When people cry they like their tears to go unobserved, but I lit match after match, and went on striking till the box was empty. Why I needed this ungracious illumination I still have no idea, but it's true that the emotionally frigid are often awkward and downright stupid.

In the end she took my arm and we left. We passed through the gate, turned right and strolled slowly down the soft, dusty road. It was dark, but after my eyes had gradually grown used to it I began to discern the silhouettes of the gaunt old oaks and limes bordering the road. Soon, on our right, dimly loomed a black streak of jagged, precipitous cliff, traversed here and there by deep chines and gullies. Near them nestled low bushes like seated human figures. The atmosphere was eerie. I squinted suspiciously at the cliff, and by now the sea's murmur and the silence of the countryside were alarming my imagination. Kitty did not speak. She was still trembling, and before we had gone a few hundred yards she was exhausted by the walk and out of breath. I too remained silent.

Less than a mile from the Quarantine is an abandoned four-storey building with a very tall chimney. Once a steam flour-mill, it stands in isolation near the cliff, and is visible from far away over sea and land in daytime. The fact that it was abandoned, had no one living in it, and possessed an echo that exactly repeated the footsteps and voices of passers-by—all this gave it an air of mystery. Picture me in the dark night, arm in arm with a woman who is running away from her husband, beside this long, tall hulk that echoes all my steps and gazes unmovingly at me with a hundred black windows. Under the circumstances any normal young man would have succumbed to romantic urges. But not I.

'This is all very impressive,' I thought, looking at the dark windows. 'But a time will come when, of that building, of Kitty and her grief, and of me and my thoughts, not one grain of dust will remain. All is emptiness and vanity.'

When we reached the flour-mill she suddenly stopped and took her arm out of mine. 'I know you're puzzled by all this, Nicholas.' She had stopped talking like a little girl and was speaking in her normal voice. 'But I'm terribly unhappy—how unhappy you can have no idea. No one could. I'm not discussing it because it's not the sort of thing you *can* discuss. Ah me, what a life, what——'

Kitty broke off, clenched her teeth and groaned as if making every effort not to scream with pain.

'What a life,' she repeated with horror in the lilting, southern, slightly Ukrainian accent that gives animated speech a singing cadence, especially a woman's. 'What a life! God, God, God, what does it mean?'

As if trying to solve the riddle of her existence, she shrugged her shoulders in bewilderment, shook her head and flung up her arms. She spoke in her sing-song voice, she moved gracefully and beautifully, and she reminded me of a certain well-known Ukrainian actress.

'God, I feel buried alive!' She was wringing her hands. 'If only I could have one minute of the sort of happiness other people enjoy! Heavens, I've sunk to running away from my husband at night in a strange man's company, like a loose woman! What good can come of that?'

As I admired her movements and voice, I suddenly found myself delighted at her being on bad terms with her husband. The idea of its being 'nice to have an affair with her' popped up—a callous notion that became fixed in my brain, haunting me all the way, and tickling my fancy more and more.

About a mile from the flour-mill we had to take a left turn past the cemetery to the town. At the corner of the cemetery is a stone windmill with the miller's small hut beside it. We passed the mill and hut, turned left and reached the cemetery gates. Here she stopped.

'I'm going back,' she said. 'You carry on, and God bless you, but I'm going back. I'm not afraid.'

'But that's ridiculous!' I was aghast. 'If you're leaving, then you'd better leave.'

'I shouldn't have been so hasty. It was all over a trifle. You and your talk reminded me of the past and put all sorts of ideas in my mind. I felt sad and wanted to cry, and my husband was rude to me in front of that officer. I lost my temper. But what's the point of my going to town to my mother's? Will it make me any happier? I must go back home.' Kitty laughed. 'Oh, all right, let's go on then. It makes no difference.'

I remembered the inscription on the cemetery gate: 'For the hour is coming, in the which all that are in the graves shall hear his voice.'

I was well aware that a time would come sooner or later when Kitty and I, her husband, and the officer in the white tunic would all lie under the dark trees beyond a wall. I knew that an unhappy, humiliated fellow-creature was walking by my side. Of all that I was clearly aware, but at the same time I was troubled by the disagreeable and unnerving fear that Kitty would turn back, and that I would lose the chance of telling her what was on my mind. At no other time have thoughts so loftily poetical been so interwoven in my brain with the lowest and most bestial prose. A dreadful business!

Not far from the cemetery we found a cab, and took it to the High Street, where Kitty's mother lived, then dismissed the driver and set off down the pavement. Kitty said nothing, while I looked at her, angry with myself. 'Why don't you start? Now's the time.' About twenty yards from my hotel she stopped near a lamp and burst into tears.

'I'll never forget your kindness, Nicholas.' She was laughing and crying at the same time, while gazing into my face with shiny, tearful eyes. 'What a fine man you are! And what splendid fellows you all are—honest, generous, sincere, clever! Isn't it marvellous!'

She saw me as an intellectual, as a thoroughly progressive man. Besides the ecstatic delight aroused in her by my person, her tear-stained, laughing face also expressed regret that she so rarely met such men, and that God had not granted her the happiness of being the wife of one. 'Isn't it marvellous?' she muttered.

The childlike joy in her expression, the tears, the gentle smile, the soft hair straying under her shawl, the shawl itself—thrown carelessly over her head—in the lamplight they reminded me of the Kitty whom I had wanted to stroke like a cat in the old days.

I could not help stroking her hair, shoulders, arms. 'Well, what is it you want, my dear?' I mumbled. 'Shall we go to the ends of the earth together? I'll take you away from this dump, I'll give you happiness. I love you. Shall we go, my darling? Well, shall we?'

Her face expressed bewilderment. She stepped back from the lamp and stared at me dumbfounded with huge eyes. I clutched her arm and began showering her face, neck and shoulders with kisses while I continued making promises and vows. Oaths and promises are practically a physiological necessity in love affairs. They are indispensable. Sometimes you know that you're lying, and that the promises aren't necessary, yet swear and promise you do. Meanwhile the astounded Kitty kept backing away and looking at me round-eyed.

'Stop, stop!' she muttered, pushing me off with her hands.

I clasped her tightly to me, but she suddenly burst into hysterical tears, and her face took on the blank, expressionless look that I had noticed when lighting matches in the summer-house. Without asking her consent, preventing her from speaking, I forcibly dragged her into my hotel. She seemed stunned and would not walk, but I took her by the arm and almost carried her. As we went upstairs, I remember, someone wearing a cap with a red band gave me a surprised look and bowed to her.

Ananyev blushed and stopped talking. He paced silently round the table, irritably scratched the back of his head, and several times hunched his shoulders and shoulder-blades convulsively, feeling a chill run down his large back. He was shamed and crushed by his memories, and he was struggling with himself.

'A bad business.' He drank a glass of wine and shook his head. 'At every introductory lecture on gynaecology medical students are said to be given this advice. "Before undressing and examining a sick woman, remember that you too have a mother, a sister, a fiancée." This advice wouldn't come amiss to anyone, medical student or not, who has any dealings with women. Oh, how well I understand it now that I have a wife and daughter myself—my God, I do! But you may as well hear the rest of it.'

Having become my mistress, Kitty viewed the matter differently from me. Above all, she loved me passionately and profoundly. What was an ordinary flirtation to me—to her it was the transformation of her whole life. I remember thinking she must have gone out of her mind. Happy for the first time in her life, looking five years younger, with an inspired, ecstatic expression, so happy that she did not know what to do with herself, she laughed and cried by turns, never ceasing to voice her dreams about us going to the Caucasus on the next day and then to St. Petersburg in the autumn, and about how we would live afterwards.

'Now, don't worry about my husband,' she said reassuringly. 'He's bound to give me a divorce. All the town knows he's sleeping with the elder Kostovich girl. We'll get a divorce and marry.'

When women are in love they become acclimatized, adapting themselves to people quickly, like cats. She had only been in the hotel room with me for an hour and a half, but she already felt at home there, and was treating my things as her own. She packed my case, told me off for not hanging my expensive new coat on a hook instead of tossing it on a chair like an old rag, and so on.

I looked at her, I listened, and I felt weary and irritated. I was rather put out to think that a decent, respectable, unhappy woman had, in some three or four hours, so readily yielded to the first man she had met. I disliked this in my own capacity as a respectable man, if you take my meaning. And then I was somewhat repelled by women of her type being shallow, superficial and too keen on having a good time, and by them even equating so essentially trivial a phenomenon as love for a man with their happiness, their suffering and the transformation of their whole existence. Besides, now that I had had what I wanted I was annoyed at my own foolishness in becoming entangled with a woman whom, like it or not, I should be compelled to deceive. May I add that, disorganized though my life was, I could not bear telling lies?

I remember her sitting at my feet, putting her head on my lap and looking at me, her eyes shining with love. 'Do you love me, Nicholas?' she asked. 'Very, very much?'

She laughed for sheer happiness. I found this sentimental, mawkish and stupid, being in a mood to make 'intellectual depth', as I called it, my main target in life.

'You'd better go home,' I told her. 'Otherwise your relatives are sure to miss you and start looking for you all over town. It's awkward, too, that it will be practically dawn when you get to your mother's.'

She agreed, and as we parted we arranged to meet at noon next day in the park, and to go on to Pyatigorsk on the day after. I went into the street to see her to the house, and I remember how tenderly and sincerely I caressed her on the way. There was a moment when her unconditional trust suddenly moved me to pity greater than I could endure, and I almost decided that I would indeed take her to Pyatigorsk. Remembering, however, that I had only six hundred roubles in my suitcase, and that it would be much harder to break things off in the autumn than now, I hastened to suppress my pity.

We came to the house where her mother lived, and I pulled the bell. When footsteps were heard behind the door Kitty suddenly looked grave, glanced up at the sky, quickly made the sign of the cross over me several times as if over a child, and then seized my hand, pressing it to her lips.

'Till tomorrow.' She vanished into the house.

I crossed to the opposite pavement and looked at the house from there. The windows were dark at first, but then one of them revealed the faint, bluish flare of a candle being lit. The light grew, emitting rays, and I saw it move from room to room accompanied by shadows. 'They weren't expecting her,' I thought.

Returning to my hotel room, I undressed, drank some Santorin, ate some fresh unpressed caviare that I had bought at the market that day, slowly went to bed and slept the tourist's deep, untroubled sleep.

Next morning I woke with a headache. I was in a bad mood, and something was bothering me. 'What's the matter,' I wondered, trying to explain my unease. 'What's the trouble?'

I ascribed my disquiet to a fear that Kitty might turn up at any moment and stop me leaving, and that I should have to dissimulate and tell lies. I quickly dressed, packed and left the hotel, telling the porter to bring my luggage to the station by seven that evening. I spent the whole day with a doctor friend, and left town in the evening. As you see, the profundity of my meditations did not prevent me from treacherously and meanly making myself scarce.

All the time I was with my friend, and later, when driving to the station, I was painfully ill at ease. I put it down to fear of Kitty meeting me and making a scene. At the station I deliberately sat in the cloak-room till the second bell rang, and on the way to my carriage I felt weighed down, felt as if I was dressed from head to foot in stolen articles. How impatiently and fearfully I awaited the third bell!

But then it rang, bringing my deliverance, and the train started. We passed the prison and the barracks, and came into open country, but the feeling of uneasiness persisted, to my great surprise, and I still felt like a thief obsessed with the urge to flee. Odd, wasn't it? To distract and calm myself I looked out of the window. The train was running along the coast. The sea was smooth, mirroring the serene turquoise sky, almost half of which was tinged with the delicate gold-crimson hue of the sunset. Black fishing boats and rafts dotted the surface here and there. Clean and spruce as a new toy, the town stood on a high cliff, and was already becoming shrouded in the evening mist. The churches' gilded domes, the windows, the greenery—all reflected the setting sun, burning and melting like molten gold. The scent of the fields blended with the delicate damp smell blowing in from the sea.

The train ran swiftly on. Passengers and conductors laughed, every-one was merry and light-hearted, but my mysterious unease kept growing and growing. I looked at the light mist veiling the town, imagining that somewhere in it, near the churches and houses, a woman was rushing here and there with a blank, expressionless look, searching for me and groaning 'Oh God, God!' in a little girl's voice, or in a sing-song cadence like a Ukrainian actress. I remembered her grave mien and large, troubled eyes when she had made the sign of the cross over me on the previous day as if I belonged to her, and I instinctively glanced at the hand that she had kissed.

'Surely I'm not in love?' I wondered, scratching my hand.

Only with nightfall, when the other passengers were asleep and I was left alone with my conscience, did I begin to see what I had been unable to grasp earlier. In the twilight of the carriage Kitty's image haunted me, and I now clearly recognized that I had committed a crime as bad as murder. My conscience tortured me. To suppress this intolerable sensation I told myself that all was emptiness and vanity, that Kitty and I would die and decay, that her grief was nothing compared to death, and so forth—and also that there was no such thing as free will in the last resort, and therefore I was not to blame. But all these considerations only irritated me, and were rapidly brushed aside by other thoughts. There was an aching sensation in the hand kissed by Kitty. I kept lying down and getting up again, I drank vodka at the stations, I forced myself to eat sandwiches, and once again took to arguing that life was meaningless. But it did no good at all. A strange and, if you like, comic ferment was working in my mind. The most heterogeneous thoughts towered up untidily on top of each other, mingling and impeding one another, while I, the thinker, bowed my head forward, understood nothing, and was simply unable to find my bearings in this clutter of notions relevant and irrelevant. It transpired that I, the great thinker, had not even mastered the elements of thinking, and that I was no more capable of deploying my own intellect than of repairing a watch. I was intently concentrating my brain for the first time in my life, and this seemed such an abnormality that I thought I was going mad. A man whose brain is active only sporadically, and at times of pressure, is often subject to delusions of insanity.

I suffered like this for a night, a day and another night. Once I had realized how little my meditations helped me, I saw the light and knew at last what kind of a creature I was. I realized that my notions weren't worth a brass farthing, and that before meeting Kitty I had never even begun thinking—had even lacked any conception of what serious thought meant. Now, having suffered so much, I realized that I possessed neither convictions nor a definite moral code, neither heart nor reason. My entire intellectual and moral resources consisted of specialized knowledge, fragments, useless memories, other people's ideas—and nothing more. My mental processes were as unsophisticated, crude and primitive as a Yakut's. If I disliked lying, stealing, murdering, while on the whole avoiding egregiously gross errors, this was not through my convictions—I had none—but only because I was bound hand and foot by nursery tales and copy-book ethics that had become part of my flesh and blood, and had guided me through life without my being aware of it, even though I considered them absurd.

I realized that I was neither a thinker nor a philosopher but simply a dilettante. God had given me a strong, healthy Russian brain and the rudiments of talent. Now, imagine this brain in its twenty-sixth year— untrained, not in the least stale, uncluttered by any kind of luggage, and just lightly besprinkled with a little information in the engineering line. The young brain instinctively craves activity and is on the look- out for it, when it is suddenly and quite arbitrarily assailed from with- out by this' lovely, juicy concept—the pointlessness of life and the darkness of the grave. The brain ravenously gulps this in, assigns it all the available space, and begins playing all sorts of cat-and-mouse games with it. The brain is innocent of systematic erudition, but no matter. It handles wide-ranging speculation on the basis of its own innate resources—typical self-taught-man stuff. Not a month passes without the brain's proprietor cooking up a hundred tasty dishes consisting exclusively of potatoes, and fancying himself a thinker.

Your generation has carried this amateurism, this toying with serious thinking, into science, literature, politics, and into every other field that it has not been too lazy to enter. Together with the dilettante approach it has also introduced emotional sterility, boredom, one- sidedness. My impression is that it has already contrived to teach the masses a new and unprecedented attitude to serious ideas.

It was through misfortune that I came to comprehend and assess my own aberrations and all-round ignorance. And my sanity, I now feel, dates only from the time when I started learning the alphabet— when my conscience drove me back to N., and when, without making any bones about it, I told Kitty how sorry I was, asked her to forgive me, as a child might, and mingled my tears with hers.

After briefly describing his last meeting with Kitty, Ananyev fell silent.

'Ah well,' the student brought out through closed teeth when Ananyev had finished. 'Such things do happen in this world.'

His face still expressed intellectual inertia, and Ananyev's story had obviously not touched him at all. Only when, after a brief pause, the engineer once more began deploying his ideas, and repeating his earlier sentiments—only then did the student frown irritably, get up from table and go to his bed. He made the bed and began undressing.

'You look as if you think you'd actually converted someone,' he said exasperatedly.

'Me—convert anyone?' asked the engineer. 'My dear fellow, do I make any such claim? May God forgive you! There's no possibility of converting you, for conversion can only come through personal experience and suffering.'

'And then your way of arguing is so grotesque,' grumbled the student as he put his nightshirt on. 'The thoughts that you so strongly dislike as fatal to the young—they're perfectly normal for the old, as you yourself admit. It's as if it were a matter of grey hairs! But why should the old enjoy this privilege? On what principle? If these thoughts indeed are poisonous, then they're equally poisonous for everyone.'

'Oh no, my dear fellow, don't say such things,' remarked the engineer with a sly wink. 'Don't, please. In the first place old men aren't dilettantes. Their pessimism doesn't reach them from outside, nor yet by accident, but from the depths of their own minds, and only after they have studied the Hegels, the Kants and so on, only after they've suffered a lot, and made no end of mistakes—in fact, only after they've climbed the entire ladder from bottom to top. Their pessimism has both personal experience and sound philosophical training behind it. Secondly, the pessimism of these elderly philosophers isn't just a lot of mumbo-jumbo, as it is with you and me—it comes from the pain and suffering of the whole world. Theirs has a Christian foundation because it springs from love of man, and from thoughts about humanity totally lacking the egoism of your typical amateur. You despise life because its meaning and purpose are hidden from you in particular, and you fear only your own death. But the true philosopher suffers because the truth is hidden from all men, and his fears are for humanity at large. For instance, there's a government forestry officer living not far from here, an Ivan Aleksandrovich—a nice old boy who was once some sort of teacher, and used to do a bit of writing. Just what he's been the devil only knows, but he's a jolly brainy sort of chap and a dab hand at philosophy. He used to read a lot, and now he reads all the time. Well, I came across him not long ago on the Gruzovo sector at a time when they were laying sleepers and rails. It was easy work, but to old Ivan, who was a non-specialist, it seemed almost like magic.

'To lay a sleeper and fix the rail to it your skilled workman needs less than a minute. Well, the men were in good form, working smartly and quickly. There was one old reprobate in particular who had the knack of catching the nail just right and driving it home with a single blow of the hammer. Now, the handle of that hammer was nearly seven foot long, and each nail was a foot long! Old Ivan looked at the workers for a long time and was enchanted by them.

' "What a pity that these splendid men will die," he said to me with tears in his eyes. Now, such pessimism I do understand.'

'All that proves nothing and explains nothing.' The young man pulled his sheet over him. 'It's all a lot of hot air. Nobody knows anything, and words can prove nothing.'

He looked out from under the sheet and raised his head. 'One is very naïve if one believes in human thought and logic, and attaches overriding significance to humanity.' He spoke rapidly, with an irritated frown. 'You can prove and disprove any proposition you like in words, and men will soon perfect verbal acrobatics to the point where they will demonstrate that twice two is seven by the laws of mathematics. I like listening and reading, but I can't manage acts of faith, with due respect, and I don't want to. I shall believe only in God. As for you, you can go on talking till the cows come home, and seduce another five hundred Kitties, but I'll only believe you when I've gone off my head. Good night.'

The young man hid his head under the sheet and turned his face to the wall to show that he did not want to hear or say any more. With this the argument ended.

Before retiring I went out of the barracks with the engineer and saw the lights again.

'We have wearied you with our chatter.' Ananyev yawned and looked at the sky. 'Ah well, never mind, old man. One's only satisfaction in this boring dump is drinking and talking about things. What an embankment, ye Gods!' he said delightedly, when we came up to it. 'It's a regular Mount Ararat.'

'These lights remind the Baron of the Amalekites, but to me they're like human thoughts,' he said after a short pause. 'Each individual's thoughts are similarly chaotic and disordered, you know, and yet they do march towards some destination in single file through darkness. They illuminate nothing, they do not make the night clear, and they vanish somewhere far beyond the bounds of old age. However, enough of this idle talk! It's time for bed.'

When we got back to the hut the engineer was insistent in offering me his own bed to sleep on. 'Do take it,' he implored me, pressing both his hands to his heart. 'I beg you to. Don't worry about me. I can sleep anywhere—and, besides, I'm staying up for a while. You'll be doing me a favour.'

I accepted, undressed and lay down, while he sat at the table and took up his drawings.

'The likes of us don't have time to sleep, old man,' he said in an undertone after I had got into bed and shut my eyes. 'A man with a wife and a couple of kids is too busy for it. It's feed and clothe them now, and save money for their future. And I've two of them—a son and a daughter. The son has a jolly little face. He's not six yet, but he's remarkably able, I can tell you. I have their photographs somewhere. Oh, my children, my children!'

He rummaged in his papers, found the pictures and began looking at them. I fell asleep.

I was woken by Azorka's barking and loud voices. Von Stenberg—in underclothes, barefoot and unkempt—was standing in the doorway talking loudly to someone. Dawn was breaking, and its mournful, dark blue light peeped through the door, the windows and the cracks in the walls, faintly illuminating my bed, the table with the papers and Ananyev. Stretched on the floor on his cloak, puffing out his beefy, hairy chest, with a leather cushion under his head, he was asleep, snoring so loudly that I felt heartily sorry for the young man who had to share the room with him every night.

'Why on earth should we take delivery?' shouted Von Stenberg. 'It's nothing to do with us. Go and see the other engineer, Mr. Chalisov. Who sent these boilers?'

'Nikitin,' a deep voice gruffly answered.

'Then go and see Chalisov. This has nothing to do with us. What the hell are you hanging around for? Be on your way.'

'Sir, we've already been to Mr. Chalisov,' said the bass voice even more gruffly. 'We was looking for the gentleman up and down the line all day yesterday, and 'twas in his hut we was told he'd gone to the Dymkovo sector, sir. Be so kind as to take delivery—we can't lug them up and down the line for ever. It's been cart them here and cart them there, there ain't no end to it.'

'What is it?' asked Ananyev in a hoarse voice as he woke and quickly raised his head.

'They've brought some boilers from Nikitin,' said the young man. 'They want us to take them, but what concern is it of ours?'

'Tell them to go to hell!'

'Do us a favour, guv'nor, and sort it out for us. The horses ain't had nothing to eat for two days, and the boss is real peeved, for sure. We can't cart them back again! The railway ordered boilers, so they should take delivery.'

'Can't you see it's no concern of ours, you oaf? Go and see Chalisov.'

'What's this? Who's there?' repeated Ananyev hoarsely. 'Oh, damn and blast them!' He got up and went to the door. 'What's up?'

I dressed and went out of the hut two minutes later. Ananyev and the student, both in their underclothes, both barefoot, were forcefully and impatiently making their explanations to a peasant who stood before them with his hat off, holding a whip, and who obviously did not understand them. Both had the air of men preoccupied with everyday trivialities.

'What do I want with your boilers?' Ananyev shouted. 'Want me to wear them on my head? If you couldn't find Chalisov, then find his assistant and leave us in peace.'

Seeing me, Von Stenberg probably remembered the previous night's conversation, for the careworn look vanished from his sleepy face, being replaced by his expression of mental inertia. He waved the peasant away, and went off to one side deep in thought.

The morning was overcast. Along the line, where the lights had shone at night, were swarming navvies who had just woken up. Voices were heard, and the creak of wheelbarrows. The day's work had begun. One little horse, in a rope harness, was already trudging off to the embankment, stretching its neck for all it was worth, and pulling a cartload of sand.

I began saying good-bye. Much had been said that night, but I had no neat solutions to take away with me. As for all the talk, nothing of it remained on memory's filter in the morning but the lights and Kitty's image. Getting on my horse, I cast a last glance at Von Stenberg and Ananyev, at the hysterical dog with its dull, tipsy-looking eyes, at the navvies glimpsed through the morning mist, at the embankment, at the little horse straining its neck.

'Nothing in this world makes sense,' thought I.

When I had struck the horse and cantered down the line, and when, a little later, I could see nothing before me but the endless, lugubrious plain and the cold, overcast sky, I remembered the questions that had been aired that night. And, while I pondered, the sun-parched plain, the huge sky, the dark oak wood looming far ahead, the misty horizons —all seemed to say that 'No, indeed, nothing in this world makes sense.'

The sun began to rise.

THE PRINCESS

THROUGH the large 'Red Gate' of the monastery at N. drove a carriage drawn by four sleek, handsome horses. Monks and novices were crowding round the part of the guest-house reserved for the gentry. Recognizing the coachman and horses from afar, they knew that the lady in the carriage was their good friend Princess Vera.

An old man in livery jumped off the box and helped the Princess down. Raising her dark veil, she slowly went up to each monk to receive his blessing, then nodded charmingly to the novices and proceeded indoors.

'Did you miss little me, then?' she asked the monks who were carrying her things. 'It's a whole month since your Princess was here. Well, here she is again, so have a good look at her. And where's the reverend abbot? Heavens, I'm just dying to see him! That wonderful, wonderful old man—you should be proud of such an abbot.'

When the abbot came in, the Princess gave an enraptured shriek, crossed her hands on her breast and went to receive his blessing.

'No, no, you must let me kiss your hand,' she said, clutching it and kissing it avidly three times. 'Delighted to see you at last, Father. I'm quite sure you've forgotten tiny me, but my thoughts have been with your dear monastery every minute of the day. Oh, isn't this wonderful! Living for God, far away from the world's vanities—it has a special charm, Father, I feel it in the very depths of my soul, though I can't put it into words.'

Her cheeks flushed, tears starting from her eyes, she spoke ardently without pausing for breath, while the abbot—an old man of seventy, grave, ugly and shy—said nothing beyond an occasional jerky utterance in military style.

'Just so, madam. Very well, madam. I understand, madam.'

'How long may we hope to be honoured by this visit?' he asked.

'I shall stay here tonight. Tomorrow I'll go and see Claudia Nikolayevna, whom I haven't met for ages, then I'll come back here the day after that and stay three or four days. I seek rest for my soul here, Father.'

The Princess loved staying at N. Monastery. She had taken a fancy to the place in the last two years, coming almost every month in summer and staying two or three days—sometimes a whole week.

The timid novices, the stillness, the low ceilings, the smell of cypress-wood, the modest fare, the cheap curtains on the windows—these things all touched her, moved her, disposing her to contemplation and good thoughts. She only had to spend half an hour in these rooms to feel that she too was timid, modest, cypress-scented. The past vanished far away, losing all meaning, and the Princess began to think that she was very much like the old abbot despite her twenty-nine years—she, like him, being born not for wealth, worldly greatness or love, but for a tranquil life of seclusion, the twilight life of these chambers.

Into the dark cell of a hermit plunged deep in prayer a shaft of light may suddenly chance to peep, or a little bird may settle on his window-sill and sing its song. The grim anchorite cannot but smile, while in that breast weighed down by penitence a stream of quiet, innocent joy suddenly gushes like a spring from behind a rock. Just such comfort, the Princess felt, as that ray of sunshine or little bird did she herself bring with her from outside. Her gay, disarming smile, her tender glance, her voice, her jokes, her whole being, so small, so well-proportioned in this simple black dress—the mere sight of her could not but awaken joyous rapture in these simple, severe men. 'An angel sent from heaven'—so everyone was bound to think on looking at her.

No one could help thinking so—which thought made her smile a smile still more disarming, and try to look like a little bird.

After tea and a rest, she went out for a stroll. The sun had already set. The monastery flower-bed breathed on the Princess the fragrant damp of freshly watered mignonette, the soft singing of male voices was wafted over from the church, seeming very agreeable and mournful from afar. Evensong was in progress. The dark windows where icon-lamps glimmered, the shadows, the figure of an old monk sitting in the church porch near the icon with a collection-box—these things expressed a calm so untroubled that the Princess somehow felt moved to tears.

Beyond the gate, in the avenue between wall and birch-trees, where the benches stood, evening had already come on, and the sky was growing darker every moment.

The Princess strolled along the avenue, and sat on a bench deep in thought.

How wonderful, she thought, to settle down for life in this monastery, where existence was quiet and untroubled as a summer evening. How wonderful to forget all about the ungrateful, dissipated Prince, her huge property, the creditors who pestered her daily, her mishaps, her maid Dasha, who had looked so pert that morning. It would be wonderful to sit out the rest of her days on this bench, gazing between birch trunks at puffs of evening mist drifting down there at the bottom of the hill, at the rooks flying over the wood like a black veil of cloud to their night's rest far, far away, and at the two novices—one on a piebald horse, the other on foot—driving the horses to their night's pasture, enjoying their freedom and frisking like small children. Their young voices rang in the still air, and every word could be heard. It was wonderful to sit and listen to the silence. A breath of wind touches the tips of the birches, a frog rustles in last year's dead leaves, a clock strikes the quarter beyond the wall.

Oh to sit still, to listen and just go on thinking.

An old woman with a knapsack passed. The Princess thought it would be wonderful to stop her and say something charming and sincere to help her on her way.

But the old woman disappeared round the corner without once looking back.

Shortly afterwards a tall, grey-bearded man in a straw hat appeared in the avenue. He took off his hat and bowed as he passed the Princess, and she knew him by his large bald patch and sharp, hooked nose as a Dr. Michael Ivanovich who had been in her service five years previously on her estate of Dubovki. The doctor's wife had died a year ago, she remembered someone telling her, and she felt the urge to offer him a little sympathy and consolation.

'I'm sure you don't recognize me, Doctor,' she said with her disarming smile.

'Indeed I do, madam,' said the doctor, once more removing his hat.

'Well, how nice of you—I thought you'd quite forgotten poor little me. People only remember their enemies, they forget their friends. And have you come here to pray?'

'I spend every Saturday night here, it's my job—I'm the doctor here.'

'Now, how are you?' sighed the Princess. 'I heard of your wife's death. How unfortunate!'

'Yes, madam, it is indeed unfortunate for me.'

'It can't be helped. We must bear misfortunes humbly. Not one hair falls from a man's head without the will of Providence.'

'No, madam.'

The Princess's sighs and sweet, disarming smile provoked from the doctor only a cold, dry 'No, madam,' and his facial expression was cold and dry too.

'What else can I say?' she wondered.

'It's so long since we met, though,' she said. 'It's five years. A lot of water has flowed under the bridge in that time. There have been so many changes, it's quite a frightening thought. I got married, you know —became a princess instead of a countess. I've already managed to become separated from my husband.'

'So I'd heard.'

'God has sent me many trials. I'm almost ruined—you've probably heard that too. My places at Dubovki, Kiryakovo and Sofyino have been sold to pay my wretched husband's debts. I only have Baranovo and Mikhaltsevo left. It's terrible to look back—so many changes and misfortunes of various kinds, so many mistakes.'

'Yes, madam, a great many mistakes.'

The Princess was slightly put out. Though she knew her own mistakes, they were all of so intimate a nature that only she could think and speak of them.

'What mistakes have you in mind?' she could not resist asking.

'Since you mention them, you presumably know what they are,' the doctor answered with a laugh. 'Why talk about them?'

'Do tell me, Doctor, I'll be most grateful. And don't stand on ceremony with me, please, I love hearing the truth.'

'I'm not your judge, madam.'

'Not my judge? If you take that tone with me, you really must know something. Tell me.'

'Very well, if you wish. But I'm not very good at putting things, unfortunately, I don't always make myself clear.'

The doctor thought for a moment.

'You've made many mistakes,' he began. 'But the main one really, I think, is the general atmosphere, er, prevailing, er, on all your country estates. As you see, I can't express myself very well. The main thing, I mean, is a dislike of other people—an absolutely all-pervading loathing. Your whole way of life's built on this loathing—a loathing for people's voices and faces, for the backs of their heads, for the way they walk—for everything, in fact, that makes a human being. At all your doors, on all your stairways, you have sleek, boorish, lazy liveried footmen to keep out improperly dressed callers. In your hall are chairs with high backs to stop the servants' heads dirtying the wall-paper during balls and receptions. Your rooms all have thick carpets to silence human footsteps. All your visitors are unfailingly warned to speak softly and as little as possible, and to make no remark which might affect the imagination and nerves adversely. You don't shake hands with people in your private room, or ask them to sit down—exactly as you didn't shake hands with me, or ask me to sit down, just now.'

'All right, if you wish,' said the Princess, holding out her hand and smiling. 'But really, to be angry over something so trivial——'

'I'm not angry, though, am I?' laughed the doctor—but at once flushed, took off his hat and waved it about as he started speaking heatedly.

'To be quite frank, I've been looking for a chance for some time to get all this off my chest. What I mean is, you're like Napoleon—everyone's so much cannon-fodder to you. But Napoleon at least had some ideas, whereas you have nothing except this loathing.'

'Me—loathe people!' smiled the Princess, shrugging her shoulders in amazement. 'Me!'

'Oh yes, you do. Want facts? Very well then. There are three of your old chefs living on charity at Mikhaltsevo after going blind in your kitchens from the heat of the ovens. You and your parasites have taken all the fit, strong, good-looking people on your countless acres to be your footmen, flunkeys and coachmen. This herd of bipeds has been trained in servility. They've stuffed themselves with food, they've grown coarse—in other words, they've lost the "image and likeness of God".

'Young medical men, experts in agriculture, teachers, professional people in general—you uproot them from an honest job of hard work, by God, and force them to earn their livelihood by acting in farcical puppet-shows embarrassing to any decent man. A young fellow hasn't served three years like this before he becomes a hypocritical toady and slanderer.

'It's not right, is it? Your Polish overseers, those scoundrelly, snooping Kazimierzes and Kajetans, prowl about your countless acres morning noon and night, trying to satisfy you by squeezing a quart out of every pint pot. I'm sorry, I'm not putting it properly, but that doesn't matter. To you common folk don't rate as human. And as for those princes, counts and bishops who've visited you—they were only an ornament to you, not living people. But the main, er, yes, the main thing—what riles me most—is that you possess a fortune of over a million roubles, yet do nothing for other people, nothing whatever.'

Astonished, shocked and offended, the Princess sat there, not knowing what to say or how to behave. No one had ever taken this tone

with her before. The doctor's disagreeable, angry voice, and his fumbling, halting speech, grated on her ears. It made her head throb, until
she felt as if the gesticulating doctor was hitting her over the head with
his hat.

'This isn't true,' she said quickly, as if pleading. 'I've done a great
deal for other people, and you know it.'

'Oh, stuff and nonsense!' the doctor shouted. 'Your work for charity
—don't tell me you still take that seriously as a useful activity, and not
a puppet-show! Why, it's been a farce all the way through—a pretence
of loving your neighbour, play-acting at its most blatant, as even
children and stupid village women could see! Take for instance your—
what's it called?—Rest Home for Lonely Old Ladies, where you made
me Head Physician or something, and you yourself were Honorary
Warden. What a charming establishment, Lord love us! They build
a house with parquet floors and a weather-vane on the roof, they
round up a dozen old women in the villages, and make them sleep
under fluffy blankets, on sheets of Dutch linen and eat fruit drops.'

The doctor snorted into his hat with malicious glee.

'It was all play-acting!' he continued in his rapid, halting speech.
'The junior staff of the Home keep the blankets and sheets locked up
to stop the old ladies soiling them—the old bitches can sleep on the
floor, damn them! The old ladies don't dare sit on a bed, put on a
jacket or walk on the smooth parquet. Everything's kept ready for
inspection and stowed away, as if the old ladies were going to steal it,
while they get their food and clothing by begging on the quiet, praying
God day and night for a speedy release from custody—and from the
improving admonishments of the fat swine you put in charge of them.
And what of your senior staff? Now, this is really priceless! Two
evenings a week up canter "thirty-five thousand couriers" to proclaim
that the Princess—you—will visit the Home on the morrow. On the
morrow, then, I have to jettison my patients, and parade in my best
suit. Very well then, I arrive. The old ladies have been put in clean,
new dresses and are waiting drawn up for inspection. Around them
prowls that retired sergeant-major type, your head warder, with his
sickly, traitorous smile. The old women yawn and look at each other
without daring to murmur. We all wait. Up gallops your under-
bailiff. Half an hour later up roars your senior bailiff, then the bailiff-
in-chief of your estates followed by someone else, and then somebody
else again—all wearing solemn, enigmatic expressions. We wait on
and on. We shift from foot to foot. We look at the clock—all this in

the deathly silence of people who are completely at loggerheads and loathe the sight of each other. One hour passes, then another—until finally your carriage appears in the distance and, and——'

The doctor uttered a shrill peal of laughter.

'You descend from your carriage,' he went on in a high-pitched voice, 'and at a word of command from the old soldier, the old witches begin singing:

"The Glory of our Lord in Zion
The tongue of man cannot describe."

Not bad, eh?'

The doctor went off into a deep chuckle, with a gesture which seemed to say that he could not speak one word for laughing. His was a heavy, harsh laugh through tightly clenched teeth, not the laugh of a kindly person. His voice, his face, his glittering eyes with their tinge of insolence—all showed how deeply he despised the Princess, her Home and her old ladies.

There was nothing amusing or light-hearted about his crude, fumbling description, but he laughed happily—gaily, even.

'And what of your school?' he went on, gasping in his mirth. 'You wanted to teach the peasant children yourself, remember? And well indeed you must have taught them, because all the boys ran away so fast, they had to be whipped or bribed to come back again. Then there was that business of the breast-fed babies whose mothers were working in the fields—you wanted to bottle-feed them yourself, remember? You went round the village in tears because no babies had been placed at your disposal, the mothers having all taken them along to the fields. Then the village elder ordered the mothers to leave their babies behind for your delectation—on a rota system! It's quite fantastic! Your favours had them all scurrying away like mice before a cat. Now, why all this? It's all very simple! It's not because of your people's ignorance and ungratefulness—your own explanation—but because not one of your projects had a grain of love or charity about it, if you'll pardon my saying so. A nice little game with live dolls—that's what you were after, and that's all there was to it.

'If you can't tell people from lap-dogs, don't go in for charity. Between people and lap-dogs there is, I assure you, a very sizeable difference.'

The Princess's heart throbbed wildly, her ears pounded, and she still felt as if the doctor was hitting her over the head with his hat. The doctor spoke rapidly, fiercely, ungracefully—stuttering, with much superfluous gesture. But all she could see was that the man talking to her was rude, ill-bred, spiteful and ungrateful. What he wanted from her and what he was talking about—that she could not see.

'Go away!' she wept, raising her hands to shield her head from the doctor's hat. 'Go away!'

'And your attitude to your employees!' went on the outraged doctor. 'You don't regard them as human, you treat them like the lowest scallywags! Why, for instance, did you dismiss me, pray? For ten years I served your father, and you after him—loyally, never taking a day off, never having any leave. I win the affection of everyone within a sixty-mile radius—then suddenly, one fine day, I'm told my services are no longer required! Why? That's what I still can't see. I'm a doctor of medicine and a gentleman, I trained at Moscow University, I'm father of a family—that is, I'm such a worm and nonentity that I can be thrown out on my ear without any explanation. Why stand on ceremony with such as me? I learnt afterwards that my wife approached you on three occasions—secretly, without my knowledge —to intercede for me, but not once did you receive her. She broke down and cried in your ante-room, I'm told. And I'll never forgive her even in her grave. Never!'

The doctor paused and clenched his teeth, racking his brains for something highly disagreeable and wounding to add. Another thought came to his mind, and suddenly his cold, frowning face lit up.

'Now, take your attitude to this monastery, for instance,' he said fiercely. 'You've never spared anyone, and the holier the place the more likely it is to fall foul of that tender, ministering angel act. Why ever do you come here? What do you want of these monks, might I ask? What's Hecuba to you or you to Hecuba? It's play-acting all over again, it's all a game—it's a mockery of human dignity, and that's all there is to it. You don't believe in the monks' God, do you? You have your own god in your heart—one attained by the light of your own intellect in spiritualist seances. You look down on the rites of the Church, you don't attend either morning or evening service, you sleep till midday—so why come here? You bring your own god to a monastery where he doesn't belong, imagining that the monastery thinks itself greatly honoured! What a hope! And you might ask, by the way, what your visits cost the monks. You were graciously pleased to arrive this evening, but two days ago there was already a messenger on horse-back here from your estate office with a warning that you were on your way. All day yesterday they were preparing your rooms and expecting you. Today your advance guard arrived—a pert maid who kept running across the yard, swishing her skirts, pestering folk with questions and giving instructions—the sort of thing I can't stand! Today the monks were on the alert all day—they'd be in trouble if they didn't greet you with due ceremony, wouldn't they? You might complain to the bishop! "Those monks don't like me, your Grace, though what I've done to annoy them I don't know. It's true I'm a great sinner, but I'm so unhappy, aren't I?" The monastery alone—it's already been in hot water on your account! The abbot's a busy man, a scholar, he hasn't a minute free, yet you keep sending for him to come to your rooms. You respect neither his age nor his rank. It wouldn't be so bad if you gave them lots of money—at least it wouldn't be so insulting—but all this time the monks haven't had a hundred roubles out of you, now have they?'

When people bothered the Princess, when they misunderstood or offended her—and when feeling at a loss what to say and do—she usually started crying. Now at last she hid her face in her hands and wept in a shrill, childish tone. The doctor suddenly paused and looked at her, his face dark and stern.

'I'm sorry, madam,' he said dully. 'I've indulged in spite, I forgot myself. It was wrong of me.'

Coughing in embarrassment and forgetting to put on his hat, he quickly left the Princess.

The stars were already twinkling in the sky. The moon must be rising on the other side of the monastery, for the sky was clear, translucent, soft-coloured. Bats swooped about silently along the white monastery wall.

A clock slowly struck three-quarters of some hour—a quarter to nine, no doubt. The Princess stood up and went slowly to the gate, feeling offended and weeping. The trees, the stars, the bats—all seemed to pity her, and that clock seemed to strike so melodiously only to show its sympathy for her. As she wept, she thought how nice it would be to spend the rest of her life in a convent. On quiet summer evenings she would stroll alone in its avenues, insulted, injured, misunderstood. God and the starry sky alone would see her tears of martyrdom.

Evensong was still proceeding in the church. The Princess stopped and listened to the singing—how good it sounded in the still, dark air. How sweet to weep and suffer to the sound of such singing!

Reaching her rooms, she looked at her tear-stained face in the mirror, put on some powder, and sat down to supper. The monks knew of her liking for pickled sturgeon, button mushrooms, Malaga wine and plain honey cakes which left a tang of cypress in the mouth, and they would serve her all these things whenever she came. Eating the mushrooms and washing them down with Malaga, she thought how she would end up utterly ruined and deserted, how all her stewards, bailiffs, clerks and maids—for whom she had done so much—would betray her and speak to her rudely, how the entire population of the globe would attack, slander, mock her. She would renounce princely title, luxury and society, she would escape to a convent without a word of reproach to a soul, she would pray for her enemies. Everyone would suddenly appreciate her, they would seek her forgiveness—but by then it would be too late.

After supper she knelt in the corner before the icon, and read two chapters of the Gospels. Then the maid prepared her bed, and she lay down to sleep. Stretching out under the white coverlet, she gave a deep, sweet sigh such as follows weeping, closed her eyes and began to drop off.

She woke up in the morning and glanced at her watch—it was half-past nine. On the carpet near her bed was a narrow, bright streak of sunlight from a beam which came through the window and faintly lit the room. Behind the black window curtain flies buzzed.

'It's early,' the Princess thought, closing her eyes.

Stretching and luxuriating in her bed, she recalled yesterday's encounter with the doctor, and all yesterday's thoughts with which she had fallen asleep. She remembered her unhappiness. Then she remembered her husband who lived in St. Petersburg, her bailiffs, her doctors, her neighbours and her acquaintances in the civil service.

A long line of familiar male faces passed before her in fancy, and she smiled, reflecting that if those men could plumb the depths of her soul and understand her, they would all be at her feet.

At a quarter past eleven she called her maid.

'Let me get dressed now, Dasha,' she said languidly. 'But first go and tell them to harness my horses. I must drive over to Claudia Nikolayevna's.'

As she left her quarters to board her carriage, she screwed up her eyes in the bright sunlight and laughed for joy—the weather was wonderfully fine. Squinting at the monks gathered by the porch to see her off, she nodded disarmingly.

'Good-bye, my friends,' she said. 'See you the day after tomorrow.'

To see the doctor by the porch with the monks was a nice surprise. His face was pale and stern.

'Madam,' said he, taking his hat off with a guilty smile. 'I have awaited you here for some time. For God's sake forgive me. Carried away by ill feeling and vindictiveness yesterday, I talked a lot of, er, nonsense. I beg your forgiveness, in other words.'

The Princess smiled disarmingly and held out her hand to his lips. He kissed it and blushed.

Trying to resemble a little bird, the Princess flitted into her carriage, nodding in all directions. She felt gay, bright, cosy. Her smile, she felt, was exceptionally charming and gentle. When the carriage had bowled up to the gates, and then along the dusty road past huts and gardens, past the long, typically Ukrainian wagon-trains, and the files of pilgrims wending their way to the monastery, she was still squinting and smiling softly. There is no higher pleasure, thought she, than to carry warmth, light and joy with one wherever one goes, forgiving wrongs and smiling disarmingly at one's enemies. Villagers bowed to her as she passed, and her carriage whirred softly, while clouds of dust blown up from the wheels drifted on the wind into the golden rye. She was floating on clouds, the Princess felt—not swaying on the cushions of her carriage. And she herself resembled an airy, transparent tuft of cloud.

'How happy I am,' she whispered, closing her eyes. 'Oh, I'm so happy.'

AFTER THE THEATRE

NADYA ZELENIN and her mother had returned from a performance *Eugene Onegin* at the theatre. Going into her room, the girl swiftly threw off her dress and let her hair down. Then she quickly sat at the table in her petticoat and white bodice to write a letter like Tatyana's.

'I love you,' she wrote, 'but you don't love me, you don't love me!' Having written this, she laughed.

She was only sixteen and had never loved anyone yet. She knew that Gorny (an army officer) and Gruzdyov (a student) were both in love with her, but now, after the opera, she wanted to doubt their love. To be unloved and miserable: what an attractive idea! There was something beautiful, touching and romantic about A loving B when B wasn't interested in A. Onegin was attractive in not loving at all, while Tatyana was enchanting because she loved greatly. Had they loved equally and been happy they might have seemed boring.

'Do stop telling me you love me because I don't believe you,' Nadya wrote on, with Gorny, the officer, in mind. 'You are highly intelligent, well-educated and serious, you're a brilliant man—with a dazzling future, perhaps—whereas I'm a dull girl, a nobody. As you're perfectly well aware, I should only be a burden to you. Yes, you have taken a fancy to me, I know, you thought you'd found your ideal woman. But that was a mistake. You're already wondering frantically why you ever had to meet such a girl and only your good nature prevents you admitting as much.'

Nadya began to feel sorry for herself, and burst into tears.

'I can't bear to leave my mother and brother,' she went on, 'or else I'd take the veil and go off into the blue, and you'd be free to love another. Oh, if only I were dead!'

Tears blurred what Nadya had written, while rainbow flashes shimmered on table, floor and ceiling, as if she was looking through a prism. Writing was impossible, so she lolled back in her arm-chair and began thinking of Gorny.

How attractive, ye gods, how seductive men were! Nadya remembered what a beautiful expression—pleading, guilty, gentle—Gorny wore whenever anyone discussed music with him and what efforts it cost him to keep a ring of enthusiasm out of his voice. In a society where coolness, hauteur and nonchalance are judged signs of breeding and good manners one must hide one's passions. Hide them he does, but without success, and it's common knowledge that he's mad about music. Those endless arguments about music, the brash verdicts of ignoramuses . . . they keep him constantly on edge, making him scared, timid, taciturn. He plays the piano magnificently, like a professional pianist, and he might well have been a famous musician had he not been in the army.

Nadya's tears dried and she remembered Gorny declaring his love to her: at a symphony concert and then by the coat-hooks downstairs, with a draught blowing in all directions.

'I'm so glad you've met my student friend Gruzdyov at last,' she wrote on. 'He is very bright and you're sure to like him. He came to see us yesterday and stayed until two in the morning. We were all delighted and I was sorry you hadn't joined us. He made many remarkable observations.'

Putting her hands on the table, Nadya leant her head on them, and her hair covered the letter. She remembered that Gruzdyov also loved her, that he had as much right to a letter as Gorny. Wouldn't it be better, actually, to write to Gruzdyov? Happiness stirred spontaneously in her breast. First it was small and rolled about like a rubber ball, then it swelled broader and bigger and surged on like a wave. Now Nadya had forgotten Gorny and Gruzdyov, her mind was muddled and ever greater grew her joy. It moved from breast to arms and legs, and she felt as if a light, cool breeze had fanned her head and stirred her hair. Her shoulders shook with silent laughter, the table and lamp-chimney trembled too, and her tears sprinkled the letter. Unable to stop laughing, she quickly thought of something funny to prove that she wasn't laughing about nothing.

'What a funny poodle!' she brought out, feeling as if she was choking with laughter. 'How funny that poodle was!'

She had remembered Gruzdyov romping with Maxim, the family poodle, after tea yesterday and then telling a story about a very clever poodle chasing a raven in some yard. The raven had turned round and spoken: 'Oh, you wretched little dog.' Not knowing that it was involved with a talking raven, the poodle had been terribly embarrassed. It had retreated, baffled, and started barking.

'No, I'd rather love Gruzdyov,' Nadya decided, tearing up the letter.

She began thinking of the student, of his love, of her love, but the upshot was that her head swam and she thought about everything at once: mother, street, pencil, piano.

She thought happily away and found everything simply wonderful. And this was only the beginning, happiness whispered to her, before long things would be even better still. Soon spring would come, and summer. She and Mother would go to Gorbiki, Gorny would have leave and he would walk round the garden with her, dancing attendance. Gruzdyov would come too. They would play croquet and skittles together, and he would make funny or surprising remarks. Garden, darkness, clear skies, stars . . . she yearned for them passionately. Once more her shoulders shook with laughter and she seemed to smell wormwood in the room, seemed to hear a bough slap the window.

She went and sat on her bed. Not knowing how to cope with the immense happiness which weighed her down, she gazed at the icon hanging at the head of her bed.

'Lord, how marvellous!' she said.

THREE YEARS

I

IT was dark, but lights had already come on in some houses, and at the end of the street a pale moon was rising behind the barracks. Seated on a bench by a gate, Laptev waited for vespers to end at St. Peter and St. Paul's. He calculated that Julia Belavin would come past on her way back from church, that he would speak to her and perhaps spend the evening with her.

He had sat for an hour and a half visualizing his Moscow flat, his Moscow friends, his valet Peter, his desk. He gazed in bewilderment at the dark, unmoving trees, astonished that he was no longer living in his Sokolniki villa but in a provincial town, in a house past which a large herd of cattle was driven every morning and evening, raising terrible clouds of dust while the herdsman blew his horn. He remembered the long Moscow discussions in which he had so recently taken part, about life without love being possible, about passionate love being a psychosis, and finally about how there's no such thing as love but only sexual attraction—that sort of thing. Recalling it, he sadly reflected that if anyone now asked him what love was he would be at a loss for an answer.

The service ended, the congregation emerged, and Laptev stared intently at the dark figures. The bishop had driven past in his carriage, the bell-ringing was over, the red and green lights on the belfry had been extinguished one after the other—special illuminations, these, to celebrate the patronal festival—and people were making their way unhurriedly, talking and pausing beneath the windows. Then at last Laptev heard a familiar voice, his heart missed a beat, and he was seized with despair because Julia was not on her own, but with two other ladies.

'That's awful, truly awful,' he whispered, feeling jealous.

She stopped at the corner of a side-road to say good-bye to the ladies, and it was then that she looked at Laptev.

'I'm on my way to your place,' he said. 'I want to talk to your father. Is he in?'

'Probably. It's too early for him to be at his club.'

The side-road was rich in gardens. By the fences grew lime trees,

now casting their broad shadows in the moonlight so that fences and
gates on one side were blanketed in darkness from which proceeded
the whisper of feminine voices, subdued laughter and the quiet strum-
ming of a balalaika. It smelt of lime trees and hay. The unseen women's
whispering and the smell aroused Laptev. He felt a sudden intense urge
to embrace his companion, to cover her face, arms, shoulders with
kisses, to burst into tears, to fall at her feet, to say how long he had
been waiting for her. She brought with her a faint, elusive whiff of
incense, reminding him of the time when he too had believed in God,
had gone to evening service, had yearned for a pure, romantic love.
But, since this girl did not love him, he now felt permanently deprived
of the prospect of that happiness for which he had then longed.

She expressed concern about the health of his sister Nina, who had
had an operation for cancer two months earlier. Now everyone was
expecting a relapse.

'I saw her this morning,' said Julia. 'And it struck me that she had
not just lost weight this last week, but all her vitality too.'

'Quite,' agreed Laptev. 'There has been no new crisis, but I see her
growing feebler every day. She's sinking before my eyes, I can't think
what's happening.'

'Goodness me, what a healthy, buxom, rosy-cheeked woman she
was,' Julia said after a short pause. 'Everyone here called her "the girl
from Moscow". How she did laugh. On holidays she would wear
peasant dress, which suited her very well.'

Doctor Sergey Belavin was at home. A stout, red-faced man in a
long frock-coat reaching below the knees, seeming short-legged, he
was pacing his study, his hands thrust into his pockets, humming a sort
of ruminating hum. His grey side-whiskers were dishevelled, his hair
was as untidy as if he had only just got out of bed. And his study—
with the cushions on the sofas, piles of old papers in the corners, and a
large, dirty poodle under the table—had an air as unkempt and
frowsty as its owner's.

'Mr. Laptev wishes to see you,' his daughter told him, going into the
study.

He hummed his ruminative hum more loudly, came into the drawing-
room, shook hands with Laptev, and asked 'what tidings?'

It was dark in the drawing-room. Laptev remained standing, kept
his hat in his hands and apologized for the intrusion. He asked what
could be done to help his sister sleep at night. And why was she so
appallingly thin? He was embarrassed because he vaguely remembered

asking the doctor these same questions already during this morning's visit. And he asked whether 'we shouldn't send for some specialist in internal diseases from Moscow'. What was the doctor's view?

The doctor sighed, shrugged, made a vague two-handed gesture.

He was offended, obviously. This was a very touchy, a very pernickety doctor, obsessed with being distrusted, not recognized, not sufficiently respected—a target, he felt, for general exploitation and his colleagues' malice. He was always mocking himself. 'Idiots like me exist only to be trampled on.'

Julia lit a lamp. The service had tired her, to judge from her pale, languid face and listless walk. Wishing to relax, she sat on the sofa, put her hands on her lap and was lost in thought, while Laptev—conscious that he was not handsome—now felt physically aware of his own ugliness. He was short, thin, with flushed cheeks, and with hair so sparse that his head felt cold. His expression wholly lacked that charm and simplicity which can make even a coarse, ugly face likeable. In women's company he was awkward, over-talkative, affected, and was almost despising himself for this at the moment. To avoid boring Julia he must say something. But what? Should he bring up his sister's illness again?

He began making trite remarks about medicine, he praised hygiene, he said that he had long wished to set up a poor people's hostel in Moscow, and already had a scheme afoot. A worker arriving in the evening was to receive for five or six copecks a portion of hot cabbage stew, bread, a warm, dry bed with a quilt, a place to dry his clothes and footwear.

Julia usually remained silent in his presence, while he—guided perhaps by the instincts of a man in love—had a strange faculty for guessing her thoughts and intentions. As she had not gone to her room to change and have tea after the service she must mean to go visiting this evening, he now calculated.

'But I'm in no hurry over the hostel,' he went on, annoyed and distressed. He was addressing the doctor, whose vague, lack-lustre and baffled gaze showed that he could not see why the man had to bring up medicine and hygiene.

'No, I don't suppose I shall carry out the project very soon,' Laptev went on. 'I fear it may fall into the clutches of Moscow's lady bountifuls and do-gooders, who ruin every initiative.'

Julia stood up, held out her hand to Laptev and asked him to excuse her. 'Time I was off. Give your sister my regards.'

The doctor hummed his ruminative hum.

Julia went out. Soon afterwards Laptev said good-bye to the doctor and set off home. What a vulgar atmosphere they do generate when one feels frustrated and unhappy—these lime trees, these shadows, these clouds, all these smug, unconcerned beauties of nature. The moon was high in the sky, clouds raced below it.

'Silly provincial moon,' Laptev thought. 'Pathetic, scraggy clouds.'

He was ashamed to have brought up medicine and that hostel just now. And he was aghast to think that he would not hold out tomorrow either, but would try to see and talk to her again, only to discover once more that he meant nothing to her. The day after tomorrow would be just the same. To what purpose? When and how would it all end?

When he arrived home he went to see his sister. Nina still looked strong, seeming a powerful, well-built woman, but her striking pallor made her corpse-like—especially when she lay on her back with her eyes closed, as now. By her sat her elder daughter, ten-year-old Sasha, who was reading to her from a school book.

'Alexis is here,' the sick woman said quietly to herself.

Between Sasha and her uncle a tacit agreement had long been reached, and they ran a shift system. So Sasha closed her reader and quietly left the room without a word. Laptev took a historical novel from the chest-of-drawers, found his place, sat down, began reading to her.

Nina had come from Moscow. Like her two brothers she had spent her childhood and youth at Pyatnitsky Road. The family was in business, and a long, boring childhood theirs had been. The father had been strict, even taking the birch to her several times, and her mother had been an invalid long before her death. The servants had been dirty, coarse, hypocritical. The house had been frequented by priests and monks no less rude and hypocritical. They drank, they ate, they crudely flattered her father, whom they disliked. The boys had had the good luck to go to a grammar school, but Nina had received no education at all, she had scrawled rather than written all her life, she had read nothing but historical novels. Seventeen years earlier, aged twenty-two, she had met her present husband Panaurov—member of a landowning family—at a Khimki villa. She had fallen in love and married him against her father's wish, in secret. Panaurov, a handsome and rather insolent person, a lighter of cigarettes from the icon lamp, a great whistler, had impressed her father as an utter nobody. Then when the son-in-law's letters had begun insisting on a dowry, the old man had written to his daughter that he would send her some fur coats at her country home, some silver and oddments left by her mother, together with thirty thousand roubles in cash, but without his blessing. He sent another twenty thousand later. This money and the whole dowry had been squandered, the estate had been sold, Panaurov and his family had moved to town, and he had taken a local government job. He had started another family in town, which caused endless discussion every day since no secret was made of this illegitimate family.

Nina adored her husband. Listening to the historical novel, she reflected how much she had experienced and suffered all this time, how poignant any account of her life would be. Since hers was a tumour of the breast she was sure that her disease had been caused by love and family life, and that jealousy and tears had laid her low.

Alexis closed the book. 'That's the end, praise be. We'll start another tomorrow.'

Nina laughed. She had always been inclined to laugh, but it had begun to strike Laptev that her mind was sometimes enfeebled by sickness, so that she laughed at mere trifles and for no reason at all.

'Julia called before dinner while you were out,' she said. 'I can see she doesn't much trust that father of hers. "Let my father treat you," says she. "But you write to the Reverend So-and-So on the quiet, get him to say a prayer for you." This is some local sage of theirs. Julia left her umbrella here—send it her tomorrow,' she went on after a short pause. 'Anyway, if this is the end, neither your doctors nor your Reverend So-and-Sos will help.'

'Why can't you sleep at night, Nina?' Laptev wanted to change the subject.

'Oh, I don't know. I can't, and that's that. I just lie thinking.'

'What about, dear?'

'The children, you, my own life. I've been through so much, haven't I, Alexis? When you start remembering, when you—heavens!' She laughed. 'It's no joke having five children and burying three of them. Sometimes I'd be on the point of having the baby, but Gregory would be with another woman and there would be no one to send for the midwife or anything. You'd go into the hall or kitchen for the servants, and you'd find Jews, tradesmen, money-lenders—all waiting for him to come home. It used to make me quite dizzy. He didn't love me, though he never said so. But now I've come to terms with it,

I'm not heart-broken any longer. It did hurt me so much when I was younger, though. I did suffer, dear. Once, when we were still living in the country, I found him in the garden with another woman, and I just left—left without caring where I went, and somehow found myself in the church porch. I fell on my knees. "Mother of God", I prayed. It was dark outside, a moonlit night.'

Exhausted, she breathed heavily. Then, after resting a while, she took her brother by the arm. 'You're so kind, Alexis,' she went on in a feeble whisper. 'You're so intelligent. What a fine man you have become.'

At midnight Laptev wished her good night, and took with him as he left the umbrella left behind by Julia. Late though the hour was servants, male and female, were drinking tea in the dining-room. What chaos. The children were still up, and they were in the dining-room too. All were talking in low voices, not noticing that the lamp was fading and would soon go out. Everyone, large and small, was troubled by an accumulation of unfavourable auguries, and they felt depressed. The hall mirror was broken, the samovar whined every day —it was at it now, confound it. And as Mrs. Panaurov had been dressing a mouse had jumped out of her shoe, or so they said. The sinister portent of these omens was already known to the children. The elder, Sasha, a thin, dark-haired little girl, sat still at the table, looking scared and downcast, while the younger, Leda—seven years old, plump, fair-haired—stood near her sister, squinting at the light.

Laptev went down to his ground-floor rooms with their stuffy atmosphere, low ceilings and permanent smell of geraniums. In his drawing-room sat Nina's husband Panaurov reading a newspaper. Laptev nodded and sat opposite him. Neither spoke. They would sometimes spend whole evenings like this, unembarrassed by their silence.

The little girls came down to say good-night. Silently, unhurriedly, Panaurov made the sign of the cross over both several times, gave them his hand to kiss. They curtsied and went up to Laptev, who also had to make the sign of the cross over them and let them kiss his hand. This kissing and curtsying occurred every evening.

When the girls had gone Panaurov put his paper on one side. 'This blessed town is such a bore.' Then he added with a sigh that he was 'frankly delighted that you've found some amusement at last, dear boy'.

'Meaning what?' Laptev asked.

'I saw you leaving Dr. Belavin's house just now. It was not on dear Daddy's account, I trust—your visit.'

'Of course it was.' Laptev blushed.

'But of course. Incidentally, what a wet blanket dear Daddy is, he must be unique. What dirty habits, what a dim, clumsy brute it is—you've no idea. Now, you Muscovites are only interested in the provinces from a romantic angle, so to speak—in the scenery, in picturesquely miserable bumpkins. But there's nothing romantic here, old man, believe you me. There's just barbarity, meanness, squalor—nothing else. Take our local lights of learning, our "professional men". Do you know we have twenty-eight doctors in this town? They've all made their fortunes, they've all bought their own houses, while the rest of the people are still in the same wretched plight as ever. For instance, Nina had to have an operation—a trivial one, actually, yet we had to have a man from Moscow because none of the local surgeons would do it. You've no idea what it's like—they know nothing, understand nothing, are interested in nothing. Ask them what cancer is, for instance—what it is, where it comes from?'

Panaurov went on to explain what cancer was. He was a specialist in all branches of learning, having a scientific explanation for everything under the sun. But he always had his own line on things. He had his own theory of the circulation of the blood, his own chemistry, his own astronomy. He spoke slowly, softly, convincingly, bringing out the words 'you haven't the remotest inkling' as if begging a favour. He screwed up his eyes, he sighed languidly, he smiled benevolently like royalty, patently self-satisfied and wholly unconcerned with being fifty years old.

'I'm a bit peckish,' said Laptev. 'I feel like something savoury.'

'But of course. That can be laid on at once.'

Soon afterwards Laptev and his brother-in-law were upstairs having supper in the dining-room. Laptev drank a glass of vodka and moved on to wine, but Panaurov drank nothing. He neither drank nor played cards, despite which he had contrived to run through his own and his wife's property, and to pile up a mass of debts. To squander so much money so quickly you need more than mere carnal appetites—you need something extra, a special flair. Panaurov liked tasty food, first-rate table appointments, music with his dinner, speeches, the bows of the waiters to whom he nonchalantly tossed tips of ten or even twenty-five roubles. He subscribed to everything, went in for all the lotteries, sent ladies of his acquaintance flowers on their name-days, bought cups, glass-holders, studs, ties, canes, scents, cigarette-holders, pipes, dogs, parrots, Japanese wares and antiques. His night-shirts were of silk, his bed was of ebony and mother-of-pearl, he had a real Bokhara dressing-gown and so on—all of which daily consumed what he called 'a mint of money'.

Over supper he kept sighing and shaking his head.

'Yes, everything in the world comes to an end,' he said quietly, screwing up his dark eyes. 'You'll fall in love and suffer. You'll fall out of love. You'll be deceived because there's no such thing as a faithful woman. You will suffer, you will despair, you too will be unfaithful. But in time all this will be only a memory, and you'll coolly reckon it as all utterly insignificant.'

Tired, slightly drunk, Laptev looked at the other's handsome head, at the clipped black beard, and felt he understood why women so loved this spoilt, confident, physically attractive man.

After supper Panaurov did not remain at home, but left for his other flat. Laptev accompanied him. Panaurov was the only man in the whole town who wore a top hat, and against the grey fences, the wretched three-windowed cottages, the clumps of nettles, his elegant, fashionable figure, top hat and orange gloves always evoked an air both strange and sad.

Laptev said good-night and returned to his quarters unhurriedly. The moon shone so brightly that every wisp of straw on the ground was visible, and Laptev felt as if the moonlight was caressing his uncovered head, which was like having his hair stroked with a feather.

'I'm in love,' he said aloud, and he suddenly felt like running after Panaurov to embrace him, forgive him, present him with a lot of money and then rush off into the fields or a wood somewhere, and run, run, run without looking back.

At home, on a chair, he saw the umbrella left behind by Julia, picked it up, kissed it passionately. It was of silk, no longer new, girded with an old piece of elastic. It had an ordinary cheap bone handle. Laptev opened it above him and felt enveloped in the very scent of happiness.

He sat down more comfortably and began writing to one of his Moscow friends while still holding the umbrella.

'My dearest Kostya,
'Here's news for you—I'm in love again. I say "again" because six years ago I was in love with a Moscow actress whom I never even managed to meet, and for the last eighteen months I've been living with the "personage" you know of, a woman neither young nor

beautiful. I've always been so unlucky in love, old friend. I never had success with women, and if I say "again" it's only because it's so sad, so painful to realize that my youth has gone by without any love at all, and that I'm now well and truly in love for the first time at the age of thirty-four. So let me say I'm in love "again".

'If you only knew what she's like. You can't call her beautiful—her face is too broad, she's very thin, but what a wonderfully kind expression! And how she smiles! When she speaks her voice sings, it's so resonant. She's never the first to speak to me, and I don't really know her, but when I'm near her I sense in her a rare, exceptional creature imbued with intelligence and high ideals. She's religious, and you can't imagine how this moves me and raises her in my estimation. On this point I'm prepared to argue with you for ever. All right, have it your own way, but I still love her church-going. She's a provincial but she went to school in Moscow, she loves our city, she dresses like a Muscovite and for that I love her, love her, love her.

'I see you frown and stand up to read me a long lecture about what love is, and whom one may and may not love, and so on and so forth. But I too knew just what love was—before I fell in love, my dear Kostya.

'My sister thanks you for your regards, and often remembers how she once took Kostya Kochevoy to join the preparatory class. She still calls you "poor Kostya" because she still remembers you as the little orphan boy. So I'm in love, poor orphan. It's a secret for now, so don't say anything there to the "personage" known to you. That business will settle itself, I think. Or as the servant says in Tolstoy, "it will sort itself out." '

The letter finished, Laptev went to bed. He was so tired that his eyes closed of themselves. But sleep he somehow could not, apparently because of the noise in the street. The herd of cattle was driven past, the horn sounded, and soon after that the bells rang for morning service. Now a cart would creak past, now a woman's voice was heard on her way to market. And the sparrows never stopped twittering.

II

The morning was bright and cheerful. At about ten o'clock Nina, wearing a brown dress, hair tidied, was led into the drawing-room where she paced about, then stood by the open window, smiling a broad, innocent smile. Looking at her, one remembered the local artist, a drunkard, who had called her face a 'countenance' and had wanted to use her as a model in a picture of a Russian Shrovetide. Everyone—children, servants, even Nina herself and her brother—was suddenly convinced that her recovery was certain. Shrieking with laughter, the little girls ran after their uncle trying to catch him, and the house was full of noise.

Visitors came to ask about her health, bringing communion bread and saying that special prayers had been offered for her today in almost all the churches. She had done much good in the town, and was much loved. Charitable deeds came as naturally to her as to her brother, who gave money very readily without bothering whether he should or not. Nina paid poor boys' school fees, took old ladies tea, sugar and jam, equipped impecunious brides with dresses, and if she chanced on a newspaper she would first look for appeals or accounts of anyone being in desperate straits.

At the moment she held a bundle of chits with which sundry indigent beneficiaries had obtained goods at the grocer's. The man had sent them along yesterday with his request to pay eighty-two roubles.

'Dear me, they've been helping themselves quite shamelessly.' She could hardly make out her own ungainly hand-writing on the notes. 'Eighty-two roubles, that's no joke, I've a good mind not to pay.'

'I'll pay it today,' said Laptev.

'But why should you?' Nina was perturbed. 'It's enough that I get two hundred and fifty roubles a month from you and our brother, God bless you,' she added quietly, so that the servants should not hear.

'Well, I spend two thousand five hundred a month,' he said. 'I tell you again, dear, you've as much right to spend money as Theodore and I. Get that into your head once and for all. Our father has three children, and one in every three copecks is yours.'

But Nina, not understanding, looked as if she had been trying to do a very complicated sum in her head. This lack of money sense always worried and embarrassed Laptev. Besides, he suspected her of having some private debts which she was ashamed to confide in him and which pained her.

They heard steps and heavy breathing. The doctor was coming upstairs, dishevelled and unkempt as ever, humming his usual ruminating hum.

To avoid meeting him Laptev stepped into the dining-room, then went down to his own quarters. To get on closer terms with the doctor, to call on him casually—that was out of the question, Laptev clearly realized. Even to meet this 'wet blanket', as Panaurov called him, was unpleasant. That was why he saw so little of Julia. If he took back her umbrella now that her father was out he would probably find her at home on her own, and his heart leapt with joy. He must hurry.

He picked up the umbrella and flew off in great excitement, on the wings of love. It was hot in the street. In the doctor's house, in the huge yard overgrown with tall weeds and nettles, a score of urchins were playing ball. These were children of tenants—workpeople who lived in the three unprepossessing old outbuildings which the doctor was going to have repaired every year, but always postponed. Healthy voices resounded. Far to one side near her porch stood Julia, arms behind her back, watching the game.

Laptev hailed her and she turned round. She usually looked coolly indifferent when he saw her, or tired, as she had been yesterday. But now she looked as vivacious and playful as the boys with their ball.

'See, they never have such fun in Moscow.' She came towards him. 'Anyway, they don't have these huge yards there, do they? There's nowhere to run about. Father has just left for your place,' she added, looking round at the children.

'I know, but it's you I've come to see, not him.'

She looked so young—that was what Laptev admired, having somehow never noticed it before today. He gazed, as if for the first time, at her slim white neck with its little gold chain. 'It's you I've come to see,' he repeated. 'My sister sent this umbrella that you left behind yesterday.'

She held her hand out to take it, but he pressed it to his breast and spoke ardently, uncontrollably, yielding once more to the delicious pleasure experienced on the previous night under the umbrella.

'I beg you, give it to me, I'll keep it in memory of you—of our friendship. It's so marvellous.'

'All right.' She blushed. 'But there's nothing marvellous about it.'

He looked at her entranced, silently, not knowing what to say.

'But why do I keep you out in the heat?' she asked after a pause, and laughed. 'Let's go inside.'

'If I won't be interrupting you.'

They went into the hall. Julia ran upstairs with a rustle of her dress, which was white with blue flowers.

'It's not possible to interrupt me.' She stopped on the staircase. 'You see, I never do anything—every day's a holiday from morning to night.'

'That's hard for me to understand.' He approached her. 'I grew up in surroundings where people work every day, all without exception, men and women.'

'But what if there's nothing to do?'

'So organize your life that work is inescapable. You can't live a decent, happy life if you don't work.'

Again he pressed the umbrella to his chest and, to his surprise, found himself speaking in a calm voice not his own. 'If you would consent to be my wife, I would give anything—anything at all. There's no price, no sacrifice I would not accept.'

She started, looking at him in surprise and fear.

'Don't, don't say such things.' She blenched. 'It's not possible, I assure you. I'm sorry.'

Then she rushed upstairs, her dress still rustling, and vanished through a door.

Laptev knew what this meant. Immediately and abruptly his mood changed, as if the light had suddenly gone out of his life. Shamed and humiliated, rejected as an unattractive, obnoxious, perhaps downright odious man shunned by one and all, he left the house.

'I would give anything.' On his way home in the heat, remembering the details of his declaration, he mocked himself. ' "Give anything"— what tradesman's talk. A lot of use your *anything* is!'

All he had just said seemed revoltingly stupid. Why had he told that lie about growing up in a family where everyone worked 'without exception'? Why had he spoken in that hectoring tone about a 'decent, happy life'? It wasn't clever or interesting, it was just eyewash, typical Moscow affectation. But then he gradually sank into the apathy of the criminal who has received a harsh sentence. Thank God it was all over and there was no more of that appalling uncertainty, he thought. No longer need he spend day after day waiting, suffering, obsessed with the one thing. Now all was clear. He must jettison every hope of personal happiness and live without desires, hopes, longings, expectations. To dispel the misery and boredom which he could no longer be bothered with, he might concern himself with other people's doings and happiness. Old age would arrive unnoticed. Life would end. That would be that. He didn't care, he wanted nothing, he could reason coolly, but his face felt somehow heavy, especially under the eyes. His forehead was taut like stretched elastic, tears seemed ready to spurt. Feeling weak all over, he went to bed. Five minutes later he was fast asleep.

III

Laptev's so unexpected proposal had plunged Julia into despair.

She didn't know him well, they had met accidentally. He was rich, he was a partner in the well-known Moscow firm Theodore Laptev and Sons, he was always very serious, he was obviously intelligent, and he was concerned about his sister's illness. He had seemed not to notice her at all, and she had been quite indifferent to him. But then there had been that declaration on the staircase, this pathetic, ecstatic face.

His proposal had upset her because it was so sudden, because the word *wife* was used, because she had had to refuse him. What she had said to Laptev she no longer remembered, but she still felt vestiges of the impulsive, disagreeable emotion with which she had turned him down. She didn't like him. He looked like a shop assistant, he was unattractive, she could only say no. Yet she still felt awkward, as if she had behaved badly.

'My God, without even going into the flat, right there on the staircase,' she said in despair, facing the icon above her bed-head. 'And he never showed any interest in me before. It's all so odd, so strange——'

In her loneliness she grew hourly more disquieted, unable to endure this oppressive sensation on her own. Someone must listen to her, tell her she had done the right thing. But there was no one to talk to. She had long ago lost her mother, she thought her father a crank and couldn't talk to him seriously. He embarrassed her with his caprices, his extraordinary touchiness, his vague gestures. Start a conversation with him and he at once began talking about himself. Even in her prayers she was not completely frank because she was unsure just what she should ask God for.

The samovar was brought in. Very pale, tired, looking helpless, Julia came into the dining-room, made tea—her responsibility—and poured her father a glass. The doctor wore that long frock-coat which reached below his knees. Red-faced, unkempt, hands in pockets, he paced the dining-room, not going from one corner to another but in random fashion like a caged beast. He would stop by the table, drink from his glass with relish, then stalk about again deep in thought.

'Laptev proposed to me this morning.' Julia blushed.

The doctor looked at her and seemed not to understand. 'What Laptev? Nina Panaurov's brother?'

He loved his daughter. She would probably marry sooner or later and leave him, but he tried not to think about that. He was terrified of loneliness. Should he be left alone in this large house he would have a stroke—so he vaguely felt without liking to say so outright.

'Then I'm delighted.' He shrugged. 'My heartiest congratulations. What a perfect chance to abandon me, how very nice for you. Oh yes, I see your point of view. To live with an aged, sick, unhinged father— what an ordeal for a girl your age. I understand you very well indeed. If only I could conk out soon, if only the foul fiend would whisk me off, how pleased everyone would be. My heartiest congratulations.'

'I refused him.'

The doctor was relieved, but had lost all self-control. 'I'm amazed. I've long wondered why I've never been put in a mad-house. Why do I wear this frock-coat and not a strait-jacket? I still believe in justice, in goodness, I'm wildly idealistic—surely that's insanity in our age! And what response do I get for being fair, for taking the decent line? I'm practically stoned in the street, I'm a general dogsbody. Even my nearest and dearest walk all over me, damn me, I'm just an old imbecile——'

'It's impossible to talk to you,' Julia said.

She abruptly stood up from the table and went to her room— furious, remembering how often her father was unfair to her. But she soon felt sorry for him, and when he left for his club she went downstairs with him and closed the door after him. The weather was disquietingly foul, the door shuddered from the wind's pressure, and in the hall there were draughts from all sides so that her candle nearly went out. Julia went all round her upstairs flat, making the sign of the cross over all windows and doors. The wind howled, someone seemed to be marching about on the roof. She had never known such depression, never felt so lonely.

She wondered whether she had been right to refuse a man solely because she did not like his looks. True, she did not love him, and marrying him would put paid to her dreams, her ideas of happiness in marriage. But would she ever meet and love the man of her dreams? She was already twenty-one. There were no eligible young men in town. She thought of all the men she knew—civil servants, schoolteachers, officers. Some were married already, and their family life was palpably empty and dreary. Others were unattractive, colourless, stupid, immoral. Now, say what you like about Laptev, he *was* a Muscovite. He had been to college, he spoke French. He lived in Moscow, where there were so many intelligent, decent, distinguished people, where things were pretty lively, what with all the splendid theatres, the musical evenings, the excellent dressmakers, the cafés.

The Bible says that a wife must love her husband, and novels attach great importance to love. But couldn't that be a bit overstated? Is family life really impossible without love? They do say that love soon passes, don't they? That it just becomes a habit, that the goal of family life isn't love and happiness, but duty—bringing up children, house-keeping and so on. Anyway, perhaps the Bible views loving a husband as 'loving one's neighbour'—being respectful and considerate, that is.

That night Julia said her evening prayers attentively. Then she knelt down, clasped her hands to her breast, looked at the burning icon-lamp and prayed fervently that the Lord and Our Lady should 'lighten my darkness'.

She had met old maids in her time, wretched nobodies haunted by bitter regrets at having once turned down their suitors. Might that happen to her? Shouldn't she enter a convent, become a nurse?

She undressed and went to bed, crossing herself and making the sign of the cross in the air around her. Suddenly a bell rang sharply and poignantly in the corridor.

'Dear God!' The sound exasperated, utterly sickened her. She lay and thought about provincial life—so uneventful and monotonous, yet so disquieting. Every now and then it made you shudder, it made you apprehensive, angry, guilt-ridden, and in the end your nerves were so frayed that you were scared to peep out from under your quilt.

Half an hour later the bell rang again no less harshly. The servants must have been asleep and not heard it. Julia lit a candle and began dressing—shivering, annoyed with them. When she had dressed and gone into the corridor the maid was closing the downstairs door.

'I thought it was the master, but it was someone about a patient,' she said.

Julia returned to her room. She took a pack of cards from her chest-of-drawers, deciding to shuffle them thoroughly and cut them. If a red card showed up that would mean *yes*—she must accept Laptev's proposal. But if it was black she should say *no*. It was the ten of spades.

That calmed her and she went to sleep. But in the morning she was back with neither yes nor no. She could change her life now if she wanted to, she reflected. Her thoughts wearied her, she felt strained and ill. But soon after eleven o'clock she dressed and went to visit Nina. She wanted to see Laptev—perhaps he might look less unattractive now, perhaps she had been on the wrong tack.

Walking into the wind was difficult, and she could hardly make headway, holding her hat in both hands and seeing nothing for dust.

IV

Entering his sister's room and unexpectedly seeing Julia, Laptev again felt the humiliation of the suitor rebuffed. If, after yesterday, she could so casually visit his sister and meet him, she must find him beneath notice, a mere nonentity, he concluded. But when he greeted her and she—pallid, with dust beneath her eyes—looked at him sadly and guiltily, he saw that she too suffered.

She was feeling out of sorts, and stayed only a brief ten minutes before taking her departure.

'Please see me home, Mr. Laptev,' she asked as she was leaving.

They went down the road without speaking, holding their hats, while he walked behind and tried to shield her from the wind. In the side-road it was calmer and they walked together.

'Please forgive me if I was unkind yesterday.' Her voice quavered as if she was about to cry. 'I was so upset I didn't sleep all night.'

'Well, I slept very well all night.' Laptev did not look at her. 'But that doesn't mean I feel all right. My life's in ruins. I'm deeply unhappy and since you refused me yesterday I've felt as if I'd taken poison. The hardest thing was said yesterday. This morning I feel at ease with you, I can talk to you directly. I love you more than my sister, more than my dead mother. Without my sister and my mother I could and did live, but life without you—it has no meaning. I can't bear——'

As usual, he had divined her intentions. He saw that she wanted to continue yesterday's conversation, that this had been her sole purpose in asking him to escort her and in taking him to her house. But what could she add to her refusal? What new thought had occurred to her? Her glances, her smile, even the way she held her head and shoulders as she walked at his side—it all said that she still did not love him, that he was alien to her. So what was there for her to add?

The doctor was at home.

'Welcome, and delighted I am to see you, my dear Theodore,' said he, getting Laptev's name wrong. 'Delighted, delighted.'

He had never been so cordial before, and Laptev concluded that he knew of the proposal—a disagreeable thought, that. He was now seated in the drawing-room, where the miserable, vulgar appointments and dreadful pictures created an odd impression. There were armchairs and a huge lamp with a shade, but it still looked like a room not lived in, being more of a capacious barn. Only someone like the doctor could feel at home in this room, that was obvious. Another room almost twice as large was called 'the ballroom', and contained nothing but chairs, as if for a dancing class. Seated in the drawing-room, talking to the doctor about his sister, Laptev was nagged by a certain suspicion. Could Julia have called on Nina and then brought him here in order to announce her acceptance of his proposal? What an awful thought, but most awful of all was to have a mind open to such suspicions. He pictured father and daughter conferring at length during the previous evening and night. They might have had a long argument and concluded that Julia had behaved foolishly in refusing a rich man. His ears even rang with such words as parents speak on these occasions. 'It's true you don't love him, but think how much good you'll be able to do.'

The doctor prepared to go on his rounds. Laptev wanted to leave with him, but Julia asked if he would please stay behind.

Having suffered agonies of depression, she was now trying to convince herself that to refuse a decent, kindly man who loved her, solely because she found him unattractive, especially when this marriage offered her the chance to change her life, the unhappy, monotonous, idle life of one whose youth was passing and who could see no bright prospects for the future—to refuse him under these circumstances was insane, it was wanton self-indulgence, and God might even punish her for it.

Her father went out. When his steps had died away she suddenly stopped in front of Laptev and spoke decisively, turning terribly pale.

'I thought things over yesterday, Mr. Laptev, and I accept your proposal.'

He bent down and kissed her hand while she awkwardly kissed his head with cold lips. This amorous declaration lacked, he felt, something vital—her love—while containing much which was anything but vital. He felt like shouting aloud, running away, leaving for Moscow then and there. But she stood near him, seeming so lovely that passion suddenly seized him. Seeing that it was too late for further discussion, he embraced her ardently, clasped her to his chest and, muttering some words or other, spoke to her intimately, kissed her neck, cheek, head.

She retreated to the window, fearing these caresses, and both regretted their declarations, asking themselves in embarrassment why this had happened.

'I'm so unhappy, did you but know.' She wrung her hands.

'What's the matter?' He went towards her, also wringing his hands. 'For God's sake tell me, my dear. But only tell me the truth, I implore you, only the truth.'

'Pay no attention.' She forced herself to smile. 'I promise to be a faithful, devoted wife. Come and see me this evening.'

Sitting with his sister and reading the historical novel afterwards, he remembered all this, and was insulted that his splendid, pure, broad sentiments had evoked a response so trivial. He was unloved, but his proposal had been accepted—probably only because he was rich, so that preference had been given to that aspect of himself which he valued least of all. Julia, being pure and believing in God, had never thought of money—that could be conceded. Still, she didn't love him, did she? That she did not, and there had obviously been an element of calculation—confused and not fully deliberate, perhaps, but calculation for all that. The doctor's house repelled him with its vulgar appointments, the doctor himself was like some miserable fat miser, a comic figure from an operetta, and the very name Julia now sounded plebeian. He imagined Julia and himself at the wedding ceremony— strangers to each other, essentially, and without a scrap of feeling on her side, as though this had been an arranged marriage. His only consolation now—one as banal as the marriage itself—was that he was neither the first nor the last, but that thousands of men and women had entered such marriages, and that Julia might come to love him in the end when she knew him better.

'Romeo and Julia.' He shut the book and laughed. 'I'm Romeo. You may congratulate me, Nina. I proposed to Julia Belavin today.'

After thinking that he was joking, Nina believed him and burst into tears. The news did not please her.

'All right, I congratulate you,' she said. 'But why does it have to be so sudden?'

'It isn't, it's been going on since March, only you never notice anything. I fell in love back in March when I met her here in your room.'

'And I thought you'd marry one of our Moscow friends,' said Nina after a pause. 'The girls from our own set are easier to get on with. But the great thing is for you to be happy, Alexis, that's what counts. Gregory never loved me, and you see how we live, there's no hiding it. Of course any woman might love you for your kindness and intelligence, but Julia went to an exclusive boarding school, didn't she? She's a lady, and intelligence and kind-heartedness won't get you far with her. She's young, Alexis, whereas you're neither young nor good-looking.'

To soften the last words, she stroked his cheek. 'You aren't good-looking, but you're a splendid fellow.'

She was so overcome that a slight flush appeared on her cheeks, and she enthusiastically discussed whether it would be proper for her to bless Alexis with an icon. She was his elder sister, after all, which made her a mother to him. And she kept trying to convince her gloomy brother that the wedding must be celebrated properly—solemnly and cheerfully so that no one should take it amiss.

As Julia's future husband he began visiting the Belavins three or four times a day, and was no longer free to take Sasha's place reading the historical novel. Julia would receive him away from the drawing-room and her father's study in her own two rooms which he liked very much. There were dark walls, there was an icon-case with its icons in a corner. There was a smell of good scent and lamp oil. She lived in the remotest part of the house, her bed and dressing-table were screened off, her bookcase doors were curtained inside in green, and she had carpets to walk on so that her steps were noiseless. All this persuaded him that she had a secretive character and liked a quiet, calm, enclosed life. Her status in the house was that of a child, she had no money of her own, and she was sometimes embarrassed during their walks because she had not a copeck on her. Her father would hand out a little cash for clothes and books, no more than a hundred roubles a year. The doctor himself hardly had any money anyway, despite his thriving practice, since he played cards at the club every evening and always lost. Besides, he was buying houses on mortgage through a mutual credit society, and renting them out. His tenants were irregular in paying their rent, but he called these housing operations highly profitable. He had mortgaged his own home, where he lived with his daughter. Having bought some derelict land with the money, he was already building a large two-storey house there so that he could mortgage that too.

Laptev was now living in a sort of haze, as though he wasn't himself but his own double, and he was doing much that he would not have ventured on before. He visited the club a couple of times with the doctor, had supper with him and offered him, unprompted, some money for his building. He even visited Panaurov in his second flat. One day Panaurov invited him to dinner, and Laptev accepted without thinking. He was welcomed by a lady of about thirty-five, tall and thin with some grey in her hair and black brows—obviously not Russian. There were white powder blotches on her face, she smiled a sickly smile, she pressed his hand impulsively, making the bracelets jingle on her white arm. Laptev felt that she used this smile to hide her unhappiness from others and from herself. He also saw two little girls, three and five years old, who resembled Sasha. The meal consisted of cream soup and cold veal with carrots, followed by chocolate. It was sickly-sweet and vaguely unpleasant, but there were gleaming gold forks on the table, pots of soy sauce and Cayenne pepper. There was a highly baroque gravy-boat and a golden pepper pot.

Only after the soup did Laptev realize how improper it was for him to dine here. The lady was embarrassed, smiling and showing her teeth all the time. Panaurov was expounding in scientific terms the meaning and origins of falling in love.

'We are confronted with a phenomenon in the electrical field.' He spoke in French, addressing the lady. 'Everyone's skin contains microscopic glands charged with current. Meet a person with currents parallel to your own and there you are—that's love.'

When Laptev was back home and his sister asked him where he had been he was embarrassed and made no reply.

Throughout the period before his marriage he felt in a false position. He loved Julia more and more each day. She seemed mysteriously sublime. Yet his love was unreturned and the plain fact was that he was buying her and she was selling herself. Sometimes, after much cogitation, he felt quite desperate and wondered whether to abandon it all. He was lying awake night after night and for ever imagining himself meeting the woman whom, in letters to his friend, he called 'a personage'—meeting her in Moscow after the wedding. And how would his father and brother, those awkward customers, react to his marriage and to Julia? He was afraid of his father saying something rude to her when they first met. And there was something odd about his brother Theodore of late. He wrote long letters about the importance of health, about the influence of illness on the psyche, about the nature of religion, but not a word about Moscow and business.

These letters irritated Laptev. His brother's character was deteriorating he thought.

The wedding was in September, and the ceremony took place after morning service at St. Peter and St. Paul's. Bride and groom left for Moscow that same day. When Laptev and his wife, in her black dress and train—no longer a girl in appearance, but a mature woman—said good-bye to Nina Panaurov the sick woman's whole face twisted, yet no tear flowed from her dry eyes.

'If I die, which God forbid, look after my little girls.'

'Yes, I promise,' Julia answered, her lips and eyelids also twitching nervously.

'I'll visit you in October.' Laptev was greatly moved. 'Get better, darling.'

They had the railway compartment to themselves. Both were sad and embarrassed. She sat in a corner without taking her hat off and pretended to be dozing, while he lay on the bunk opposite, perturbed by sundry thoughts—about his father, about the 'personage'. Would Julia like his Moscow flat? Looking at the wife who did not love him, he despondently wondered why it had all come about.

V

In Moscow the Laptevs had a wholesale haberdashery business dealing in fringes, ribbons, braid, knitting material, buttons and so on. The turnover was two million a year. As for the net profit, no one knew that except the old man. The sons and clerks reckoned it a cool three hundred thousand, saying that it would be a hundred thousand more if the old man hadn't 'dissipated his efforts' by allowing indiscriminate credit. In the last ten years they had collected nearly a million in worthless promissory notes, and when this topic cropped up the chief clerk would give a sly wink and use language which many found obscure.

'It's the psychological aftermath of our age.'

Their main business was done in the city's commercial district, in the building called the warehouse. It was approached from a yard sunk in gloom, smelling of matting. Dray-horse hooves battered the asphalt. The modest-looking door was iron-bound and led from the yard into a room where the walls, brown with damp, were bescribbled in charcoal. This was lit by a narrow iron-grilled window. Then there was another room on the left—larger, cleaner, with a cast-iron stove and two tables, but also with its prison-style window. This was the office, and from it a narrow stone stairway led to the first floor, the main centre of activity. It was a fairly large room, but being in permanent twilight, low-ceilinged and cluttered with crates, bales and scurrying people, it struck those new to it as no more prepossessing than the two lower ones. Up here, as also on the office shelves, were goods in stacks, bundles and cardboard boxes. There was no order or beauty in the arrangements, and had it not been for purple threads, tassles and bits of fringe peeping out of the paper-wrapped bundles here and there, no one could have divined at a glance what goods they dealt in. Looking at these rumpled paper-wrapped bundles and boxes, one could not believe that such trifles brought in millions, and that fifty persons, not counting buyers, were active in this warehouse every day.

When Laptev arrived at the warehouse at noon on the day after reaching Moscow, workmen were packing up goods and banging crates so loudly that no one in the first room or office heard him enter. A postman known to him came downstairs with a bundle of letters, frowning in the din, and he didn't notice Laptev either. First to greet him upstairs was his brother Theodore, who so closely resembled him that they were believed to be twins. This similarity regularly reminded Laptev of his own appearance. He now saw before him a short, red-cheeked man, thin on top, with narrow haunches of the lowest pedigree —so unprepossessing, so unprofessional-looking.

'Do I really look like that?' he wondered.

'And glad I am to see you.' Theodore exchanged kisses with his brother and firmly shook his hand. 'I've been so much looking forward every day to seeing you, my dear fellow. When you wrote that you were getting married I suffered agonies of curiosity. I have missed you, old man, as you can imagine—we haven't met for six months. Well, how are things, eh? How is Nina? Very bad?'

'Yes.'

'It's God's will,' sighed Theodore. 'And then your wife? I'll bet she's beautiful. I love her already—she's my dear little sister, isn't she? We'll both spoil her.'

Laptev glimpsed the long familiar, broad, bent back of his father, also a Theodore. The old man was sitting on a stool near the counter talking to a buyer.

'God has sent us great joy, Father,' shouted the younger Theodore. 'Alexis is here.'

Laptev Senior was tall and very powerfully built, so that he still looked a strong, healthy man for all his wrinkles and his eighty years. He spoke in a ponderous, deep, rumbling voice which came booming out of his broad chest as from a barrel. He shaved his chin, wore a clipped military moustache, smoked cigars. Never feeling the cold, he wore a roomy canvas jacket in the warehouse and at home, whatever the season. Having recently undergone a cataract operation, he had poor sight and no longer handled business, but just talked and drank tea with jam.

Laptev bent forward to kiss his father's hand and then his lips.

'It's a mighty long time since we met, sir,' said the old man. 'Aye, that it is. Now, you'll expect congratulations on your marriage, eh? Very well, then. Congratulations.'

He disposed his lips for a kiss, and Laptev bent forward to kiss him.

'And have you brought the young lady with you?' asked the old man. Then, without waiting for an answer, he addressed the buyer. '"I hereby inform you, Dad old man, that I'm marrying a Miss Such-and-Such." Aye. But as for asking our dear old Dad's blessing and advice, that's not our way. Oh, we do things our own way nowadays. Now, when I married I was over forty and I threw myself at my father's feet and asked his advice. There's none of that now.'

Glad to see his son, the old man thought it unseemly to show him affection or display pleasure. His voice, his style of speaking and that 'young lady' business put Laptev into the bad mood that the warehouse always did evoke. Every detail reminded him of the old days when he had been whipped and given bread and water to eat. That boys were still whipped and punched on the nose till they bled, that when these same boys grew up they would punch others in turn—of these things he was aware. And he had only to spend five minutes in the warehouse to expect to be shouted at or punched on the nose.

Theodore clapped the buyer on the shoulder and spoke to his brother. 'Let me present Gregory Timofeyevich, the old firm's main support in Tambov. What an example to today's young men! He's in his sixth decade but he has children who are no more than babies.'

The clerks laughed and the customer, an emaciated, pale-faced middle-aged man, laughed too.

''Tis flying in the face of nature,' remarked the chief clerk, standing behind the same counter. 'Things come out the way they go in.'

The chief clerk, a tall, dark-bearded, bespectacled man of about fifty with a pencil behind his ear, usually expressed his thoughts obscurely, in distant hints, his sly smile indicating that he attached some special, subtle meaning to his words. He liked to obfuscate his speech with bookish expressions which he understood in his own way, and he often gave ordinary words a sense different from their true meaning—for example, the word 'otherwise'. When stating an idea dogmatically and not wanting to be contradicted, he would hold out his right hand before him and give tongue.

'Otherwise!'

Oddest thing of all, the other clerks and the buyers understood him very well. His name was Ivan Pochatkin and he came from Kashira. Congratulating Laptev, he expressed himself as follows.

'Highly meritorious and courageous of you, for bold and proud is woman's heart.'

Another warehouse notability was the clerk Makeichev—a stout, fair-haired worthy with receding hair and side-whiskers. He came up and congratulated Laptev respectfully in a low voice.

'I have the honour, sir. The Lord has hearkened to the prayers of your good father, sir. The Lord be praised, sir.'

Then other clerks came up to congratulate him on his marriage—all fashionably turned out, all with the air of utterly decent, educated men. From their speech they were northerners, and since their every other word was 'sir', their swiftly delivered congratulations whistled through the air like so many whiplashes. 'Sir, here's wishing you every blessing, sir.'

Laptev was soon bored with it all, and felt like going home, but it was awkward to leave, for propriety dictated that he spend at least two hours at the warehouse. Stepping aside from the counter, he asked Makeichev whether they had had a successful summer, and whether there was any news, and the man answered respectfully without looking Laptev in the eye. A boy with close-cropped hair, wearing a grey shirt, gave Laptev a glass of tea without a saucer. A little later another boy knocked into a crate as he was passing, nearly falling over, and the sedate Makeichev suddenly adopted a fearful, vicious, ogre-like look.

'You watch your step!' he yelled.

The clerks were glad that the young master had married and was back again at last. They gave him inquisitive, friendly glances, each feeling obliged as he passed to make some agreeable and respectful remark. But Laptev was sure it was all false, that they flattered him from fear. He could not forget one mentally ill clerk. Fifteen years ago the man had run into the street in his underclothes, bare-footed, shaking his fist at the boss's windows and shouting that they had made his life hell. Long after the poor fellow had been cured people had teased him, reminding him how he had called the bosses 'brutoclats' instead of 'plutocrats'. The Laptev employees had a bad time of it on the whole —such had long been the talk of the entire commercial district. The worst thing was that old Mr. Laptev handled them with oriental duplicity. Thus no one knew what salary his favourites Pochatkin and Makeichev received—it was no more than three thousand a year each with bonuses, actually, but he pretended to pay them seven. Bonuses were paid to all the clerks each year, but secretly, so that those who got little were compelled by pride to say they'd had a lot. None of the office boys knew when he would be promoted to clerk, no employee knew whether the boss was satisfied with him or not. Nothing was directly forbidden to the clerks, and so they had no idea what was permissible and what was not. Though not actually forbidden to marry, they did not do so, fearing to displease the boss and lose their jobs. They could have friends, they could pay visits, but at nine in the evening the gate was locked. Every morning the boss suspiciously scrutinized all his employees, testing them to see if they smelt of vodka. 'Hey, let me smell your breath.'

Every saint's day employees had to attend early service and stand in church where the boss could see them all. The fasts were strictly kept. On special days, on the boss's and his family's name-days, for instance, the clerks had to subscribe for a cake from Fley's or an album. They lived on the ground floor of the house in Pyatnitsky Road and in an outbuilding, three and four to a room. They ate their meals from a common bowl, though each had his own plate before him. If any of the boss's family came in at mealtimes they all stood up.

Only those ruined by the old man's schooling could seriously regard him as their benefactor, Laptev realized. To the rest he was an enemy and a 'brutoclat'. Now, after six months' absence, he saw no improvements, and one innovation even boded ill. His brother Theodore— previously quiet, thoughtful, very sensitive—now had a great air of bustle and efficiency. Pencil behind ear, he scuttled round the warehouse clapping buyers on the shoulder and hailing the clerks as his 'old pals'. He was playing some part, obviously, a part in which Alexis found him unrecognizable.

The old man's voice rumbled on and on. Having nothing to do, he was instructing a buyer in the art of living and managing his affairs, and constantly invoked himself as a model. This boasting, this crushingly authoritative tone—Laptev had heard it ten, fifteen, twenty years

ago. The old man adored himself. From his words it always transpired
that he had made his deceased wife and relatives happy, bestowed
advantages on his children, lavished benefactions on his clerks and
employees, put the entire street and his whole acquaintanceship
eternally in his debt. Whatever he did was excellent, and if others'
dealings went awry, that was only because they wouldn't take his
advice, without which no enterprise could succeed. In church he always
stood in front of the rest of the congregation and even reprimanded the
priests when he considered their performance of the ritual incorrect.
All this he thought pleasing to God, since God loved him.

By two o'clock everyone in the building was at work except the
old man, who was still booming away. Not wanting to be idle, Laptev
took some braid from a female employee, dismissed her, and then
listened to a buyer—a Vologda trader—and told a clerk to deal with
him.

Since the prices and serial numbers of goods were denoted by letters,
cries of 'T–V–A' or 'R–I–T' could be heard.

On his way out Laptev said good-bye to Theodore alone. 'I'll bring
my wife to Pyatnitsky Road tomorrow. But I warn you I shan't stay a
minute if Father says one rude word to her.'

'You're just the same as ever,' sighed Theodore. 'Marriage hasn't
changed you. You must be nice to the old man, lad. All right, be there
by eleven tomorrow. We'll look forward to it, you can come straight
from church.'

'I don't go to church.'

'Then never mind. Just don't be later than eleven so as to leave time
to worship the Lord before lunch. My regards to my dear sister-in-law,
kiss her hand for me. I'm sure I shall like her,' Theodore added with an
air of complete sincerity.

'How I envy you, old man,' he shouted when Alexis was already on
his way downstairs.

Oh, why did the man cringe so humbly, as if he felt naked? Walking
down Nikolsky Road, Laptev puzzled over the change in Theodore.
Then there was this new style of speaking—this 'old man', 'dear
brother', 'God's mercy', 'worship the Lord' stuff. What sickening
humbug!

VI

At eleven next day, a Sunday, Laptev was driving down Pyatnitsky
Road with his wife in a one-horse trap. Fearing some outburst by his

father, he felt ill at ease before he had even arrived. After two nights in her husband's house Julia thought her marriage a disastrous mistake. Had life with him taken her to any town but Moscow she did not think she could have endured such a horror. Moscow amused her, though. The streets, houses, churches delighted her. Could she have driven about Moscow in this splendid sledge pulled by expensive horses—driven all day from morning to evening, careering at full tilt and breathing the cool autumn air—then perhaps she would have felt less miserable.

Near a white, newly plastered two-storey house the coachman halted the horse and turned right. Here they were awaited. At the gate stood the doorkeeper in a new caftan, high boots and galoshes, and two police constables. The whole area, from the middle of the street to the gate and down the yard to the porch, had been strewn with fresh sand. The doorman doffed his cap, the constables saluted. At the porch brother Theodore greeted them with an earnest air.

'So pleased to meet you, sister.' He kissed Julia's hand. 'Welcome.'

He led her upstairs by the arm, and then down a corridor through a group of men and women. Then came a vestibule, also crowded and smelling of incense.

'I shall now present you to our Dad,' whispered Theodore amid the solemn, tomb-like silence. 'A venerable old gent, the pater.'

In a large hall, by a table prepared for divine service, stood in evident anticipation old Mr. Laptev, a priest in his high purple hat, and a deacon. The old man gave his hand to Julia without a word. No one spoke. Julia was embarrassed.

The priest and deacon put on their vestments. A censer, scattering sparks and smelling of incense and charcoal, was brought. Candles were lit. Clerks tiptoed into the hall and stood by the wall in two ranks. It was quiet, no one even coughed.

'Bless us, O Lord,' began the deacon.

They celebrated the service solemnly, omitting nothing and intoning the prayers 'Sweetest Jesus' and 'Holy Mother of God'. The choir sang only from sheet music, and took its time about it. Laptev had noted how embarrassed his wife had been just now. While the prayers were read and the choristers were delivering their diversely harmonized triple 'Lord Have Mercy', he agonizingly expected the old man to look round at any moment and utter some reprimand like 'don't you know how to make the sign of the cross?' He was annoyed. Why all these people? Why this ceremony, these clergymen, this choir? Here was your old-fashioned Russian merchant style with a vengeance. But when Julia and the old man together allowed the Gospel to be laid on their heads, and when she several times genuflected, he saw that she liked all this and was relieved.

At the end of the service, during the anthem 'Long Life', the priest gave the old man and Alexis the cross to kiss, but when Julia came up he covered the cross with his hand and looked as if he wanted to speak. They waved to the choir to be quiet.

'The prophet Samuel came to Bethlehem at the Lord's command,' said the priest. 'And elders of the town besought him, trembling. "Comest thou peaceably, O prophet?" And the prophet said, "Peaceably: I am come to make sacrifice unto the Lord: sanctify yourselves, and rejoice this day with me." Shall we too question thee, O servant of the Lord Julia, whether thou dost come in peace unto this house?'

Deeply moved, Julia blushed. When he had finished, the priest gave her the cross to kiss and spoke in quite a different voice.

'Now it's time young Mr. Theodore was married, high time.'

The choir sang again, the congregation stirred, there was noise and bustle. Greatly touched, eyes brimming with tears, the old man kissed Julia three times and made the sign of the cross in front of her face.

'My house is yours,' he said. 'I'm old, I need nothing.'

The clerks offered congratulations and said something, but the choir was singing so loudly that nothing could be heard. Then they had lunch and drank champagne. She sat by the old man while he told her that it was wrong to live asunder, and right to live together in one house. Divisions and disagreements led to ruin.

'I made money, my children only spend it,' he said. 'Now, you must live in the same house with me and make money. I'm old, it's time I had a rest.'

Julia kept catching sight of Theodore. He looked so like her husband, but was more restless in his movements, more diffident. He fussed about near her and kept kissing her hand.

'We're just ordinary folk, sister dear.' Red blotches appeared on his face. 'We lead ordinary Russian, Christian lives, dear sister.'

On the way home Laptev was delighted that all had gone well, and that nothing untoward had occurred as he had feared.

'You wonder that a hefty, broad-shouldered father should have such small, narrow-chested children as me and Theodore,' he told his wife. 'Well, that's no problem. My father married my mother when he was forty-five and she was only seventeen. She would go white and tremble in his presence. Nina was born first, when Mother was comparatively healthy, so she turned out stronger and better than us. But Theodore and I were begotten and born when my mother was already worn out by a reign of terror. I remember that Father began teaching or, to put it bluntly, beating me before I was five. He birched me, boxed my ears, clouted my head, and when I woke up each morning my main worry was whether I'd be beaten that day. Theodore and I were forbidden to play and lark about. We had to attend matins and morning service, kiss the hands of priests and monks, recite the prescribed prayers at home. You're religious, you like all this, but I fear religion, and when I pass a church I remember my childhood and feel scared. When I was eight they took me on at the warehouse. I was an ordinary office boy, which was hard for me because I was beaten almost daily. Then, after I'd started school, I'd do my homework before dinner, and from then until night I'd be cooped up in the same old warehouse. So it went on till I was twenty-two and met Yartsev at the university. He persuaded me to leave my father's house. Yartsev has done me a lot of good. I tell you what.' Laptev laughed gleefully. 'Let's go and see Yartsev. He's a very fine man, and he'll be so touched.'

VII

On a Saturday in November Anton Rubinstein was conducting at the Conservatoire. The place was packed, and it was hot. Laptev stood behind some columns while his wife and Kostya Kochevoy sat far away in front, in the third or fourth row. When the interval began the 'certain personage'—Polina Rassudin—unexpectedly came by. Since marrying, he had often been worried by the thought of a possible meeting with her. As she glanced at him, frankly and openly, he remembered that he hadn't even got around to offering her any explanation or writing her a couple of friendly lines. It was as if he was hiding from her. He felt ashamed, he blushed. She shook his hand firmly and impulsively, and asked whether he had seen Yartsev.

Not waiting for his reply, she swept on with long strides as if impelled from behind.

She was very thin, ugly, long-nosed, she always looked utterly exhausted, as if it cost her enormous effort to keep her eyes open and not fall over. She had lovely dark eyes and a clever, kind, unaffected expression, but her movements were jerky and harsh. She was hard to talk to because she could not listen or speak calmly. And loving her had been an ordeal. When staying with Laptev she would sometimes go off in long, loud peals of laughter, hiding her face in her hands and claiming that love was not the basis of her existence. She was as coy as a maid of seventeen, and one had to put out all the candles before kissing her. She was thirty and had married a schoolmaster, but had not lived with her husband for many years. She made her living by teaching music and playing in quartets.

During the Ninth Symphony she again passed by, as if by accident, but a packed group of men standing behind the columns held her up, and she paused. Laptev noticed that she wore the same velvet bodice in which she had attended last year's concerts and those of the year before. Her gloves were new. So was her fan, but cheap. She would have liked to dress well but, lacking the knack and grudging the expense, rigged herself out so tastelessly and sloppily that she could easily have been mistaken for a young monk when striding swiftly down the street on her way to a lesson.

The audience applauded, there were shouts of encore.

Polina went up to Laptev, looked him sternly over. 'You are to spend this evening with me. We're going to have tea together when this is over, do you hear? I insist on it. You owe me a lot, and you have no moral right to deny me this trifle.'

Laptev agreed. 'All right then.'

The symphony evoked endless encores. The audience stood up and left very slowly. Since Laptev could not go without a word to his wife he had to wait by the door.

'I'm dying for some tea,' Polina Rassudin complained. 'I'm all parched inside.'

'We can get some here,' said Laptev. 'Come to the bar.'

'No, I've no money to waste on barmen. *I'm* not a tradesman's wife.'

He offered her his arm but she refused, pronouncing a long wearisome sentence which he had often heard from her, to the effect that she did not classify herself as one of the 'weaker' or 'fair' sex, and did not require the services of any male persons, thank you very much.

While talking to him she kept glancing at the audience, often greeting friends. These were fellow-alumnae of Guerrier's courses and the Conservatoire, and also her pupils, male and female. She shook hands firmly and impulsively with a sort of jerkiness. But then she began twisting her shoulders and trembling like a fever victim. In the end she spoke quietly, looking at Laptev with horror.

'What kind of wife have you married? Where were your eyes, maniac? Whatever did you see in that silly, insignificant little bitch? I loved you for your mind, for what you really are, didn't I? Whereas that little china doll only wants your money.'

'Let's forget that, Polina,' he begged. 'Anything you could say about my marriage I've told myself umpteen times already. Don't hurt me more than necessary.'

Julia appeared wearing a black dress and the large diamond brooch which her father-in-law had sent her after that prayer service. She was followed by her suite—Kochevoy, two doctors of her acquaintance, an officer and one Kish—a stout young man in student uniform.

'You go with Kostya, I'll come on afterwards,' Laptev told his wife.

Julia nodded and went off. Trembling all over and cringing nervously, Polina pursued her with a look of revulsion, hatred and pain.

Laptev feared to go to her room, foreseeing some disagreeable confrontation, with harsh words and tears. He suggested tea in a restaurant. But 'No, no, no', she said. 'Come to my place. Don't you restaurant me.'

She disliked restaurants because their air seemed poisoned with tobacco and male breath. She was oddly biased against strange men. To her they were all debauchees capable of leaping upon her at any moment. Besides, tavern music irritated her, gave her headaches.

Leaving the Gentry Club, they took a cab to Ostozhenka Road and Savelovsky Street where Polina lived. On the way there Laptev thought about her. He really did owe her a great deal. Laptev had first met her at his friend Yartsev's when she had been teaching him musical theory. She had fallen very much in love with him, with no thought of personal advantage. After becoming his mistress, she had gone on giving her lessons and working until she collapsed. Thanks to her he had begun to understand and love music, which had barely interested him before.

'Half my kingdom for a glass of tea,' she said hollowly, covering her mouth with her muff to avoid catching cold. 'Five lessons I've just given, blast it. My pupils are such dolts and dunderheads, I nearly died of rage. When this hell will end I don't know. I'm dead beat. When I've saved three hundred roubles I shall give it all up, go to the Crimea, lie on the beach and gulp oxygen. How I love, love, love the sea.'

'You won't go anywhere,' said Laptev. 'First, you won't save anything. And secondly, you're too mean. I'm sorry, but I'll ask you again—is it really less humiliating to amass your three hundred roubles copeck by copeck from idlers who study music with you because they have nothing else to do, than to borrow it from your friends?'

'I have no friends.' She was annoyed. 'So I must ask you not to talk nonsense. The working class, to which I belong, has one privilege—the consciousness of being incorruptible, together with the right to despise shopkeepers and not to borrow from them. No sir, I am not for sale. I'm not one of your Julias!'

Laptev did not pay the cabman, knowing that this would unleash a spate of all-too-familiar words. She paid herself.

She rented a small furnished room with board in a single lady's flat. Her Becker grand piano was at Yartsev's house on Great Nikitsky Road for the time being, and she went there every day to play. Her room contained armchairs in covers, a bed with a white summer quilt, flowers provided by the landlady. There were oleographs on the walls, and there was nothing to remind one that the tenant was a woman and a graduate. There was no dressing-table, there were no books, there was not even a desk. It was obvious that she always went straight to bed on arriving home, and that she left the house at once after getting up in the morning.

The cook brought the samovar, and Polina made tea. Still trembling, for it was cold in her room, she began criticizing the choir which had sung in the Ninth Symphony. Closing her eyes through excess of emotion, she drank one glass of tea, then another, then a third.

'So you're married,' she said. 'But don't worry, I shan't mope. I shall contrive to wrench you out of my heart. I'm just annoyed and upset to find you as worthless as everyone else, not wanting a woman's intellect and brains, but her body, her beauty, her youth. Youth, youth!' She spoke through her nose, as if mimicking someone, and laughed. 'You need purity, *Reinheit*.' She laughed aloud, lolling against the back of her chair. '*Reinheit*, I ask you!'

When she had finished laughing her eyes were full of tears. 'Are you at last happy?'

'No.'

'Does she love you?'

'No.'

Agitated, feeling miserable, Laptev got up and paced the room.

'No,' he repeated. 'I'm very unhappy, Polina, since you must know. But what can I do? I've done something foolish, but it can't be mended now. I must be philosophical. She married me without love, stupidly perhaps. She did marry me for money, yes, but without really thinking what she was doing. Now she obviously realizes she was wrong. She suffers, I can see that. We sleep together at night, but she's afraid to be alone with me for five minutes in daytime. She seeks entertainment, a social life. She's ashamed to be with me. Scared too.'

'But she still takes your money, doesn't she?'

'Don't be silly, Polina,' shouted Laptev. 'She takes my money because she simply doesn't care whether she has money or not. She's a decent, honourable woman. She just married me because she wanted to leave her father, that's all.'

'But are you sure she'd have married you if you hadn't been rich?' Polina asked.

'I'm not sure of anything at all,' said the agonized Laptev. 'I can't make sense of anything. For God's sake, let's stop talking about it, Polina.'

'Do you love her?'

'Madly.'

Silence ensued. She drank a fourth glass while he paced about, and reflected that his wife was probably having supper at the Doctors' Club at this moment.

'But can one really love without knowing why?' Polina asked with a shrug. 'No, that's just the voice of animal passion. You're intoxicated—poisoned by that beautiful body, all that *Reinheit*. Leave me, you're dirty. Go to your woman.'

She dismissed him with a gesture, took his hat, threw it at him. He put on his fur coat silently and went out, but she ran into the hall, frantically clutched his upper arm and burst into sobs.

'Stop it, Polina, do.' He could not unclench her fingers. 'Please calm yourself.'

She closed her eyes, she grew pale, her long nose turned an unpleasant, waxen, corpse-like colour, and Laptev still could not unclench her fingers. She had fainted. He carefully lifted her, laid her on her bed, sat by her for ten minutes until she came round. Her hands were cold, her pulse was weak and irregular.

She opened her eyes. 'Do go home, please, or I'll start howling again. I must pull myself together.'

After leaving her he did not go to the Doctors' Club, where he was expected, but went home. All the way there he asked himself reproachfully why he had set up house with someone else instead of this woman who so loved him, this true wife and friend. She was the only person who was attached to him. And in any case it would surely have been a rewarding, worthwhile undertaking—to provide this intelligent, proud, toil-worn creature with happiness, with a peaceful haven.

'Are they really my style?' he asked himself of these hankerings after beauty, youth and that unattainable bliss which, by keeping him so miserably depressed for three months, seemed to punish or mock him.

The honeymoon had long been over, but he was still absurdly ignorant of his wife's true nature. She sent her old school-friends and father long letters on five sides of paper, and so she must find things to write about. But what did she speak to *him* of? The weather, that it was lunch time or supper time. When she said her long prayers before going to bed, and then kissed her wretched crosses and icons, he looked at her with hatred.

'She prays,' he reflected, 'but what, what does she pray about?' He insulted both of them, as he went to bed with her and took her in his arms, by telling himself that this was what he was paying for, and a revolting thought it was. He wouldn't have minded if she had been a lusty, bold, bad sort of woman, but there was all this youth, religious feeling, tenderness. There were those pure, innocent eyes.

During their engagement her devotions had touched him, but now the very conventional and explicit nature of her views and convictions seemed a barrier between him and the real truth. Everything in his domestic life was torture to him now. When his wife sighed or laughed unaffectedly as they sat together in the theatre, he was hurt that she should enjoy herself on her own, without sharing her pleasure with him. And she had hit it off with all his friends, oddly enough. *They* all knew what she was like, while he had no idea. He just sulked, said nothing. He was jealous.

Reaching home, Laptev donned dressing-gown and slippers, sat in his study and read a novel. His wife was out, but within half an hour the bell in the hall rang, followed by the hollow thud of Peter's steps as he ran to answer it. It was Julia. She came into the study in her fur coat, cheeks red with cold.

'There's a large fire at Presnya,' she gasped. 'There's a huge glow. I'm going there with Kostya Kochevoy.'

'Then good luck to you.'

Seeing her health, her freshness, the childlike panic in her eyes, Laptev calmed down. He read for another half hour and went to bed.

On the next day Polina sent two books once borrowed from him to the warehouse together with all his letters, his photographs and a note consisting of the one word *basta*.

VIII

At the end of October Nina had an unmistakable relapse. She was losing weight rapidly, her face was changing. Despite the agonizing pain she thought that she was recovering, put on her clothes every morning as if she was well—and then lay in bed all day fully dressed. By the end she had become downright garrulous. She would lie on her back and talk quietly away, panting with the effort. Her death came suddenly and these were its circumstances.

It was a clear, moonlit night and there was sleighing on the newly fallen snow in the street, the noise being borne into the room from outside. Nina lay on her back. Sasha, the only person to sit with her now, sat dozing by her side.

'I don't remember his second name,' said Nina quietly. 'But they called him Ivan. The surname was Kochevoy. He was a poor clerk and the most awful drunkard, may he rest in peace. He visited us, and we'd give him a pound of sugar and a small packet of tea every month. And sometimes money, of course. Ah, well. Now, here's what happened next. Our Kochevoy embarked on the most almighty bender and snuffed it—went out like a light. He left a son, a little boy of seven, a poor little orphan. We took him in and hid him in the clerks' quarters, where he survived for twelve months after a fashion, without Father knowing. When Father did see him he just dismissed him with a gesture and said nothing. When the little orphan was eight I tried to get him into a high school—this was when I was engaged to be married. I took him here, I took him there, but they wouldn't have him anywhere. He kept crying. "Why cry, you silly boy?" I asked. Then I took him to the Second High School on Razgulyay Square, where they accepted him, God bless them. The little lad would walk from Pyatnitsky Road to the Square and back every day. Alexis paid the fees. The boy was good at his lessons, he had a feel for them and he's turned out all right, praise be. Now he's a lawyer in Moscow, he's Alexis's friend, and they're each as brainy as the other. There's someone we didn't despise, we took him in, and now he mentions us in his prayers, sure enough. Ah, well——'

Nina spoke more and more quietly, with long pauses. After one brief silence she suddenly raised herself and sat up.

'I, er, I don't feel so grand,' she said. 'Oh mercy, I can't breathe.'

Sasha knew that her mother must die soon, and seeing the sudden pinched look on her face, she guessed that the end had come and took fright.

'No, Mother, no,' she sobbed. 'You mustn't.'

'Run into the kitchen, tell them to send for your father. I really do feel awful.'

Sasha ran through the whole house calling, but no servants were in. There was only Leda asleep on a chest in the dining-room—fully dressed, with no pillow. Just as she was, without galoshes, Sasha ran into the yard and then into the street. On a bench outside the gate sat her nanny watching the sleigh-riding. From the river, where there was a skating rink, a brass band could be heard.

'Mother's dying, Nanny,' Sasha sobbed. 'We must fetch Father.'

Nanny went up to the bedroom, looked at the patient, placed a lighted wax candle in her hand. Sasha was appalled and dashed about imploring someone, anyone, to fetch her father. Then she put her coat and kerchief on, and ran into the street. She knew from the servants that her father had another wife and two little girls with whom he lived in Market Street. From the gate she ran to the left, weeping, afraid of the strange people, and was soon getting stuck in the snow and shivering.

A free cab approached her, but she did not take it—perhaps the man would drive her out of town, rob her and throw her into the grave-yard. (There had been such an incident, the servants had spoken of it at tea.) She walked and walked—out of breath, weary, weeping. Emerging in Market Street, she asked where Mr. Panaurov lived. Some unknown woman gave her a long explanation and then, seeing that she wasn't taking it in, led her by the hand to a one-storey house with a porch. The door was not locked. Running through the hall and down the corridor, Sasha at last found herself in a light, warm room where her father sat over a samovar, and with him a lady and two little girls. By now Sasha could not get out a single word, she only sobbed. Panaurov understood.

'Mother's unwell, isn't she?' he asked. 'Tell me, dear, is Mother unwell?'

He was alarmed and sent for a cab.

When they arrived home Nina sat supported by pillows, candle in hand. Her face looked dark, her eyes were shut. In the bedroom, bunched near the door, were Nanny, cook, the chambermaid, the peasant Prokofy and others of the servant class—strangers. Nanny was whispering orders which were not understood. Pale and sleepy, Leda stood at the far end of the room by the window sternly surveying her mother.

Panaurov took the candle from Nina's hands and tossed it behind the chest-of-drawers, frowning with disgust.

'This is terrible.' His shoulders trembled. 'You must lie down, Nina,' he said kindly. 'Do lie down, dear.'

She looked at him without recognizing him. They laid her down.

When the priest and Dr. Belavin arrived the servants were piously crossing themselves and praying for her.

'What a to-do.' The doctor pensively emerged into the drawing-room. 'And so young, you know—not yet forty.'

The little girls' loud sobs were heard. Pale, with wet eyes, Panaurov went up to the doctor.

'Do me a favour and send a telegram to Moscow,' he said in a feeble, suffering voice. 'I'm just not up to it, old son.'

The doctor obtained ink and wrote the following telegram to his daughter.

> NINA DIED EIGHT PM   TELL HUSBAND HOUSE ON DVOR-
> YANSKY STREET IS FOR SALE WITH TRANSFERABLE MORTGAGE
> NINE THOUSAND TO PAY   AUCTION IS ON THE TWELFTH
> ADVISE YOU NOT TO MISS CHANCE

IX

Laptev lived in a side-street off Little Dmitrovka Street, not far from Old St. Pimen's Church. Besides a large house facing the street he also rented a two-storey cottage on the premises for his friend Kochevoy, a junior barrister known to all the Laptevs by the familiar name 'Kostya' because they had watched him grow up. Opposite that cottage stood another, also two-storeyed, occupied by a French family —husband, wife, five daughters.

It was twenty degrees below, and the windows were frosted up. When he awoke in the morning, Kostya swallowed fifteen drops of medicine with a worried air, then took two dumb-bells from his bookcase and did his exercises. He was tall, very thin, with large, reddish whiskers. But his most remarkable features were his extraordinarily long legs.

Peter, a middle-aged odd-job man in a jacket, his cotton trousers tucked into jack-boots, brought in the samovar and made tea.

'It's mighty fine weather today, Mr. Kochevoy,' he said.

'Fine it is. But you and I aren't managing too brilliantly, old son.' Peter sighed from politeness.

'What are the children doing?' asked Kochevoy.

'The priest ain't here yet. Mr. Laptev's teaching 'em himself, like.'

Kostya found an ice-free part of the window and looked out through binoculars. He pointed them at the French family's windows, but said that he couldn't see anything.

Meanwhile Laptev was giving Sasha and Leda a scripture lesson downstairs. They had now been living in Moscow for six weeks with their governess, on the ground floor of the cottage. A priest and a municipal schoolmaster came and taught them three times a week. Sasha was on the New Testament, Leda had just started the Old. Last time Leda had been told to revise everything up to Abraham.

'So Adam and Eve had two sons,' said Laptev. 'Very good, but what were their names? Try and remember.'

Leda, stern as ever, said nothing, staring at the table and just moving her lips while her elder sister Sasha looked at her face and suffered agonies.

'You know it all right—just don't be nervous,' said Laptev. 'Now then, who were Adam and Eve's sons?'

'Able and Cable,' whispered Leda.

'Cain and Abel,' corrected Laptev.

A large tear crawled down Leda's cheek and fell on the book. Sasha lowered her eyes and blushed, also ready to weep. Laptev felt so sorry for them that he was speechless. Tearfully gulping, he got up from the table and lit a cigarette. Then Kochevoy came down carrying a newspaper. The children stood up and curtsied without looking at him.

'For God's sake, Kostya, you teach them,' said Laptev. 'I'm afraid I'll cry as well, and I must pop over to the warehouse before lunch.'

'All right.'

Laptev went out. Frowning and looking most serious, Kostya sat at the table and drew the Bible towards him.

'Well, what are you on?'

'She knows the flood,' said Sasha.

'The flood? Fine, we'll cook something up on that. The flood it is.' Kostya ran through the short description of the flood in the Bible.

'I must observe that no flood like this actually took place,' he then added. 'Nor was there any Noah. Several thousand years before

Christ the earth experienced a remarkable inundation which is mentioned not only in the Hebrew Bible but also in the books of other
ancient peoples, to wit the Greeks, the Chaldees and the Hindus.
Whatever form this inundation took it can't have flooded the whole
earth. It did fill the valleys if you like, but you can bet the mountains
were still there. By all means read the nice book if you want, but don't
take it too seriously.'

Leda's tears welled up again. Turning away, she suddenly burst out
sobbing so loudly that Kostya shuddered and stood up from his seat
in utter dismay.

'I want to go home to Daddy and Nanny,' she said.

Sasha also burst out crying. Kostya went up to his room and
telephoned Julia. 'The girls are crying again, dear. This is beyond me.'

Wearing a knitted kerchief, with nothing over her dress, Julia ran
across from the big house. Nipped by the frost, she comforted the girls.

'You must, you must believe me,' she pleaded, clutching first one
and then the other to her. 'Your Daddy *will* be here today, he's sent a
telegram. You're grieving for your mother, and so am I, my heart's
breaking in two. But it can't be helped. What God has willed we
can't unwill, can we?'

When they had stopped crying she wrapped them up and took
them for a drive. They drove down Little Dmitrovka Street, then past
the Strastnoy Boulevard to the Tver Road. At the Iverian Chapel they
stopped and each set up a candle and knelt in prayer. On their way
back they called at Filippov's Café and bought lenten cracknels with
poppy seed.

The Laptevs would lunch between two and three, the meal being
served by Peter. By day this Peter ran errands to the post office, to the
warehouse or to the District Court for Kostya, and generally made
himself useful. In the evenings he packed cigarettes, at night he was
on the run opening the door, and between four and five in the morning
he did the stoves. When he slept no one knew. He adored opening
bottles of soda water, which he did easily and silently, not spilling a
drop.

'Cheers!' said Kostya, and drank a glass of vodka before his soup.

Julia had not liked Kostya at first. That deep voice, those slangy
sayings—all that 'shove off', 'sock on the jaw', 'scum of the earth',
'activate the samovar' stuff—his habit of clinking glasses and waxing
maudlin over his vodka, it all seemed so puerile. But when she knew
him better she felt very much at ease with him. He was open with her,

liked talking to her quietly in the evenings, and even lent her novels of his own composition, which had so far been kept even from such close friends as Laptev and Yartsev. She read them, she praised them so as not to offend him, and he was pleased because he hoped to become a famous writer one day. His novels were all about the countryside and manor houses, though he only saw the country very occasionally when visiting friends who had a holiday cottage. And he had only been in one manor house in his life, on a visit to Volokolamsk over a court case. He shunned the theme of love as if ashamed of it, and he went in for nature descriptions, favouring such expressions as 'the hills' fussy silhouettes', 'the clouds' grotesque forms', 'a chord of mysterious harmonies'.

That his novels were never published he put down to censorship.

He liked being a lawyer. But it was those novels, not the law, that he considered his main life's work. He thought himself a subtle artistic organism. Art held a permanent fascination for him. He neither sang nor played a musical instrument, he had no ear for music at all, but he attended all the symphonic and philharmonic concerts, he organized charity performances and cultivated singers.

There was conversation at lunch.

'It's quite amazing,' said Laptev. 'Brother Theodore has completely floored me yet again. We must find out, says he, when our firm's centenary will be so that we can apply to be registered as gentlefolk. And he's completely serious! What *is* up with him? Frankly, I'm worried.'

They talked about Theodore, and about how posturing was all the rage nowadays. For instance, Theodore was trying to ape an old-style merchant, though he wasn't a merchant at all any more. And when the teacher—from the school where old Laptev was patron—called for his salary, Theodore even spoke and walked in a different way, behaving like the man's superior officer.

As there was nothing to do after lunch they went into the study. They spoke of modernism in the arts and *The Maid of Orleans*. Kostya delivered an entire soliloquy—he fancied himself at taking off Mariya Yermolov. Then they played bridge. Instead of going back to their cottage, the little girls sat on, pale and sad, both on the same armchair, listening to the street noises and hoping to hear their father arrive. In the dark and candlelight of evening they felt miserable. The talk over bridge, Peter's steps, the crackling in the fireplace—it all irritated them and they didn't want to look at the fire. In the evenings they no longer even wanted to cry, but felt on edge and sick at heart. How could people talk and laugh when their mother was dead? That was beyond them.

'What did you see through your binoculars this morning?' Julia asked Kostya.

'Nothing, but yesterday the old Frenchman himself had a bath.'

At seven o'clock Julia and Kostya left for the Maly Theatre. Laptev stayed behind with the girls.

'It's time your father was here.' He looked at his watch. 'His train must be late.'

The girls sat in the armchair, silently clinging to each other like little animals who feel the cold, while he paced the rooms, looking impatiently at his watch. The house was quiet. Then, just before ten, there was a ring, and Peter answered the door.

Hearing the well-known voice, the children shrieked, burst out sobbing, rushed into the hall. Panaurov wore a sumptuous fur coat. His beard and whiskers were white with frost.

'Yes, yes—in a moment,' he muttered while Sasha and Leda, sobbing and laughing, kissed his cold hands, his cap, his fur coat. Handsome, languid, spoilt by love, he unhurriedly caressed the children and went into the study.

'I shan't stay long, friends.' He rubbed his hands. 'I'm off to St. Petersburg tomorrow, they've promised me a transfer to another city.'

He had put up at the Hotel Dresden.

X

A frequent visitor at the Laptevs' was Ivan Yartsev, a well-built, powerful, black-haired man with a clever, pleasant face. He was considered good-looking, but had put on weight lately, which spoilt his face and figure, as did his habit of wearing his hair cropped almost to the scalp. His powerful build and his strength had once earned him a nickname, 'the Bruiser', at the university.

He had done an arts course with the Laptev brothers, had then transferred to science, and now held a master's degree in chemistry. He was not banking on a professorial chair, he had never even been a laboratory assistant, but taught physics and biology at a boys' secondary school and two girls' high schools. Enchanted by his pupils, especially the girls, he would say that the rising generation was wonderful. Apart from his chemistry he also studied sociology and Russian history at home, and sometimes published short articles in newspapers and magazines, signing them 'Y'. When he talked about botany or zoology he resembled a historian, but when he discussed a historical problem he looked like a scientist.

Another member of the Laptev inner circle was Kish, the 'eternal student'. He had read medicine for three years before going over to mathematics, and spending two years on each year of that course. His father, a provincial pharmacist, sent him forty roubles a month, while his mother sent him ten without his father knowing. This sufficed for his living expenses, and even for such luxuries as a cloak trimmed with Polish beaver, gloves, scent and photography—he often had his picture taken and would give copies to his friends. A neat, balding fellow with golden whiskers round his ears, modest, he always looked poised to be of service. He was for ever doing people's errands, dashing round collecting subscriptions, or freezing at dawn outside some theatrical box-office to buy a ticket for a lady of his acquaintance. Or he would go and order a wreath or bouquet at someone's behest. The word was always 'Kish will fetch it, Kish will do it, Kish will buy it'. These errands were ill-managed on the whole, Kish being showered with reproaches while people often forgot to pay for what he had bought them. But he never said anything. In crises he only sighed. He was never greatly pleased or greatly grieved, he was always telling long, boring stories, and his jokes always made people laugh—but only because they weren't funny. For instance, he once addressed the following would-be witticism to Peter. 'You, Peter, are no sturgeon.' Everyone roared with laughter, and Kish himself joined in for quite a time, delighted to have launched a shaft so felicitous. At professors' funerals Kish would walk in front with the torch-bearers.

Yartsev and Kish usually came over for afternoon tea, and if the host and hostess were not going to the theatre or a concert that tea would drag on till supper time. One February evening the following conversation took place in the dining-room.

'A work of art is significant and useful only when its theme embraces a serious social problem,' said Kostya with an angry look at Yartsev. 'If a work protests against serfdom, if the author tilts against the smugness of high society, then that work is significant and useful. But novels and stories full of moaning and groaning, all about her falling in love with him and him falling out of love with her—such works are insignificant, say I. To hell with them.'

Julia told him that she agreed. 'These lovers' meetings, these acts of infidelity, these separations followed by assignations—is there nothing else to say? There are plenty of ill, unhappy, desperately poor people, aren't there? It must disgust them to read all this.'

Laptev disliked his wife discussing love so earnestly and coolly—a young woman not yet twenty-two. But he could guess why she did it.

'If poetry doesn't solve the problems you think important, then refer to technical works,' said Yartsev. 'Look up your criminal and financial law, read scientific articles. Why should *Romeo and Juliet* discuss educational freedom, say, or prison hygiene instead of love, when you can find all that stuff in specialist articles and reference works?'

'That's a bit steep, old man,' interrupted Kostya. 'We aren't talking about giants like Shakespeare or Goethe, we're talking about a hundred odd gifted and not so gifted writers who'd do a sight more good if they left love alone and tackled the popularization of knowledge and humane ideals.'

In a slightly nasal voice, pronouncing his 'rs' like a Parisian, Kish began telling the plot of a story which he had recently read. He related the details without haste. Three minutes passed, then five, then ten, and he was still at it, though no one knew what he was on about. His expression grew more and more apathetic, his eyes had lost their lustre.

Julia could not contain herself. 'Do get it over with, Kish, this is sheer agony.'

'Give over, Kish,' shouted Kostya.

Everyone, Kish included, burst out laughing.

Then Theodore came in, with red blotches on his face, rapidly greeted them and took his brother into the study. He had been avoiding crowded gatherings of late, preferring to talk to one person at a time.

'Let the young folk laugh, you and I must have a proper talk.' He sat in a low armchair away from the lamp. 'It's ages since we met, old son. How long is it since you were at the warehouse? A week, I reckon.'

'Yes, there's nothing there for me to do, and I'm frankly fed up with the old man.'

'They can manage without us two there of course, but you must have some sort of job. "In the sweat of thy face shalt thou eat bread", as the saying goes. Labour is pleasing to God.'

Peter brought a glass of tea on a tray. Theodore drank it without sugar and asked for more. He was a great tea drinker, and could put away ten glasses in an evening.

'I tell you what, old man.' He stood up and approached his brother. 'Why don't you simply go ahead and put up for the City Council, then we'll gradually winkle you on to the Executive Committee, and you'll end up as Deputy Mayor. The further you go the bigger you'll get. You're an intelligent, educated man, you'll be noticed and invited to St. Petersburg. Local government people are all the rage there, old son, and—hey presto!—you'll be an under-secretary or something before you're fifty and wear a ribbon round your neck.'

Laptev did not answer. Realizing that all this, the under-secretary-ship, the ribbon, were Theodore's own ambitions, he didn't know what to say.

The brothers sat in silence. Theodore opened his watch and stared at it for an unconscionable time as if wanting to check the movements of the hands. To Laptev his expression seemed strange.

They were called in for supper, and Laptev went into the dining-room while Theodore stayed in the study. The argument was over, and Yartsev was talking like a professor lecturing.

'Differences of climate, energy, taste and age render human equality a physical impossibility. But civilized man can neutralize this in-equality just as he has tamed swamps and bears. A scientist has con-trived to teach a cat, a mouse, a falcon and a sparrow to eat from the same bowl. Education will do the same for people, one hopes. Life marches on, culture is visibly striding ahead, and a time will obviously come when the current position of factory-hands, say, will seem as absurd as serfdom—when they swopped girls for dogs—seems to us.'

'That won't be soon, oh dear me no,' Kostya laughed. 'It will be quite a while before Rothschild finds his gold vaults absurd, and until that day the worker must bend his back, starve till his stomach swells. Take it from me, old chap—we mustn't stand idly by, we must fight. A cat eating from the same bowl as a mouse—is *that* due to social consciousness? Not on your life. It was forced to do it.'

'Theodore and I are rich, our father's a capitalist, a millionaire, so we're the ones you have to struggle against.' Laptev wiped his forehead with his palm. 'A struggle against me—my consciousness finds that a bit hard to swallow. I am rich, but what have I got out of it so far? What has this power bestowed on me? In what way am I happier than you? My childhood was sheer hell, and money never saved me from the birch. My money was no use to Nina when she fell ill and died. If I'm not loved I can't make anyone love me even if I spend a hundred million.'

'But think how much good you can do,' said Kish.

'Good? What do you mean? Yesterday you asked me to help some mathematician who's looking for a job. I can do no more for him than you can, believe me. I can give him money, but that's not what he wants, now, is it? I once asked a famous musician to find a post for an indigent violinist, and he told me that only a non-musician would have made such a request. I give you the same answer—the reason you ask my help so assuredly is that you've never been in a rich man's shoes yourself.'

'But why this parallel with the famous musician?' Julia blushed. 'Why drag the famous musician in? It beats me.'

Her face shook with hate, and though she lowered her eyes to conceal this emotion, her expression was understood not only by her husband but by everyone at the table.

'Why drag in the famous musician?' she repeated quietly. 'Nothing's easier than to help the poor.'

Silence ensued. Peter served grouse, but no one would eat it, they only took salad. Unable to remember, now, what he had said, Laptev realized that it had not been his words, it had been the fact that he had taken part in the conversation at all which had aroused her hatred.

After supper he went to his study. Tensely, with pounding heart, anticipating further humiliations, he listened to the proceedings in the drawing-room. They had started another argument. Then Yartsev sat at the piano and sang a sentimental ditty. He was very versatile—sang, played, even did conjuring tricks.

'I don't know about you, gentlemen, but I don't want to stay at home,' said Julia. 'Let's go out.'

They decided on a trip out of town and sent Kish to the Merchants' Club for a troika. Their reason for not inviting Laptev was that he didn't usually go on such excursions and that he had his brother with him. But he took it that he bored them, and was utterly out of place among such jolly young people. Such was his annoyance, his resentment, that he almost wept. He even took pleasure in being treated so unkindly, in being this despised, stupid, boring husband, this mere moneybags. And should his wife betray him that night with his best friend, should she confess as much with a look of hatred—then he would be still more pleased.

The students, actors and singers whom she knew, Yartsev, even her casual encounters—all made him jealous to the point where he now yearned for her to be unfaithful. He wanted to surprise her with

someone, then poison himself and be rid of the whole nightmare once
and for all. Theodore drank tea, swallowing noisily, but then he too
made to leave.

'Something must be up with the old man,' he said, putting on his
fur coat. 'His eyesight's very bad.'

Laptev also put on his coat and went out. He saw his brother as far
as the Strastnoy Boulevard, then took a cab to the Yar Restaurant.

'So that's your married bliss, is it?' he taunted himself. 'That's love
for you.'

His teeth chattered, whether from jealousy or something else he
couldn't tell. At the Yar he paced about near the tables and listened to
a cabaret singer in the big room. He hadn't one sentence prepared in
case his wife and friends should appear, realizing in advance that if she
did show up he would only give a pathetic, silly smile, and everyone
would sense what emotions had brought him here. The electric
lighting, the noisy band, the smell of powder, the staring women—it
all confused him. He stopped by the door, trying to eavesdrop and spy
on the private rooms, and feeling as if he, the singer, the women—all
were playing some base and despicable role. Then he went on to the
Strelna, but saw none of them there either, and only when he was
approaching the Yar again on his way back did a troika noisily over-
take him with shouts from the drunken coachman and roars of
laughter from Yartsev.

When Laptev reached home after three in the morning Julia was in
bed. Seeing that she was not asleep, he went up to her.

'I understand your revulsion, your hatred,' he snapped. 'But you
might spare me in front of strangers, you might conceal your feelings.'

She sat up in bed with her feet hanging down, her eyes huge and
black in the lamplight.

'Please forgive me,' she said.

Agitated, trembling all over, he could not get a word out, but stood
silent in front of her. She too was shaking, and sat there like a criminal
waiting for him to state the case against her.

'I've been hurt so much,' he said at last, clutching his head. 'It's
sheer hell, I feel I've gone mad.'

'Do you think I find it easy?' Her voice shook. 'God only knows
how I feel.'

'You've been my wife for six months, but you haven't a spark of
love for me in your heart. There's no hope, no gleam of it. Why ever
did you marry me?' Laptev went on desperately. 'Why? What devil

drove you to my arms? What were you hoping for, what did you want?'

She looked at him in horror, as if fearing that he would kill her.

'Did you like me, did you love me?' He choked for breath. 'No. Then what? What? Tell me, what?' he shouted. 'It was that damned money, blast it.'

'It wasn't that, I swear,' she exclaimed. She crossed herself, flinching at the insult, and for the first time he heard her weep.

'As God is my witness, no,' she went on. 'I wasn't thinking of money, I don't need that. I simply felt I'd be wrong to refuse you. I was afraid I might ruin both your life and mine. And now I'm suffering for my mistake, suffering unbearably.'

She sobbed bitterly. Seeing how hurt she was, he sank on the carpet before her at a loss for words.

'Do stop, please,' he muttered. 'I insulted you because I love you so madly.' He suddenly kissed her foot and embraced her passionately. 'Just a tiny spark of love,' he muttered. 'Come on then, lie to me. Don't say it was a mistake.'

But she went on crying, and he felt that she only tolerated his caresses as the inevitable consequence of her mistake. As for the foot which he had kissed, that she had tucked beneath her like a bird. He felt sorry for her.

She lay down, covered herself up. He undressed and lay down too. In the morning both felt awkward, not knowing what to talk about, and he even sensed that she trod unsteadily on that kissed foot.

Before lunch Panaurov came to say good-bye, and Julia felt an irresistible urge to go back to her home town. How good to leave, she thought, to recover from married life, from this embarrassment and constant awareness of having behaved badly. It was decided at lunch that she would go with Panaurov and stay at her father's for two or three weeks until she was bored.

XI

She and Panaurov travelled in a private railway compartment, he wearing an odd-looking lambskin cap.

'Well, Petersburg was a disappointment,' he sighed, articulating deliberately. 'They promise you everything, but nothing specific. Yes, my dear, I've been a Justice of the Peace and a Permanent Secretary, I've chaired the local appeal court, and finally I've been a consultant to the County Council. I've served my country, I think, and I do have some claim to attention. But, do you know, I just can't get a transfer to another town.'

He shut his eyes, shook his head.

'I'm not recognized,' he went on sleepily. 'I'm no ace administrator of course, but I am a decent, honest man, and nowadays even that's a rarity. I confess I've deceived women a bit, but in my relations with the Russian government I've always been the perfect gentleman. Still, enough of that.' He opened his eyes. 'Let's discuss you. Why this sudden urge to visit your dear papa?'

'Oh, I'm not getting on too well with my husband.' Julia looked at his cap.

'Yes. Funny chap, isn't he? All the Laptevs are odd. Your husband's not that bad, he can pass at a pinch, but brother Theodore's a real nit-wit.'

Panaurov sighed. 'And do you have a lover?' he asked in all seriousness.

Julia looked at him in amazement, laughed. 'Heavens, what a question!'

At about half-past ten both got out at a large station and had supper. When the train moved off Panaurov took his overcoat and cap off, and sat by Julia's side.

'You're very lovely, I must say,' he began. 'You remind me of a freshly salted gherkin, if you'll excuse the snack-bar simile. It still has the whiff of the forcing bed, so to speak, but it has already absorbed a little salt and smells of dill. You're gradually shaping into a magnificent woman—a splendid, elegant creature. If this trip had taken place five years ago'—he sighed—'I'd have thought it my agreeable duty to place myself on the register of your admirers. But now, alas, I'm in retirement.'

Smiling a sad, yet compassionate smile, he put his arm round her waist.

'You must be mad.' She blushed, so scared that her hands and feet went cold. 'Stop it, Gregory.'

'What's so frightening, my dear?' he asked softly. 'What's so terrible? You're not used to it, that's all.'

To him a woman's protests only meant that he had impressed and attracted her. Holding Julia's waist, he firmly kissed her cheek, then her lips, in absolute certainty that he was affording her great pleasure. Recovering from her terror and embarrassment, she began laughing. He kissed her again.

'That's all you get from the old warrior.' He was putting on that comic hat. 'A certain Turkish pasha, a nice old boy, was once presented with—or, more probably, inherited—an entire harem. When his beautiful young wives paraded before him he inspected them, telling each one as he kissed her that this was "all I'm able to bestow on you now". Those are my sentiments too.'

She found it all foolish and unusual, it amused her. Feeling a little skittish, she stood on the seat, humming, and took a box of chocolates from the rack.

'Catch!' she shouted. And threw him one.

He caught it. She threw him another, loudly laughing, and then a third. He caught them all and put them in his mouth, looking at her with eyes full of yearning. There was much about his face, features and expression that was feminine and childlike, she felt. When she sat down out of breath, still looking at him and laughing, he touched her cheek with two fingers and pretended to be annoyed.

'Bad, bad girl!'

'Take it.' She gave him the whole box. 'I don't like sweets.'

He ate every single one and shut the empty box in his trunk, liking boxes with pictures on them.

'Enough of the horseplay,' said he. 'It's the land of Nod for the old warrior now.'

He took out his Bokhara dressing-gown and a cushion from a hold-all, lay down and covered himself with the gown.

'Good night, dearest lady,' he said, quietly sighing as if his whole body ached.

Soon his snores were heard. Feeling no constraint, she too lay down and was soon asleep.

As she drove home from the station next morning in her native town the streets seemed abandoned and deserted, the snow grey, the houses small and squashed. She encountered a funeral procession. The body was borne in an open coffin with banners.

'They say a funeral means good luck,' she thought.

In the house where Nina had once lived the windows were now pasted with white notices.

With sinking heart she drove into the yard, rang the door-bell. It was opened by a maid—a buxom, sleepy stranger in a warm quilted blouse. On her way upstairs Julia remembered Laptev declaring his love for her there. But the stairs were unwashed now, with footmarks everywhere. In the cold first-floor corridor waited fur-coated patients, and for some reason her heart thumped—she was almost too agitated to walk.

Stouter than ever, brick-red, hair dishevelled, the doctor was drinking tea, and even shed a tear in his delight at seeing his daughter. She was the old man's only joy, she reflected. Greatly touched, she embraced him heartily, and said that she would stay a long time, till Easter. After changing in her room, she went to the dining-room to drink tea with him, while he stalked about, hands in pockets, humming that ruminating hum which meant that he was vaguely annoyed.

'You have lots of fun in Moscow,' said he. 'I'm overjoyed for your sake, but I don't need anything myself, being old. I'll soon conk out and free you all. Why is my hide so tough, why am I still alive? Amazing, isn't it? Astonishing.'

He said he was a sturdy old donkey, not to say dogsbody. He had been saddled with treating Nina, with caring for her children, with her funeral, while this popinjay Panaurov would have nothing to do with it all, and had even borrowed a hundred roubles from him which still hadn't been returned.

'Take me to Moscow, put me in the mad-house,' the doctor said. 'I must be certifiable, seeing I'm naïve and infantile enough to go on believing in truth and justice.'

Then he reproached her husband with lack of foresight in not buying houses when they were on advantageous offer. No longer could Julia feel that she was the old man's only joy. While he received patients and did his rounds she stalked the house, not knowing what to do or think. She had grown away from her town and her home. She had no urge to go out in the street or visit people she knew, and when she remembered her former girl friends and her own life as a girl she neither felt sad nor hankered for the past.

That evening she dressed up and went to church. But the congregation consisted of no one in particular, and so her magnificent fur coat and hat went unappreciated. She felt as if the church and she herself had both undergone some change. At one time she had enjoyed hearing the canon recited at vespers, and listening to the choir sing anthems like 'I shall open my lips'. She had once enjoyed slowly drifting with the congregation towards the priest who stood in the centre of the church, she had liked the feel of holy oil on her forehead. But now she was just waiting for the service to end. Leaving church, she feared being accosted by beggars. It would be tedious to stop and search her pockets. She had no small change, anyway, only roubles.

She went to bed early, but fell asleep late and kept dreaming of certain portraits and that morning's funeral procession. They bore the open coffin with the body into a yard, stopped by a door, tossed the corpse on sheets for a time. Then they banged it full tilt into the door. Julia woke, leapt up in terror. There actually was a banging on the door downstairs. The bell-wire rustled on the wall, but she heard no ring.

The doctor coughed. Then the maid was heard going down and coming back.

'Madam!' It was the maid knocking at Julia's door.

'What?'

'A telegram.'

Julia went out carrying a candle. Behind the maid stood the doctor wearing his overcoat over his underclothes, also with a candle.

'The bell's broken.' He yawned, half asleep. 'It should have been mended ages ago.'

Julia opened the telegram and read it.

WE DRINK YOUR HEALTH

YARTSEV   KOCHEVOY

'Oh, how silly of them.' She laughed aloud, feeling relaxed and cheerful.

Returning to her room, she quietly washed and dressed, then spent some time packing until it was light. At noon she left for Moscow.

XII

In Easter week the Laptevs went to the School of Art to see a picture exhibition. They went as a family, Moscow fashion, taking both little girls, their governess and Kostya.

Laptev knew all the famous artists by name, and never missed an exhibition. He sometimes painted landscapes himself, at his country cottage in summer, thinking that he had excellent taste and might have made a fine artist had he studied. When abroad he would visit antique shops, inspect the wares with a knowing air, express an opinion, make some purchase. The dealer would charge whatever price he liked, and the object would then be stuffed in a box and lie around the coach-house before vanishing who knows where. Or he would go into a print-shop, scrutinize the pictures and bronzes carefully at length, make various observations—then suddenly buy some rough frame or box of worthless paper. The pictures in his home were of generous dimensions but poor quality, with some good ones which were badly hung. He had often paid a lot for what had turned out to be crude forgeries. Now, why should one so timid about life in general be so very bold and brash at picture exhibitions? Odd.

Julia looked at the pictures as her husband did—making a peep-hole of her fingers or through opera glasses—and was surprised that the people in them seemed alive and that the trees looked real. But they made no sense to her. She felt that many pictures at the exhibition were more or less the same, and that the whole aim of art came down to making the persons and objects depicted look real when observed through your fingers.

'This wood is a Shishkin,' her husband explained. 'He paints the same things over and over again. Now, you'll observe that real snow is never as mauve as this. And this boy has a left arm shorter than the right.'

When all were tired and Laptev had gone in search of Kostya so that they could return home, Julia stopped by a small landscape and idly looked at it. The foreground was a stream crossed by a wooden bridge with a path merging into dark grass on the far side. On the right was part of a wood with a bonfire near it—there must be grazing horses and watchmen hereabouts. Far away the sunset's last fires smouldered.

Julia imagined going over the bridge, and then further and further down the path. It was quiet there, sleepy landrails cried. A light winked far away. Suddenly she vaguely felt that she had often seen them long ago—those clouds spanning the red of the sky, that wood, these fields. She felt lonely, she wanted to walk on, on, on down the path. There, at the sunset's end, lay reflected an eternal, unearthly Something.

'How well painted.' She was surprised at her sudden understanding of the picture. 'Look, Alexis—see how quiet it is.'

She tried to explain why the landscape had so taken her fancy, but neither her husband nor Kostya understood. Sadly smiling, she continued to gaze at the scene, disturbed to find that the others saw nothing special in it. Then she began going round the gallery again, looking at the pictures, wanting to understand them, and no longer did the exhibition seem to contain so many identical works. Returning home, and noticing for the first time in her life the large picture above the grand piano in the hall, she felt animosity towards it.

'Who wants that sort of picture?'

After this the golden cornices, the Venetian mirrors with their flowers, the pictures like that above the grand piano, her husband's and

Kostya's debates on art—all depressed and irritated her, even arousing her occasional hatred.

Life went on as usual from day to day, promising nothing in particular. The theatre season was over, the warm weather had begun and was set fair. One morning the Laptevs were to go to the District Court and hear Kostya as defence counsel appointed by the court. After being held up at home they arrived when the cross-examination of witnesses had begun. A private of the reserve was charged with breaking and entering. Among the witnesses numerous laundresses testified that the accused often visited their employer, the laundry manageress. On the thirteenth of September—the day before the Exaltation of the Cross—he had turned up late in the evening with a hangover, demanding money for a drink, but no one had given him any. Then he had gone away, but had come back an hour later with beer and peppermint cakes for the girls. They had drunk and sung almost till dawn, but on looking round in the morning had found the lock on the loft entrance broken and some laundry missing—three men's nightshirts, a skirt, two sheets. Kostya ironically asked each witness whether she had drunk any of the beer brought by the accused that night. Obviously he was trying to make it look as if they had robbed their own laundry. He delivered his speech without the least emotion, looking angrily at the jury.

He explained what breaking and entering was, and what petty larceny was. He spoke circumstantially, convincingly, revealing a remarkable gift for solemnly retailing a long string of earnest platitudes. Just what was he driving at, though? From his oration a juror could only conclude either that there had been breaking and entering without larceny—in that the proceeds of the linen had been consumed by the laundresses—or else that there had been larceny without breaking and entering. Yet he was saying just the right things, evidently, since his speech greatly affected the jury and the public, being highly popular. Julia nodded to Kostya when the acquittal was brought in, and later gave him a hearty hand-shake.

In May the Laptevs moved to a cottage at Sokolniki, Julia now being pregnant.

XIII

More than a year passed. At Sokolniki, not far from the Moscow-Yaroslavl railway line, Julia and Yartsev sat on the grass. A little to one side lay Kochevoy, his hands under his head, looking at the sky. All three had walked far enough, and were waiting for the six o'clock excursion train to pass so that they could go home for tea.

'All mothers think their children are unusual, that's nature's way,' said Julia. 'A mother stands by the cot for hours observing her baby's little ears, eyes, nose, and delighting in them. If a stranger kisses baby the poor woman thinks this affords him the utmost pleasure. And a mother can talk only of her baby. I know this maternal weakness and guard against it. But my Olga *is* special, honestly. The look she gives when she's feeding! And her laugh! She's only eight months old, but I've honestly never seen such intelligent eyes, even in a child of three.'

'Which do you love more, by the way,' Yartsev asked. 'Your husband or your baby?'

Julia shrugged. 'I don't know. I never did love my husband much, and Olga's really my first love. I didn't marry Alexis for love, as you know. I used to be so silly, suffering agonies and obsessed with having ruined both our lives. But now I see that one doesn't need love, that's all nonsense.'

'Then what feeling does attach you to your husband, if not love? Why do you stay with him?'

'I don't know—well, habit, I suppose. I respect him, I miss him when he's away for a while. But that's not love. He's an intelligent, decent man, and that's enough to make me happy. He's very kind and unaffected.'

'Alexis is intelligent, Alexis is kind.' Kostya lazily raised his head. 'This intelligence, this kindness, this charm of his—until one's known him for donkeys' years one doesn't even notice them, my dear. And what use are his kindness and intelligence? He'll shell out all the cash you want, that *is* within his range. But when it comes to force of character, and standing up to some boor or bounder, then he jibs and loses heart. People like dear kind Alexis are all very well, but they're utterly unfit for struggle. They're no use for anything, actually.'

At last the train appeared. Steam, bright pink, surged from the funnel and soared above the wood. Two windows in the last carriage suddenly flashed blindingly in the sun.

'Tea time.' Julia stood up.

She had put on weight recently, and now walked in leisurely, matronly style.

'Still, it's a poor look-out without love.' Yartsev followed her. 'We keep talking and reading about love, but we do precious little loving. A poor look-out, say I.'

'None of that matters, Ivan,' said Julia. 'That's not where happiness lies.'

They had tea in the garden where mignonette, stocks and tobacco flowers were blooming, with the early gladioli opening out. Julia was going through a blissful phase of spiritual calm and equilibrium, as Yartsev and Kochevoy could tell from her expression. She needed nothing beyond what she had, and they too began to feel gloriously at peace with themselves. Things were panning out so nicely—just right, there was no denying that. The pines were wonderful, there was a uniquely splendid aroma of resin, the cream was delicious, Sasha was a clever, good little girl.

After tea Yartsev sang ditties to his own piano accompaniment while Julia and Kochevoy sat listening silently, except that Julia stood up now and then, and quietly went out to look at her baby and at Leda, who had had a temperature for two days and had eaten nothing.

'My love, my gentle love,' sang Yartsev. He shook his head. 'Well, friends, I don't know what you have against love, cross my heart I don't. If I wasn't busy fifteen hours a day I'd fall in love myself. Definitely.'

Supper was laid on the terrace. It was warm and quiet, but Julia huddled in her shawl and complained of the damp. When it grew dark she felt vaguely uneasy, couldn't stop shivering, and asked her guests to stay on. She plied them with wine, and had cognac brought in after supper to stop them leaving. She didn't want to be left alone with the children and servants.

'We—the ladies staying in the resort, that is—are putting on a show for the children,' she said. 'We already have everything—the theatre, the actors. All we lack is a play. We've been sent a score of odd plays, but none of them's any good.' She turned to Yartsev. 'Now, you like the theatre, you know your history. So write us a historical play.'

'Very well.'

The guests drank up the cognac and made to leave. It was past ten o'clock, late by holiday standards.

Julia saw them through the gate. 'It's so dark, pitch black. How you'll find your way I can't think, friends. It is cold, I must say.'

She wrapped herself up tighter and returned to the porch. 'Alexis must be playing cards somewhere,' she shouted. 'Good night.'

Coming out of the brightly-lit house, Yartsev and Kostya could see nothing, but blindly groped their way to the railway line and crossed it.

'Can't see a bloody thing.' Kostya spoke in a deep voice, pausing to look at the sky. 'And the stars, look at them. Just like new fifteen-copeck pieces, they are, Hey, Yartsev!'

'What?' replied Yartsev's voice.

'I can't see, I say. Where are you?'

Yartsev went up to him whistling, took his arm.

'Hey, everyone round here!' Kostya suddenly shouted at the top of his voice. 'We've caught a socialist.'

In his cups he was always rather rowdy—shouting, picking quarrels with policemen and cabbies, singing, laughing crazily.

'To hell with Mother Nature!' he shouted.

Yartsev tried to calm him. 'Now, that's enough of that. Please.'

The friends soon grew used to the dark, and began to make out the silhouettes of the tall pines and telegraph poles. From Moscow's stations occasional whistles were heard, wires whined piteously. But the wood itself gave off no sound—the silence had a proud, powerful, mysterious air. The tips of the pines almost seemed to brush the night sky. The friends found the right cutting in the forest, and walked down it. It was pitch dark. Only the long strip of sky festooned with stars, and the trodden earth beneath their feet, showed that they were on a path. They walked silently side by side, both fancying that people were approaching from the other direction. Then their intoxicated mood subsided. Yartsev had the idea that the wood might be haunted by the ghosts of Muscovy's Tsars, boyars and patriarchs. He wanted to tell Kostya so, but refrained.

When they came to the city gate the sky was faintly paling. Still silent, Yartsev and Kochevoy marched down a paved road past cheap holiday cottages, taverns, timber-yards. Under the bridge of a branch line they felt a sudden dampness—pleasant, with a smell of lime trees. Then a long, broad street opened up without a soul or a light on it.

Dawn was breaking when they reached Krasny Prud.

'Moscow town has many agonies in store.' Yartsev gazed at St. Alexis's Convent.

'What put that into your head?'

'I don't know, I love Moscow.'

Yartsev and Kostya were both Moscow-born. They adored it, being vaguely hostile to other towns. That Moscow is a wonderful city and Russia a wonderful country they were convinced. In the Crimea, in the Caucasus, in foreign parts they felt bored, out-of-place, frustrated. Dear old Moscow's drab weather was the nicest and healthiest kind they found. The days when cold rain raps the windows, when twilight comes on early, when the walls of houses and churches take on a sombre brown hue, when you don't know what to wear when you go out—those days were an agreeable stimulus to them. They found a cab near the station in the end.

'It really would be nice to write a historical play,' said Yartsev. 'But without all the—you know—the Lyapunovs and Godunovs. I'd take Yaroslav's and Monomakh's times. I hate all Russian historical plays, Pimen's soliloquy excepted. When you handle a historical source, when you read a Russian history text-book, even, everything Russian strikes you as phenomenally accomplished, proficient and fascinating. But when I see a historical play at the theatre, Russian life seems so drab, morbid, tame.'

At Dmitrovka Street the friends parted and Yartsev went on to his lodgings in Nikitsky Road. He was dozing and swaying, he kept thinking about the play. Suddenly he imagined an appalling racket, a clanging, shouts in an incomprehensible language like Kalmuck. Then there was some village engulfed in flames, while near-by woods, decked with hoar frost and delicately pink in the fire's glow, were so clearly visible far and wide that every fir tree stood out. Savages, mounted and on foot, careered through the village, both they and their horses as crimson as the sunset.

'Those are Polovtsians,' thought Yartsev.

One of them—old, terrifying, bloody-faced, charred all over—was tying a young girl with a white, typically Russian face to his saddle. The old man was shouting furiously and the girl had a sad, intelligent look.

Yartsev shook his head and woke up.

'My love, my gentle love,' he sang.

Paying the cabby and then going upstairs to his room, he could not shake off his hallucination, but saw the flames move into the trees. The wood crackled and started smoking. Crazed with fear, a huge wild boar hurtled through the village.

The girl tied to the saddle kept watching.

When Yartsev entered his room it was light. On the grand piano near open music books two candles were burning low. On the sofa lay Polina in a dark dress with a sash, holding a newspaper, fast asleep. She must have been playing for a long time waiting for him, and had fallen asleep before he arrived.

How utterly worn out she looked, he thought.

Carefully removing the paper from her grasp, he covered her with a rug, put out the candles, went into his bedroom. As he lay down he thought about the historical play and he couldn't get the tune 'My love, my gentle love' out of his head.

Two days later Laptev looked in for a moment to say that Leda had diphtheria, and that Julia and the baby had caught it from her. Then, five days later, came news that Leda and Julia were recovering, but the baby had died and the Laptevs had fled from their Sokolniki villa to the city.

XIV

Laptev disliked spending much time at home these days. His wife often went over to the cottage in their yard, saying that she must help the girls with their studies, but he knew that she didn't go there for that but to cry at Kostya's place. Came the ninth day, the twentieth, the fortieth and he kept having to go to the St. Alexis Cemetery to attend the requiems, and then suffer agonies for twenty-four hours, thinking only of this unhappy baby and uttering sundry common-places to console his wife. He rarely visited the warehouse nowadays, charitable activity being his sole occupation. He invented odd chores and troubles for himself, and he was glad when he had to spend a whole day driving about on some trivial errand.

He had recently been intending to go abroad and study the organiza-tion of hostels for the poor, and this idea now diverted him.

It was autumn. Julia had just gone over to the cottage to weep, while Laptev lay on his study sofa trying to think of somewhere to go. Then Peter announced Polina Rassudin. Laptev delightedly jumped up to greet the unexpected guest—his former, now almost forgotten, friend. She had not changed at all since the evening when he had last seen her.

'It's been ages, Polina.' He held out both hands. 'I'm so glad to see you, you've no idea. Do come in.'

She greeted him with a snatch of the hand, entered the study, sat down without removing hat or coat.

'I only dropped in for a moment, I've no time for small talk. Pray sit down and listen. Whether you are or are not glad to see me I don't in the least care, not giving a rap for the condescending attentions of personages of the male tribe. If I am here now it is because I've been in five places already today and been turned down in all of them, and the matter is urgent. Now, then.' She looked him in the eye. 'Five students of my acquaintance, persons of limited intelligence but indubitable poverty, have failed to pay their fees and are being sent down. Your wealth imposes the obligation to go to the university this instant and pay up.'

'I'll be glad to, my dear.'

'Here are the names.' She gave Laptev a note. 'Off with you this instant, you can bask in domestic bliss later.'

A vague rustle came from the door into the drawing-room—the dog scratching itself, most likely. Polina flushed and jumped up.

'Little Miss Whatnot's listening at the key-hole,' she said. 'How revolting!'

Laptev was offended on Julia's behalf.

'She's not here, she's over at the cottage,' he said. 'And don't talk about her like that. Our baby died and she's dreadfully unhappy.'

'Then you can set her mind at rest.' Polina laughed and sat down again. 'She'll have a dozen more.

> "A person well may stupid be,
> Yet still engender progeny." '

Laptev remembered often hearing this or something like it in days gone by, and caught the evocative scent of time past, of his free bachelor existence—when he had felt young and capable of anything, when love for his wife and memories of his child still lay ahead of him.

He stretched himself. 'Let's go together.'

When they reached the university Polina waited by the gates while Laptev went to the registry. Returning soon afterwards, he handed her five receipts.

'Now where are you off to?' he asked.

'Yartsev's.'

'Well, I'm going with you.'

'You'll interrupt his work, you know.'

'No, I assure you.' He gave a pleading look.

She was wearing a black mourning hat with crêpe trimmings and a very short, threadbare overcoat with bulging pockets. Her nose seemed longer than ever, there was no colour in her face despite the cold. Laptev enjoyed following her, obeying her, listening to her complaints. What inner resources the woman must have, he reflected on the way—ugly, angular, restless, lacking all dress sense, with hair always dishevelled, always vaguely ungainly, she was yet enchanting.

They reached Yartsev's room by the servants' entrance through the kitchen, where they were greeted by the cook, a trim old girl with grey curls. Much embarrassed, she gave a sweet smile which made her tiny face look like a pie.

'Come in, do.'

Yartsev was out. Polina sat at the piano and embarked on some boring, difficult exercises after telling Laptev not to interrupt. Not seeking to distract her with talk, he sat on one side leafing through *The European Herald*. After playing for two hours, her daily stint, she ate something in the kitchen and went off to give her lessons. Laptev read an instalment of some novel, then just sat for a while, neither reading nor feeling bored, delighted that he would be late for dinner at home.

'Ha, ha, ha.' That was Yartsev's laugh, and he followed it in person—healthy, hearty, red-cheeked, in a new tail-coat with bright buttons.

The friends dined together. Then Laptev lay on the sofa while Yartsev sat by him and lit a cigar. Twilight fell.

'I must be getting old,' said Laptev. 'Ever since my sister died I keep thinking about death for some reason.'

They spoke of death and immortality. How nice it indeed would be to be resurrected and then fly off to Mars or somewhere, to be for ever idle and happy, and above all to think in some special non-terrestrial manner.

'But I don't want to die,' said Yartsev quietly. 'No philosophy can reconcile me to death, I look at it simply as annihilation. I want life.'

'Do you enjoy life, old friend?'

'Indeed I do.'

'Now, in that sense I just don't understand myself. My mood varies from dejected to apathetic. I'm timid, I lack self-confidence, my conscience makes me craven, I just can't adapt to life and master it. Some people talk nonsense or behave like scoundrels—and with what zest! Yet I sometimes consciously perform good works while feeling only anxiety or utter indifference. I put it all down to being a slave, old man—the grandson of a serf. A lot of us plebeians will come to grief before we find the right path.'

'That's all very well, my dear chap.' Yartsev sighed. 'It just shows once again how rich and varied Russian life is. Ah, rich indeed it is. You know, I'm more convinced every day that we're on the brink of some colossal achievement. I'd like to live to see it, have a part in it myself. Believe it or not, we have a wonderful new generation now, that's my view. Teaching children, especially girls, is sheer delight—those children are superb.'

Yartsev went to the piano and struck a chord.

'I am a chemist,' he went on. 'I think like a chemist, I shall die a chemist. But I'm greedy, I fear to die without glutting myself. Chemistry alone, that's not enough. I clutch at Russian history, at the history of art, at the theory of education, at music. This summer your wife told me to write a historical play, and now I'd like to write, write, write. I think I could sit in one place for three days and three nights, just writing. Images have drained me, they crowd my head—I feel my pulse pounding in my brain. It isn't that I want to make anything extraordinary out of myself or achieve greatness. Not a bit of it—I just want to live, think, hope, be everywhere at once. Life is short, my dear chap, and one must do one's best to live it.'

After this friendly conversation, which ended only at midnight, Laptev took to visiting Yartsev almost daily. He felt drawn there. He usually arrived in the late afternoon, lay down and waited patiently for Yartsev to arrive, not in the least bored. Yartsev would come back from his job, have his meal and sit down to work, but Laptev would ask a question, conversation would start up, work would lose its interest. The friends would part at midnight, delighted with each other.

It didn't last long, though. Reaching Yartsev's one day, Laptev found Polina there on her own. She was doing her piano exercises. She gave him a cold, almost hostile, look and did not shake hands.

'Tell me, pray, when will all this end?' she asked.

'All what?' Laptev did not understand.

'You come here every day, you stop Yartsev working. Now, he's not some damned tradesman, he's a scholar. Every moment of his life is precious. I should have thought you might see that and show at least *some* sensitivity.'

'If you think I'm interfering I shall discontinue my visits,' said Laptev shortly. He was embarrassed.

'A very good thing too. And leave now, or he'll come and find you here.'

Polina's tone, her look of indifference, completed his embarrassment. She felt nothing for him, she just wanted him to hurry up and go—what a change from their former love. He went out without shaking hands, expecting her to call him back. But the scales rang out again. Slowly making his way downstairs, he knew that they were strangers now.

Three days later Yartsev came over for the evening.

'I have news.' He laughed. 'Polina has moved in with me.' Somewhat embarrassed, he went on in a low voice. 'Well, we're not in love of course, but I, er, I don't think that matters. I'm glad to offer her a peaceful refuge and a chance to give up work if she falls ill. Now, *she* feels that by living with me she'll bring order into my life, that I'll become a great scholar under her influence. That's her view, so let her keep it. They have a proverb down south—"if wishes were horses, beggars would ride." Rather funny, that.'

Laptev said nothing. Yartsev paced the study—looking at the old, familiar pictures, sighing.

'Yes, my friend, I'm three years older than you. It's too late for me to think of real love now. A woman like Polina—that's a stroke of luck for me, in fact, and naturally I shall live happily with her until my old age. But I still have vague regrets, damn it, and vague yearnings. I keep seeing myself lying in a valley in the Caucasus, I dream I'm at a ball. Man's never satisfied with what he has, in other words.'

He went into the drawing-room and sang some songs as if he had no care in the world, while Laptev sat in his study with his eyes shut and tried to understand why Polina had taken up with Yartsev. How sad to think that all attachments lacked solidity and permanence. Polina's liaison with Yartsev annoyed him. He was annoyed with himself too because his feelings for his wife had completely changed.

XV

Laptev sat in an armchair reading and rocking himself. Julia was also in the study, reading. There seemed to be nothing to say, and both had been silent since morning. He cast her occasional glances over his book. You marry because you're passionately in love, he thought, or you marry without love at all. It makes no difference, does it? The jealous, emotional, suffering phase—how distant it seemed to him now. He had already fitted in a foreign trip which he was now recovering from, reckoning to return to England in the spring. He had liked England.

Having come to terms with her grief, Julia no longer went over to the cottage to cry. She did not visit shops or attend theatres and concerts that winter, but stayed at home. Disliking large rooms, she was always in her husband's study or in her own room where she kept her icon-cases—part of her dowry—and where the landscape she had so fancied at the exhibition hung on the wall. She spent hardly any money on herself, and her expenses were now as small as they had been back in her father's house.

The winter passed cheerlessly. People were playing cards all over Moscow, but when an alternative entertainment was conceived— singing, reciting or sketching, say—that turned out an even greater bore. The scarcity of accomplished persons in the city, the participation of the same old singers and lecturers at the same old functions—it gradually made the joys of artistic appreciation pall and become a tedious, monotonous obligation for many.

Besides, no day passed without tribulations for the Laptevs. Old Mr. Laptev's eyesight was very poor. He had stopped going to the ware-house, and the eye specialists said he would soon be blind. Theodore didn't go there any more either for some reason, but spent all his time at home writing. Panaurov had obtained his transfer to another town with promotion to a higher rank, and was now staying at the Dresden Hotel and visiting Laptev almost daily to borrow money. Finally, Kish had left the university and was hanging round the Laptevs' place for days on end telling long, boring stories and expecting them to find him a job. It was all irksome and tiring, and it took the zest out of life's daily round.

Peter came into the study and announced a lady visitor unknown to them and described on the card which he presented as a 'Joséphine Milan'.

Julia stood up lazily and went out, slightly limping from pins and needles in the leg. In the doorway appeared a woman—thin, very pale, dark-browed, dressed all in black. She clenched her hands on her breast.

'Monsieur Laptev, save my children,' she pleaded.

The jangle of bracelets and powder-blotched face were familiar to Laptev, and he recognized the woman at whose home he had once so maladroitly chanced to dine before his marriage. This was the second Mrs. Panaurov.

'Save my children!' she repeated. Her face quivered, and she suddenly looked old and pathetic. Her eyes reddened. 'Only you can save us. I've spent all I have on this visit to Moscow. My children will starve.'

She made to sink to her knees while Laptev, panic-stricken, clasped her arms above the elbows.

'Sit down, I beg you,' he muttered, offering her a chair.

'We have no money left for food,' she said. 'Gregory is going off to his new job, but he doesn't want to take me and the children with him. All the money you've sent in your generosity—he spends it on himself. So what can we do, I ask you? My poor, unfortunate children.'

'Calm down, I beg you. I'll tell the office to send the money to you personally.'

She burst into sobs. Then she calmed herself and he noticed the tear furrows running down her powdered cheeks. And she had a moustache.

'You're infinitely generous, Monsieur Laptev. But do be our guardian angel, our fairy godfather—do persuade Gregory not to abandon me, to take me with him. I love him so much, I'm crazy about him. He is my joy in life.'

Laptev gave her a hundred roubles and promised to talk to Panaurov. He saw her to the hall, terrified of her bursting into sobs again, or falling on her knees.

Kish arrived next. Then Kostya turned up with a camera. He had recently taken up photography, and would snap everyone in the house several times a day, an occupation which caused him much distress. He had even lost weight.

Before tea Theodore arrived. Sitting in a corner of the study, he opened a book and spent some time looking at one page, obviously not reading it. Then he dawdled over his tea, his face red. He depressed Alexis, whom even his brother's silence irked.

'You may congratulate Russia on acquiring a new pundit,' said Theodore. 'Quite seriously, though, I have given birth to a certain little article, old man, just to try out the old pen as it were, and I've brought it to show you. Read it, my dear chap, and tell me what you think. But do be frank.'

He took an exercise book from his pocket and gave it to his brother. The article was called 'The Russian Soul'. It was written in the flat, featureless style commonly cultivated by persons with no talent and much secret conceit. The main idea was as follows. An intellectual has the right not to believe in the supernatural, but has the duty to conceal his scepticism so as not to create a stumbling-block and shake the faith of others. Without faith there can be no idealism, and idealism is destined to save Europe and show Man his true path.

'But you don't say what Europe is to be saved *from*,' Laptev remarked. 'It's obvious.'

'Not at all.' Laptev strode up and down excitedly. 'I can't see why you wrote it. Still, that's your business.'

'I want to publish it as a pamphlet.'

'That's your business.'

They said nothing for a minute, and Theodore sighed. 'I profoundly, I infinitely regret that we don't see eye to eye. Oh, Alexis, my dear brother Alexis. We're Russians, you and I, we belong to the Orthodox Church, we have a certain breadth. All these wretched German and Jewish ideas, how ill they suit us. We aren't a couple of mountebanks, you and I, we represent an illustrious merchant house.'

'An illustrious house—fiddlesticks!' Laptev tried to contain his irritation. 'An illustrious house! Our grandfather was always being kicked around by the nobs, and the most wretched little jack-in-office used to slap his face. Grandfather beat Father, Father beat you and me. What did your "illustrious house" ever give either of us? What kind of nerves and blood have we inherited? For nearly three years you've been maundering on like some canting cleric, mouthing miscellaneous clap-trap. As for what you've just written—why, it's the ravings of a flunkey! And what of myself? Well, just look at me. I lack adaptability, audacity, strength of mind. I'm as scared of taking the smallest step as if I risked a flogging. I quail before nobodies, imbeciles and swine, my utter inferiors intellectually and morally. I fear hall porters, janitors, policemen of all kinds, I fear them all because I was born of a mother who was hounded to death, and because I have been beaten and terrorized from infancy. We'd do well not to have children, you and I. Oh, let's hope your illustrious merchant house ends with the two of us.'

Julia came into the study and sat by the desk.

'Were you arguing?' she asked. 'Am I interrupting?'

'No, sister dear,' answered Theodore. 'We're discussing matters of principle. Now, you'—he turned to his brother—'say our family is this that and the other. Yet this family created a business worth millions. That means quite a bit!'

'To hell with your business worth millions. A man with no special intelligence or ability accidentally becomes a trader, makes his pile. He does business day in day out without system, without purpose, without even any lust for money, operating like some machine, and the money flows towards him without his taking a step. He's at his business all his life, only liking it because he can boss his clerks and mock his customers. He's a church elder because he can bully the choir and make them dance to his tune. He's a school trustee because he likes to see the schoolmaster as an underling and can boss him around. It's not business, it's throwing his weight about your merchant likes, and that warehouse of yours is no commercial enterprise, it's a torture chamber. Oh yes, for your kind of business you need clerks devoid of personality, with no stake in anything, and that's how you breed them. From infancy you make them grovel for every bite of food, from infancy you condition them to believe you their benefactors. You'd never take a university man into the warehouse, that's for sure.'

'Graduates are no use in our business.'

'Untrue!' shouted Laptev. 'Lies!'

'I'm very sorry, but you seem to be spitting on your own doorstep.' Theodore stood up. 'You hate our business, but you benefit from our profits.'

'Ah, so we've reached the point at last, have we?' Laptev laughed and looked angrily at his brother. 'Certainly—if I didn't belong to your illustrious house, if I had a jot of will-power or courage I'd have jettisoned your "profits" years ago, I'd have gone and earned my own living. But you and your warehouse have sapped my individuality since infancy. I am your creature.'

Theodore looked at his watch and hurriedly said goodnight. He kissed Julia's hand and made to leave, but instead of going into the hall he went into the drawing-room and then into a bedroom.

'I'd forgotten which room was which.' He was most embarrassed. 'This is an odd house. Odd, eh?'

As he put on his furs he seemed struck by something and his face expressed pain. Laptev was no longer angry. He felt scared, and also sorry for Theodore. That good, deep love for his brother which seemed to have dimmed inside him during the last three years—it now awoke, and he felt a strong desire to express it.

'Come to lunch tomorrow, Theodore.' He stroked his brother's shoulder. 'How about it?'

'All right then, but give me some water.'

Laptev ran into the dining-room himself, and picked off the sideboard the first thing that came to hand, a tall beer jug, poured some water and took it to his brother. Theodore began drinking thirstily, but suddenly bit into the jug, and was then heard gnashing his teeth and sobbing. The water spilt on his fur coat and frock-coat, and Laptev —who had never seen a man cry before—stood there confused and scared, not knowing what to do. Gazing in perplexity at Julia and the maid who had removed Theodore's coat and taken him back into the house, he followed them, feeling guilty.

Julia helped Theodore to lie down and sank to her knees beside him. 'It's all right, it's just nerves,' she said soothingly.

'My dear, I feel so awful,' said he. 'I'm so, so unhappy, but I've been trying and trying to hide it.'

He put his arm round her neck. 'I dream of Nina every night,' he whispered in her ear. 'She comes and sits in the armchair by my bed.'

An hour later he was putting on his coat again in the hall, smiling and embarrassed in the maid's presence. Laptev drove with him to Pyatnitsky Road.

'Do come to lunch tomorrow,' he said on the way, holding his brother's arm. 'And at Easter we'll go abroad together. You need an airing, you've rather gone to seed.'

'Yes, yes, yes—certainly I'll come. And we'll take sister Julia along.'

Returning home, Laptev found his wife highly distraught. This business of Theodore had shocked her, and she just could not get over it. She was not weeping, but was very pale—tossing about in bed, tightly grasping her quilt, her pillow and her husband's hands in cold fingers. Her eyes were dilated with fear.

'For heaven's sake don't leave me,' she said to her husband. 'Tell me, Alexis, why don't I say my prayers any more? Where's my faith? Oh, why did you have to discuss religion in my presence? You've confused me, you and your friends. I don't say my prayers any more.'

He placed compresses on her forehead, warmed her hands, gave her tea, while she huddled up to him in terror.

By morning she was tired, and she fell asleep while Laptev sat holding her hand. So he had no sleep. All next day he felt crushed, deadened and vacuous, wandering listlessly through the house.

XVI

The doctors said that Theodore was mentally ill, but what was happening at Pyatnitsky Road Laptev had no idea. The gloomy warehouse, where neither the old man nor Theodore were to be seen any more—it seemed just like a morgue. Whenever his wife told him he must visit the warehouse and Pyatnitsky Road every day, he either gave no answer or spoke irritably about his childhood—about how he couldn't forgive his father for the past, about how he loathed Pyatnitsky Road and the warehouse. And so on.

One Sunday morning Julia went to Pyatnitsky Road herself. She found the old man in the same large room where that service had once been held to celebrate her arrival. In his canvas jacket, without a tie, in slippers, he sat unmoving in an armchair, blinking his blind eyes.

'It's me, your daughter-in-law.' She went up to him. 'I came to see how you are.'

He breathed heavily, overcome by emotion. Touched by his unhappiness and loneliness, she kissed his hand while he felt her face and head. Then, having so to speak assured himself that it was really she, he made the sign of the cross over her.

'Thank you indeed,' he said. 'My eyes have gone, I see nothing. I can just make out the window, and the light too, but I don't notice people and objects. Yes, I'm going blind, and Theodore's ill. Aye, 'tis a bad business with no boss's eye on them. With no one to keep them up to scratch the lads will get out of hand if things go wrong. And what's this illness of Theodore's, a chill or something? Now, I've never been ill myself, never gone to the doctor. Nay, I've had no truck with doctors.'

The old man had started bragging as usual. Meanwhile servants were swiftly laying the table in the same room, putting out the *hors d'œuvre* and bottles of wine. They brought a dozen bottles, one shaped like the Eiffel Tower. They served a dishful of hot pasties smelling of boiled rice and fish.

'Help yourself, dear,' said the old man.

She took his arm, led him to the table, poured him vodka.

'I'll come back tomorrow,' she said. 'I'll bring your grandchildren Sasha and Leda. They'll love you and be nice to you.'

'Don't you bring them here, they ain't legitimate.'

'What do you mean? Their father and mother were married, weren't they?'

'Not with my permission. I never blessed them and I want nothing to do with them, confound them.'

'That's a strange way to speak, Father.' Julia sighed.

'Children should respect and fear their parents, the Gospels say.'

'Not at all. The Gospels say we should forgive even our enemies.'

'You can't forgive people in our business. Start forgiving everyone and you'll go bust in three years.'

'But to forgive, to say a kind, friendly word, even to someone who's done wrong—that's more important than business and making money.'

Julia wanted to mollify the old man, to instil compassion and evoke contrition, but he only heard her out with the condescension of an adult listening to a child.

'You're an old man, Father.' Julia spoke decisively. 'Soon God will call you to Himself. He won't ask you what your business was, or whether your affairs prospered, but whether you showed mercy to others. Were you harsh with those weaker than yourself—your servants and clerks, for instance?'

'I've always been good to my workpeople, and they should always mention me in their prayers.' The old man spoke with assurance. But, touched by Julia's air of sincerity and wishing to please her, he added that it was all right—she could bring his little granddaughters tomorrow. 'I'll have some presents bought.'

The old man was untidily dressed, and had cigar ash on chest and lap. No one was keeping his boots or clothes clean, obviously. The rice in the pasties was under-cooked, the table-cloth smelt of soap, the servants no longer trod quietly. The old man, the whole house in Pyatnitsky Road—they looked neglected. Julia sensed this and felt ashamed on her own and her husband's behalf.

'I'll definitely be back tomorrow,' said she.

She marched round the house telling them to tidy up the old man's bedroom and light his icon lamp. Theodore was in his own room gazing at an open book, not reading. Julia spoke to him, told them to tidy his room as well and then went down to see the clerks. In the middle of the room where they had their meals stood an unpainted wooden post to shore up the ceiling. The ceilings were low, the wallpaper was cheap, there was a smell of stove fumes and cooking. As it was Sunday the clerks were all at home, and were sitting on their beds waiting for their meal. When Julia came in they jumped up and answered her questions diffidently, looking at her as sullenly as convicts.

'Heavens, you *are* badly housed.' She threw up her hands. 'Don't you feel cramped?'

'Aye, cramped we be, but we ain't no worse for that,' Makeichev said. 'We are most grateful to you, and we lift up our prayers to merciful God.'

'In proportion commensurate to the dimensions of the personality,' said Pochatkin.

Seeing that Julia had not understood Pochatkin, Makeichev hastened to explain. 'We're humble folk and must live as fits our station.'

She inspected the boys' quarters and kitchen, she met the house-keeper—and was most dissatisfied.

Returning home, she spoke to her husband. 'We must move to Pyatnitsky Road as soon as we can. And you'll visit the warehouse every day.'

Then both sat in the study side by side, not speaking. He felt depressed, not wanting to go to Pyatnitsky Road or the warehouse, but he had guessed what was in his wife's mind and lacked the strength to gainsay her.

He stroked her cheek. 'I feel as if our life was over,' he said. 'It's as if a dim half-life was beginning. I wept when I learnt that brother Theodore's illness was incurable. We spent our childhood and youth together, I loved him dearly once. But then came this catastrophe, and I feel as if losing him means a complete break with my past. And when you just said we must move to Pyatnitsky Road, that prison, I began to feel I'd have no future either.'

He stood up and went over to the window. 'Anyway, I can say good-bye to any hope of happiness.' He gazed at the street. 'There's no such thing. I've never had it, so it must be an impossibility. I was happy once in my life, though—the night I sat under your umbrella. Remember leaving your umbrella at Nina's?' He turned towards his wife. 'I was in love with you then, I remember sitting under that umbrella all night, experiencing a state of bliss.'

In the study near the bookcases was a mahogany chest-of-drawers with bronze fittings where Laptev kept various unneeded objects, including that umbrella. He took it out and gave it to his wife.

'There it is.'

Julia looked at the umbrella, recognized it and smiled sadly.

'I remember,' she said. 'You were holding it when you told me you loved me.'

'Please come back early if you can,' she added, noticing that he was just going out. 'I miss you.'

Then she went to her room and gazed at the umbrella for a while.

XVII

There was no accountant at the warehouse, despite the complexity of the business and huge turnover, nor could any sense be made of the book-keeper's records. Buyers' agents, German and English, visited the warehouse every day and discussed politics and religion with the clerks. There was a genteel alcoholic—a sick, pathetic creature—who came and translated the foreign correspondence in the office. The assistants called him the Midget, and put salt in his tea. By and large the entire operation was, to Laptev, just one vast exercise in eccentricity.

He visited the warehouse every day, trying to introduce new methods. He forbade them to whip boys and mock customers, he was furious when laughing clerks merrily consigned useless, shop-soiled goods to the provinces as if they were new and in fashion. He was now the boss, but he still did not know how large his property was, whether his business was flourishing, what salary his senior clerks received. And so on. Pochatkin and Makeichev thought him young and inexperienced, kept a great deal from him, exchanged mysterious whispers with the blind old man every evening.

One day in early June, Laptev and Pochatkin went to Bubnov's Inn for a business lunch. Pochatkin had worked at Laptev's for years—he had gone there at the age of eight. He was very much at home there, enjoying complete trust. When, on leaving the warehouse, he removed all the takings from the cash-box and filled his pockets with them, this aroused no suspicion. He was the senior person in the warehouse, in the house and also at church, where he functioned as elder in the old man's place. His cruelty to subordinates had earned him the nickname 'Old Nero' from the clerks and boys.

When they reached the tavern he nodded to the waiter. 'Bring us half a cynosure, my good man, and a couple of dozen indelicacies.'

A little later the waiter brought half a bottle of vodka on a tray and several dishes of *hors d'œuvre*.

'Now, my man,' said Pochatkin. 'Bring a portion of the main author of slander and calumny with mashed potatoes.'

Not understanding, the waiter became embarrassed and made to say something, but Pochatkin looked at him sternly and spoke.

'Otherwise!'

The waiter racked his brains and went to consult his colleagues, but guessed right in the end and brought a helping of tongue.

When each had drunk two vodkas and had a bite, Laptev spoke. 'Tell me, Pochatkin, is it true that our business has been declining in recent years?'

'Not at all.'

'Tell me frankly and openly—what are the profits, past and present? What's the extent of the property? One can't go round blindfold, after all. The warehouse was recently audited, but I don't believe that audit, I'm sorry. You think fit to hide things from me, the only person you tell the truth to is my father. You've been steeped in chicanery since infancy, and now you can't do without it. But what use is that? Now, please be frank, I beg you. What is our business position?'

'That depends on credit fluctuation,' Pochatkin answered after some thought.

'And credit fluctuation means what?'

Pochatkin began explaining, but Laptev understood nothing and sent for Makeichev. He reported at once, said grace, ate some *hors d'œuvre*, and held forth in his portentous, fruity baritone—largely about the clerks' duty to pray for their benefactors night and day.

'All right then, but permit me not to consider myself one of your benefactors,' Laptev said.

'Every man must remember what he is, must be conscious of his station. You are our father and benefactor by God's grace, and we are your slaves.'

'Once and for all I'm sick of all this.' Laptev was angry. 'Will *you* please be *my* benefactor now, and explain our business situation to me. Pray cease treating me as a child, or I shall close down the warehouse tomorrow. My father's blind, my brother's in the mad-house, my nieces are still young. I hate the business, and I'd like to get out of it, but there's no one to take my place, you know that. So leave out the jiggery-pokery, for God's sake.'

They went to the warehouse to do the accounts, and they were still at it in the house that evening, helped by the old man. As he initiated his son into his business secrets, his tone suggested that he had not been practising commerce, but the black art. It transpired that the profits were increasing ten per cent per annum, and that the Laptevs' fortune, in cash and securities alone, totalled six million roubles.

When Laptev went out for some fresh air after doing the accounts it was nearly one o'clock in the morning, and he felt mesmerized by the figures. The night was quiet, moonlit, fragrant. The white walls of the houses in south-bank Moscow, the sight of the heavy locked gate, the quiet, the silent, black shadows—they produced the general impression of a fortress. All it needed was an armed sentry. Laptev went into the garden and sat on a bench near the fence—there was a garden next door too. The bird-cherry was in bloom. Laptev remembered this cherry being just as gnarled and just as big when he had been a boy—it hadn't changed since then. Every corner of the garden and yard reminded him of the distant past. As a boy he had been able, just as now, to see through the sparse trees the whole premises bathed in moonlight with shadows as enigmatic and stern as ever. A black dog lay in the middle of the yard, just as before, and the clerks' windows were wide open. But none of these were cheerful recollections.

Beyond the fence light footsteps were heard in the next-door yard.

'My darling, my dear one,' a man's voice whispered, so close to the fence that Laptev could even hear breathing.

A kiss followed. These millions of roubles, that so uncongenial business—they would ruin Laptev's life and enslave him in the end, of that he was certain. He imagined himself gradually adjusting to his situation, gradually assuming the role of head of a commercial house. He would grow dim and old, he would finally die, as dullards generally do die—in a dirty, sloppy fashion inducing melancholia in their associates. But what was there to stop him giving up these millions and that business, abandoning this garden and yard which he had loathed since boyhood?

The whispering and kissing behind the fence disturbed him. He went into the middle of the yard, unbuttoned his shirt, gazed at the moon. He felt like asking for the garden gate to be unlocked, going out and never coming back. The thought of freedom was a delicious pang in his heart. He laughed happily, imagining what a wonderful and romantic—perhaps, even, saintly—life that might be.

But he still stayed where he was, wondering what on earth kept him there. He was annoyed, both with himself and with the black dog which lay sprawled on the cobbles without escaping into the woods and fields where it would be independent and happy. He and the dog, both were prevented from leaving the yard by the same thing, obviously—the habit of bondage and slavery.

At noon next day he went to see his wife, asking Yartsev along as an insurance against boredom. Julia was staying at a cottage at Butovo, and it was five days since he had visited her. Reaching the station, the friends got into a carriage, and Yartsev sang and rhapsodized about the wonderful weather as they drove along. The cottage was in a large park not far from the station, and Julia sat under a broad old poplar awaiting the guests just where the main avenue began, about twenty yards from the gate. She wore an elegant lace-trimmed dress, light cream in colour, and she was holding the same old umbrella. After greeting her, Yartsev went towards the cottage, whence Sasha's and Leda's voices were heard, while Laptev sat down beside her to talk business.

'Why have you been so long?' she asked, not releasing his hand. 'I've been waiting here and looking out for you for days on end. I do miss you so.'

She got up, passed a hand through his hair, gazed at his face, shoulders and hat with lively interest. 'I do love you, you know.' She blushed.

'You're very dear to me. Now you're here, now I can see you, I'm happier than I can say. Let's talk, then. Say something.'

While she declared her love he felt as if they had already been married ten years. He also wanted his lunch. She put her arms round his neck, tickling his cheek with the silk of her dress. He carefully removed her hand, stood up, went wordlessly towards the cottage. The children ran to meet him.

'How they've grown,' he thought. 'And what changes there have been during these three years. But then I may have another thirteen or thirty years to live. What else has the future in store? Time alone will tell.'

He embraced Sasha and Leda, who hung round his neck.

'Grandfather sends his regards,' he told them. 'Uncle Theodore will soon be dead, Uncle Kostya has written from America and sends his regards. He's bored with the Exhibition and will soon be home. And Uncle Alexis is hungry.'

Then he sat on the terrace and watched his wife sauntering down the path towards the cottage. She looked pensive, she had an expression of bewitching sadness, and tears shone in her eyes. She was no longer the slim, brittle, pale-faced girl, but a mature, beautiful, strong woman. Laptev noticed how ecstatically Yartsev gazed at her, and how her own new, beautiful expression was reflected on Yartsev's face—also sad and entranced. This was like looking at her for the first time in his life, Laptev felt. As they lunched on the terrace Yartsev smiled a vaguely happy, shy smile, and could not take his eyes off Julia and her beautiful neck. Laptev observed him involuntarily, thinking of the thirteen or thirty years which might lie ahead.

What experiences awaited him during that time? What has our future in store?

'Time alone will tell,' he thought.

THE ARTIST'S STORY

I

SIX or seven years ago I was staying in a country district of T——
Province on the estate of a young landowner called Belokurov. He
was a very early riser who wore a peasant jerkin, drank beer in the
evenings and was forever complaining that no one appreciated him.
He had a cottage in the garden, while I lived in the old manor-house in
a huge colonnaded ballroom with no furniture except the wide sofa
on which I slept and the table where I played patience. Even in calm
weather the ancient pneumatic stoves were always droning away and
in a storm the whole house shuddered as if shaking to bits. It was rather
frightening, especially at night when a blaze of lightning suddenly lit
the ten large windows.

Being one of nature's idlers, I simply did nothing at all, but looked
out of my windows at sky, birds and avenues for hours on end. I
read everything that came from the post-office, slept, and sometimes
went outdoors and strolled about till late evening.

Once on my way home I chanced to stray into the grounds of a
house where I had never been before. The sun was setting and evening
shadows lay across the ripening rye. Two rows of towering, closely
planted old fir-trees stood as compact as walls and formed a fine,
sombre avenue. I climbed the fence easily and set off down the avenue,
slipping on a carpet of fir-needles an inch or two deep. It was quiet
and dark. Only an occasional vivid golden gleam quivered high in the
tree-tops and made rippling rainbows of the spiders' webs. I was
almost choked by the smell of resin.

Then I turned into a long avenue of lime-trees. Here too was an air of
age and neglect with last year's leaves rustling sadly underfoot and
shadows lurking in the dusk amongst the trees. In the old orchard
on my right an oriole was singing half-heartedly in a faint voice as if
he too was old. Now the limes ended. I passed a white house with a
terrace and a sort of penthouse or attic-storey on top. Then suddenly
a view unfolded—a courtyard, a small lake with a bathing-hut, a
clump of green willows and a village on the far bank. There was a tall,
narrow bell-tower with a cross on it, glittering in the setting sun. For
a second I caught the enchanting breath of something dear and familiar
as if I had seen this landscape as a child.

A white gate led from yard to open country. It had sturdy, old-fashioned stone gateposts with lions on them and two girls were standing by it. One, the elder, was slim, pale and very pretty, with auburn hair stacked high on her head and a small, stubborn mouth. Her expression was severe and she barely glanced at me. But the other girl, very young—no more than seventeen or eighteen and also slim and pale with a large mouth and large eyes—gave me a surprised look as I passed. She said something in English and seemed rather put out. I felt as if I had known those two lovely faces for a very long time, and as I went home it all seemed like a wonderful dream.

Soon after this Belokurov and I happened to be strolling near the house about noon one day when a carriage drove unexpectedly into our yard and whirred over the grass. One of the girls was in it—the elder. She was collecting money for some peasants whose homes had burnt down. Without looking at us, she gave a most earnest and circumstantial account, telling us how many dwellings had been burnt in the village of Siyanovo and how many men, women and children had been left homeless. She was on the relief committee and she told us what emergency measures they had in hand.

Having got us to subscribe she put her list away and started saying goodbye there and then.

'You've quite forgotten us, Mr. Belokurov,' she said as she gave him her hand. 'Do come and see us. And if Mr. N.' (she mentioned my name) 'wants to meet some admirers of his work and cares to look us up, Mother and I will be delighted.'

I bowed.

When she had gone Belokurov told me about her. He said that she was of good family and was called Lydia Volchaninov. The estate where she lived with her mother and sister was called Shelkovka—the same name as the village on the other side of the lake. The father had once had an important job in Moscow and had been high up in the civil service when he died. The Volchaninovs were well off, but never left the countryside winter or summer and Lydia taught at their own village school in Shelkovka at a salary of twenty-five roubles a month. She lived on her earnings and took pride in paying her own way.

'Charming family,' said Belokurov. 'We might go over there one day. They'll be very pleased to meet you.'

One afternoon—it was a Sunday or some other holiday—we thought of the Volchaninovs and went over to Shelkovka to see them. They were all at home—the mother and her two daughters. The mother, obviously once a good-looking woman, but now short-winded, sad, vague and overweight for her age, tried to entertain me with talk about painting. Having heard from her daughter that I might be visiting Shelkovka, she had hurriedly called to mind two or three of my landscapes that she had seen at Moscow exhibitions. Now she wanted to know what I was trying to express in them.

Lydia, or Leda, as the family called her, talked more to Belokurov than me. Earnest, unsmiling, she asked why he was not on the local council and had never been to a council meeting.

'It's not right, Mr. Belokurov,' she said reproachfully. 'Not right at all. You should be thoroughly ashamed.'

'True, Leda, true,' her mother agreed. 'It's not right at all.'

'Balagin has the whole district in his pocket,' Lydia went on, turning to me. 'He's chairman of the council himself and he's handed out all the local jobs to nephews and in-laws. And he has everything his own way. We must fight back. The younger people should form a pressure group, but just look what our young people are like. You should be thoroughly ashamed of yourself, Mr. Belokurov.'

While we spoke of local government affairs the younger sister, Zhenya, said nothing. She never joined in serious conversations because the family did not think her quite grown up. They treated her as a child and called her 'Missy', the name she had given to her English governess when she was little. She kept watching me curiously. 'This is uncle . . . that's godfather,' she would tell me as I looked at their photograph album. She moved her finger over the photographs, touching me with her shoulder like a child and I could see her slight, undeveloped bosom, her slender shoulders, her plait and her slim, tightly belted waist.

We played croquet and tennis, strolled round the garden and drank tea followed by a leisurely supper. After my large, empty room with its pillars I somehow felt at home in this small, comfortable house where there were no oleographs on the walls, and where they were polite to the servants. Lydia and Zhenya were so young, and they seemed like a breath of fresh air about the place—it was all thoroughly civilized.

At supper Lydia once more talked to Belokurov about the council and Balagin and school libraries. She was a vigorous, sincere girl who held strong views. And she was interesting to listen to, though she talked a lot in a loud voice, perhaps because she was used to speaking at school. But friend Belokurov, who could not open his mouth without arguing—an undergraduate habit that was still with him—spoke tediously, feebly and long-windedly, obviously eager to pass as intelligent and progressive. He waved his arms about and knocked over a gravy-boat with his sleeve, spilling a pool of gravy on the table-cloth, but no one except me seemed to notice.

It was dark and quiet as we went back.

'The sign of good breeding,' sighed Belokurov, 'is not that you don't spill gravy on the table-cloth, but that you don't notice if someone else does. Yes, what a splendid, cultured family. I'm out of touch with nice people, sadly out of touch. It's all this work, work, work.'

He talked about what a lot of work there is in running a model farm while I thought what a disagreeable, lazy fellow he was. When he spoke about anything serious he dragged out his words laboriously with lots of 'er, er, erring' and he worked as he talked, slowly, always behindhand, always in arrears. I had a pretty poor opinion of his efficiency if only because when I gave him letters to post he went round with them in his pocket for weeks on end.

'The worst thing,' he mumbled as he walked by my side, 'is getting no appreciation however hard you work. None whatever.'

II

I took to calling on the Volchaninovs and usually sat on the bottom step of the terrace, depressed, dissatisfied with myself, and full of regrets about my life passing so rapidly and unexcitingly. My heart felt heavy within me and I kept thinking how wonderful it would be if I could only rip it out of my breast somehow. Meanwhile there would be talk on the terrace and the rustle of dresses, or someone would turn the pages of a book.

I soon grew used to Lydia seeing patients and handing out books in the daytime. She was always going off to the village with a parasol and no hat, and in the evenings there was all her noisy talk about the council and schools.

'This won't interest you,' I was coldly told by this slim, handsome, always severe girl with the small, exquisitely outlined mouth, whenever conversation turned to some practical matter.

She did not like me. She disliked me as a landscape painter who did not portray peasant hardship in my pictures and because she thought all her most cherished beliefs meant nothing to me.

I remember once driving along the shores of Lake Baikal and meeting a Buryat girl on horseback wearing a shirt and blue cotton trousers. I asked her to sell me her pipe, but as we spoke she looked scornfully at my European face and hat, then suddenly grew tired of talking to me, gave a wild yell and galloped off. Lydia was like that. She despised me because we had nothing in common. She did not express this dislike at all openly, but I sensed it, and sometimes felt exasperated as I sat on the bottom step of the terrace and said that dosing peasants was a fraud if you were not a doctor. After all, who couldn't play lady bountiful on five thousand acres of her own land?

Her sister Zhenya was a carefree person. Like me she lived a life of utter idleness. She would pick up a book first thing in the morning and sit reading in a deep armchair on the terrace with her feet hardly touching the ground. Or she would take refuge with her book in the lime-tree avenue or go off into the open country outside the gate. She read all day, poring avidly over her book, and only the occasional dazed, fatigued look in her eyes and her extreme pallor showed what a strain this reading was. When I called she always blushed slightly on seeing me and put her book down. She would look into my face with her enormous eyes and tell me eagerly about the latest happenings. The chimney in the servants' quarters might have been on fire or one of the men might have caught a big fish in the pond. On week days she usually wore a pastel-coloured blouse and navy blue skirt. We went for walks together, picked cherries for jam and went boating, and when she jumped up to reach the cherries or pulled on the oars, her slender, delicate arms showed through her full sleeves. Sometimes I sketched while she stood by and watched admiringly.

One Sunday at the end of July I went over to the Volchaninovs' house at about nine in the morning and strolled round the park, keeping well away from the house. I was looking for mushrooms—there were a lot that summer—and marking their position so that Zhenya and I could pick them later. A warm breeze was blowing and I saw Zhenya and her mother come home from church. Both wore bright Sunday dresses and Zhenya held her hat in the wind. Then I heard them breakfasting on the terrace.

For a feckless person like me, forever seeking to excuse his inveterate idleness, these Sunday mornings on our country estates in summertime have always had a special charm. The green garden is still wet with dew and glows in the sun, seeming to radiate happiness, there is a scent of mignonette and oleander near the house, the young people are just back from church and are breakfasting in the garden, and everyone is so gay, so delightfully dressed. And you know that all these healthy, well-nourished, good-looking people are going to do nothing all day long. At such times you find yourself wishing that life was always like this. I thought so now as I strolled round the garden, prepared to wander in this way, aimless and unoccupied, all day or all summer.

Zhenya came out with a basket, looking as if she had known or sensed that she would find me in the garden. We picked mushrooms and talked, and when she asked a question she always stepped ahead so as to see my face.

'Yesterday there was a miracle in the village,' she said. 'Pelageya, the cripple, has been ill a whole year. Doctors and medicines did her no good at all, but yesterday an old woman whispered a spell and she got better.'

'That doesn't mean much,' I said. 'You mustn't look for miracles only among sick people and old women. Isn't health a miracle? And life itself? Anything we can't understand is a miracle.'

'But aren't you afraid of things you can't understand?'

'No. When I meet such things I face them boldly and don't give in to them. I'm above them. Man should realize that he's a cut above lions, tigers, stars and everything else in nature—even things he can't understand and thinks of as miracles. Otherwise he's not a man at all, but a frightened little mouse.'

Zhenya thought that, being an artist, I must know a lot and have a sound intuition about what I did not know. She wanted me to lead her to the realm of the Eternal and the Beautiful, that higher sphere to which she thought I had the entrée. She talked to me about God, immortality and miracles. Now I refuse to believe that I and my imagination will perish for all time after death, so I answered, 'Yes, men are immortal', 'Yes, eternal life awaits us.' She listened, believed and did not ask for proof.

We were going back to the house when she suddenly stopped.

'Leda's a wonderful person, isn't she?' she said. 'I love her so much, I'd gladly die for her without a moment's hesitation. But tell me' (Zhenya touched my sleeve with her finger), 'tell me, why are you two always quarrelling? Why do you get so annoyed?'

'Because she's wrong.'

Zhenya shook her head and tears came into her eyes.

'I can't make sense of it,' she said.

Lydia had just returned home and stood by the porch holding a whip, graceful and handsome with the sun shining on her. She was giving orders to one of the men. She quickly saw two or three patients, talking in a loud voice, then marched round the house with a busy, preoccupied air, opening one cupboard after another before going off to the attic. For a long time no one could find her to tell her that dinner was ready and by the time she came down we had finished our soup.

Somehow I remember and love all these little details and have vivid memories of that whole day, though not very much happened.

After lunch Zhenya lay back in a deep armchair reading, while I sat on the bottom step of the terrace. We did not speak. The sky had clouded over, and a fine drizzle had set in. It was hot, the wind had dropped long ago and it seemed as if the day would never end. Mrs. Volchaninov came out onto the terrace with a fan, looking half asleep.

'Oh, Mother,' said Zhenya, kissing her hand, 'it's bad for you to sleep during the day.'

They adored each other. When one went into the garden the other would stand on the terrace looking towards the trees and shouting, 'Hallo there, Zhenya!' or, 'Where are you, Mother?' They always said their prayers together and shared the same faith, understanding each other perfectly without even having to speak. And they felt the same about people. Mrs. Volchaninov also took to me very quickly and grew fond of me. When I did not appear for two or three days she would send someone round to see if I was well. She also admired my sketches, chattered away as readily as Zhenya about the latest happenings, and often told me family secrets.

She stood in awe of her elder daughter. Lydia never showed any sign of affection, spoke only of serious things, and lived a life apart. In the eyes of her mother and sister she was a revered, somewhat enigmatic personage—they thought of her as sailors think of an admiral who never leaves his cabin.

'Leda's a wonderful person, isn't she?' her mother often said.

And now as the drizzle came down we talked about Lydia.

'She's a wonderful person,' said her mother. 'Her sort are few and far between,' she added in hushed, conspiratorial tones with a frightened glance over her shoulder. 'But I am getting a bit worried, you know. The school, dispensaries, books—isn't it all a bit too much of a good thing? She is twenty-three, after all, and it's time she took herself seriously. As it is, what with books and dispensaries her life will be over before it's begun. . . . It's high time she got married.'

Pale from her reading, her hair disarranged, Zhenya raised her head slightly. 'It's all in God's hands, Mother,' she said, as if to herself, but looking at her mother. And she plunged back into her book.

Belokurov came over in his jerkin and embroidered smock and we played croquet and tennis. Then, after dark, we had a leisurely supper and Lydia talked about schools again and about this Balagin who had the whole district in his pocket.

As I left the Volchaninovs that evening I took away the impression of a long, long, idle day, and realized sadly that everything in this world, however long, does come to an end. Zhenya saw us to the gate, and—perhaps because she had spent all day with me from morning till night —I felt that life without her was somehow dreary, and I realized how fond I was of this whole delightful family. For the first time that summer I felt the urge to paint.

'Tell me, why do you live such a drab, tedious life?' I asked Belokurov as we walked home. 'My life's dull, tiresome, monotonous—but then I'm an artist, an oddity. Since I was quite young I've been racked with envy, fed up with myself and disillusioned with my work. I'm always poor. I'm a kind of tramp, but you now—you're a normal, healthy man, a landowner, a squire. So why lead such a dull life? Why get so little out of it? Why have you never fallen in love with Lydia or Zhenya, for instance?'

'You forget that I love another woman,' Belokurov answered.

Here he was speaking of his 'friend' Lyubov Ivanovna who shared his cottage. Every day I saw the lady—podgy, stout and solemn, not unlike a fattened goose—walking in the garden in traditional Russian dress complete with beads. She always carried a parasol and the servants kept calling her in for meals or a cup of tea. About three years earlier she had taken one of the cottages for the holidays and just moved in with Belokurov, evidently on a permanent basis. She was some ten years older than he and kept him on a tight rein—he had to put in for leave of absence whenever he left the premises. She often sobbed in a voice like a man's, and then I would send word that I should move out if she didn't stop. And stop she did.

When we reached home Belokurov sat on my sofa with a brooding frown, while I paced the room in a state of subdued excitement as if I was in love. I wanted to talk about the Volchaninovs.

'Lydia,' said I, 'could only love a welfare worker as much taken up with hospitals and schools as she is. You know, for a girl like that a man might do more than welfare work, he might take a tip from Russian folk tales and wear out a pair of iron boots. And then there's Zhenya. Isn't she adorable!'

Drawling and 'er-er-erring', Belokurov embarked on a long-winded harangue about the disease of the age—pessimism. He spoke with assurance and his tone implied that I was arguing with him. Hundreds of miles of desolate, monotonous, burnt steppe are less demoralizing than one man sitting and talking if you have no idea when he is going to leave you in peace.

'Pessimism and optimism are neither here nor there,' I said irritably. 'It's just that ninety-nine per cent of people have no sense.'

Thinking this was aimed at him, Belokurov took umbrage and left.

III

'The prince is staying at Malozyomovo and sends his regards,' Lydia told her mother. She had just come in and was taking off her gloves. 'He had a lot of interesting things to say. . . . He promised to raise this question of a clinic for Malozyomovo with the council again, but he says there's not much hope.'

Then she turned to me.

'Sorry,' she added. 'I keep forgetting this sort of thing doesn't interest you.'

That annoyed me.

'And why shouldn't it interest me?' I asked with a shrug. 'You don't care what I think, but I assure you the matter does interest me a great deal.'

'Really?'

'Yes. Really. In my view Malozyomovo doesn't need a clinic.'

My irritation infected her. She looked at me, her eyes half-closed.

'What does it need then? Landscape paintings?'

'It doesn't need landscapes either. It needs nothing at all.'

She finished taking off her gloves and opened a newspaper which had just been collected from the post-office.

'Last week Anna died in childbirth,' she said quietly a little later, obviously trying to control herself. 'And if there had been a clinic anywhere near, she'd still be alive. I should have thought that even landscape painters, however high and mighty, ought to have some views about that.'

'I do have a very specific view about it, I can tell you,' I answered, and she hid behind her paper as if she did not want to hear. 'My view is this. As things are, clinics, schools, and all those cosy little libraries and dispensaries only help to enslave people. Our peasants are in heavy chains, but you don't break their chains. You just add new links. That's my view.'

She raised her eyes and smiled derisively, while I went on, trying to get a grip on my main point.

'What matters isn't that Anna died in childbirth, but that all these Annas, Mavras, Pelageyas and other peasant women are hard at work every minute of the day. They fall ill from working too hard, they spend all their lives trembling with anxiety for their sick, famished children, in terror of death and illness. They're always being treated for some complaint, they wither and age before their time, and they die in stench and filth. Then their children grow up and start off on the same old grind. And so it goes on for hundreds of years, with untold millions of people living worse than beasts, wondering where their next meal's coming from, in constant fear. Placed as they are—and this is what's so horrible—they've no time to think of their souls or remember in Whose image and likeness they were created. Famine, cold, blind terror and overwork—those are the avalanches that seal off all roads to spiritual activity, the one thing that distinguishes men from animals and makes life worth living.

'You go to their aid with hospitals and schools, but that's not freeing them from their shackles, oh dear me no. It's only a worse form of slavery, because by bringing these new fads into their lives you increase their needs, quite apart from their having to pay the council for these poultices and books and so having to work even harder.'

'I shan't argue with you,' said Lydia, lowering her newspaper. 'I've heard all that before. I'll only say this—we can't just sit around twiddling our thumbs. It's true we're not saving mankind and we may be getting a lot of things wrong, but we *are* doing what we can and we're on the right lines. Serving one's fellow men—a civilized person can't do anything finer or nobler than that, and we are trying to serve. We're doing our best. You don't like it, but one can't please everybody, can one?'

'True, Leda,' said her mother. 'True.'

She was always a little scared when Lydia was around. And when she spoke she kept giving Lydia nervous little glances, fearing to say something out of turn and put her foot in it. She never contradicted her daughter, but always agreed, with a 'true, Leda, true'.

'Teaching peasants to read, books of wretched maxims and tags, clinics—these can't reduce ignorance or the death-rate any more than the lamps from your windows can light up this huge garden,' I said. 'You don't give these people anything and by meddling in their lives you only create new needs and more claims on their work.'

'But good God, one must *do* something!' Lydia was annoyed and sounded as if she thought my arguments beneath all contempt.

'Free them from heavy manual work,' I said. 'Lighten their load. Give them a breathing space, so that they don't spend their whole lives at the stove and wash-tub, or in the fields, but also have time to think about their souls, about God, and to develop the life of the spirit. The spiritual life, the constant search for truth and the meaning of existence—these are man's real calling. So save them from this rough work that makes them like brutes, and let them feel free—and then you'll see what a farce these books and dispensaries really are. Once a man knows his true vocation, only religion, science and the arts will satisfy him—not all that rubbish.'

Lydia gave a sardonic laugh. 'Free them from work! Can that be done?'

'Yes. Do some of their work yourself. If all we townspeople and country folk, every man jack of us, agreed to share the work done by mankind as a whole to satisfy physical needs, we might not have to do more than two or three hours' work a day each. Imagine us all, rich and poor, doing only three hours' work a day and having the rest of the time free. And imagine us inventing machines to work for us and trying to keep our needs to the minimum so as to depend less on our bodies and have less work to do. We'd train ourselves and our children not to fear hunger and cold, so that we shouldn't always be panicking about their health like these Annas, Mavras and Pelageyas. If we didn't take medicine and had no doctors, chemists, tobacco factories or distilleries, what a lot of leisure that would give us in the end. And we'd all join in devoting our leisure to science and the arts. We'd unite in a communal quest for truth and the meaning of life, just as peasants sometimes club together to mend a road. And I'm quite sure that truth would quickly be found and that man would be freed from this constant, agonizing, oppressive fear of death—even from death itself.'

'But you contradict yourself,' Lydia said. 'You keep on about science, but say people shouldn't be taught to read.'

'Knowing how to read when your only reading matter is pub signs and occasional books that you can't understand—that sort of reading's been with us Russians from time immemorial. Gogol's Petrushka has been reading for goodness knows how long, yet our villages haven't changed since the time of the Vikings. It's not reading our people need, it's freedom to develop their spiritual powers. We need universities, not schools.'

'You reject medicine too.'

'Yes. It would only be required for the study of disease as a natural phenomenon, not for its cure. If anything needs curing, it's not illness, but its cause. Remove the main cause—manual work—and there won't be any illness.

'I don't recognize a science of healing,' I went on excitedly. 'Real science and real art don't have short-term, particular aims. They seek the eternal and the universal—truth and the meaning of life, God and the soul. Drag them down to the level of the latest craze or such things as dispensaries and libraries, and they just complicate life and clutter it up. We've lots of doctors, chemists, lawyers, lots of people who can read and write, but no biologists, mathematicians, philosophers or poets. All our intellectual and spiritual energies go to satisfy temporary, transient needs.

'Scholars, writers and artists work madly away and, thanks to them, amenities improve daily and physical needs increase. But we're still pretty far from the truth and man's still, as before, the greediest and dirtiest of animals. The tendency is for most people to degenerate and lose their vitality once and for all. An artist's life means nothing at all in these conditions. The more gifted he is, the more strange and baffling is the part he plays, since it comes down to this—he works to amuse a dirty, greedy animal and maintain the *status quo*. So I don't want to work and I'm not going to. . . . We don't need anything. The world can go to hell!'

'Zhenya dear, leave the room,' said Lydia to her sister, clearly thinking my words bad for a girl of her age.

Zhenya went out with a sad look at her sister and mother.

'Those are the sort of charming things people usually say to excuse their own apathy,' said Lydia. 'Rejecting hospitals and schools is easier than healing or teaching.'

'True, Leda,' her mother agreed. 'True.'

'You threaten to give up working,' Lydia went on. 'You put a high value on your work, that's very evident. But let's stop arguing. We shall never agree, because though you've just been sneering so hard at all these libraries and dispensaries, I rate the least perfect of them higher than all the landscapes ever painted.'

She turned to her mother and went straight on in a different tone of voice.

'The prince looks very thin, and he's changed a lot since he was last here. They're sending him to Vichy.'

She told her mother about the prince to avoid talking to me. Her face was flushed. To hide her feelings she bent low over the table, as if short-sighted, and pretended to read the paper.

My presence was unwelcome. I said good night and set off home.

IV

It was quiet outside. The village beyond the lake was asleep already. Not a light could be seen and only the pale reflections of the stars glinted faintly on the water. By the gates with the lions Zhenya was standing quite still, waiting to see me off.

'Everyone's asleep in the village,' I told her, trying to make out her face in the darkness and seeing her sad, dark eyes fixed on me. 'Inn-keeper and horse-thieves sleep peacefully, while we respectable citizens quarrel and get on each other's nerves.'

It was a sad August night—sad because there was already a smell of autumn. The rising moon, wrapped in crimson cloud, cast a dim light on the road and on the dark fields of winter corn to both sides of it. There were a lot of shooting stars. Zhenya walked along the road by my side, trying not to look up at the sky because she did not want to see the shooting stars. Somehow they frightened her.

'I think you're right,' she said, shivering in the damp night air. 'If people would all co-operate in spiritual activity they would soon know everything.'

'Of course. We're superior beings, and if we truly recognized the full force of human genius and lived only for higher things, we might be like gods in the end. But that will never be. Mankind will degenerate and genius will vanish without trace.'

When we were out of sight of the gates, Zhenya stopped and quickly shook hands.

'Good night,' she said with a shiver. She was wearing a thin blouse, and was huddled up because she was cold. 'Do come tomorrow.'

I dreaded being left alone, overwrought and annoyed with myself and people in general. Now I too tried not to look at the shooting stars.

'Do stay a bit longer,' I begged.

I loved Zhenya. I must have loved her for meeting me and coming to see me off, and for looking at me so fondly and admiringly. Her pale face, her slender neck, her slim arms, her helplessness, her idleness, her reading—there was something touching and beautiful about these things. And what of her mind? She was highly intelligent, I felt, and I was delighted by her breadth of vision, perhaps because she thought differently from the severe, handsome Lydia, who disliked me. Zhenya liked me as an artist. Having won her love by my art, I longed to paint for her alone. I thought of her as my young princess who would reign with me over these trees and fields, over this mist and sunset, and over this wondrously enchanting world of nature where I had so far felt utterly lonely and unwanted.

'Stay a bit longer,' I said. 'Please.'

I took off my overcoat and put it over her chilled shoulders. Afraid of looking silly and unattractive in a man's coat, she laughed and threw it off as I put my arms round her and began to cover her face, shoulders and hands with kisses.

'See you tomorrow,' she whispered, embracing me cautiously as if fearing to disturb the silence of the night. 'We have no secrets from each other, so I must tell Mother and Leda at once. . . . I'm so frightened. Mother's all right, she likes you, but Leda. . . .'

She ran off towards the gates.

'Good night,' she shouted.

After that I could hear her running for a minute or two. I did not want to go home and there was no point in going anyway. I stood and thought for a moment, then slowly wandered back for another look at the house that she lived in—the dear, innocent old house, which seemed to stare at me as if its attic windows were eyes, understanding everything. I walked past the terrace, sat on a bench in the darkness under the old elm near the tennis-court and looked at the house. In the windows of the attic where Zhenya slept, a bright light flashed, changing to a subdued green as the lamp was covered with a shade. The shadows quivered.

I was full of tenderness and peace. And I was pleased with myself—pleased that I had been carried away by my feelings and fallen in love. Meanwhile I was embarrassed to think that only a few yards away Lydia had a room in that house—Lydia, who disliked, perhaps hated me. I sat waiting in case Zhenya should come out. As I listened I seemed to hear voices in the attic.

About an hour passed. The green light went out and the shadows vanished. The moon was high above the house now, lighting the sleeping garden and the paths. The dahlias and roses in the bed in front of the house could be clearly seen, and all looked the same colour. It was growing very cold. I left the garden, picked up my overcoat from the road, and strolled slowly home.

When I went to see the Volchaninovs next afternoon, the french windows into the garden were wide open. I sat for a while on the terrace, expecting to see Zhenya any moment behind the flower-bed on the lawn or on one of the paths, or to hear her voice from the house. Then I went into the drawing-room and the dining-room. There was no one about. From the dining-room I walked down the long corridor to the hall and back. There were several doors in the corridor and through one of them I heard Lydia's voice.

' "A crow . . . picked up . . ." ' she said, loudly and deliberately, probably dictating, ' "picked up a piece of cheese. . . . A crow . . . picked up. . . ." Who's there?' she suddenly called, hearing my steps.

'It's me.'

'Oh! Sorry, but I can't come out now, I'm busy with Dasha.'

'Is your mother in the garden?'

'No. She and Zhenya left this morning to stay at my aunt's in Penza Province.' She paused. 'They'll probably go abroad this winter,' she added. ' "A crow picked up . . . a pie-iece of chee-eese. . . ." Got that?'

I went into the hall and stood staring at the lake and the village, my mind a blank.

' "A piece of cheese . . ." ' the voice went on. ' "A crow picked up a piece of cheese. . . ." '

I left the grounds by the path that I had taken when I first came, but the other way round—first from the courtyard into the garden and past the house, then down the avenue of lime-trees. . . . Here a boy came running after me with a note. I read as follows:

I've told Leda everything. She says I mustn't see you again, and I could never bring myself to distress her by disobeying. May God give you happiness. Forgive me. Mother and I can't stop crying, you can't imagine how miserable we are.

Then came the dark avenue of fir-trees and the broken-down fence. Cows and hobbled horses were grazing in the field where once I had seen the ripening rye and heard the call of quails. The slopes were dotted with bright green patches of winter corn. A sober, workaday mood came over me—I felt ashamed of all I had said at the Vol-chaninovs' and as bored with life as ever before. I packed when I got home, and left for St. Petersburg that evening.

I have never seen the Volchaninovs again, but I did run across Belokurov in the train on my way to the Crimea not long ago. He still wore that jerkin and embroidered smock. When I asked how he was he said 'fine, thanks'.

We talked. He had sold his estate and bought a smaller one in Lyubov Ivanovna's name. He could not tell me much about the Volchaninovs. Lydia was still living at Shelkovka, he said, and teaching at the school. She had gradually managed to collect a group of fellow spirits, who had formed a pressure group, and at the last council elections they had 'turfed out' Balagin, who had always had the whole district in his pocket. As for Zhenya, he could only tell me that she was not living at home. He did not know where she was.

I am beginning to forget the Volchaninovs' house, and only now and then, when I am painting or reading, the green light in the win-dow suddenly comes to mind—or the sound of my steps in the fields at night as I walked home so much in love, rubbing my hands in the cold. Even more rarely, at sad, lonely moments, vague memories awake, and gradually I seem to feel that I am remembered and ex-pected—that we shall meet again. . . .

Zhenya, where are you?

HOME

I

THE Donets Railway Line. A gloomy station, lone and white in the steppe, quiet, with its walls baking in the heat. There is no shade and the place seems deserted, the train has gone on and left you behind and its faint rumble dies away at last.

There is no one about near the station and the only horses are your own. You get in your carriage—which makes a pleasant change from the train—and bowl off down the road through the steppe. Vistas gradually open up, vast, infinite, enchanting in their very monotony— the sort of thing that you won't find anywhere near Moscow. There is a great expanse of plain with nothing in sight but an old burial mound or windmill far away and a team of oxen hauling coal.

Solitary birds skim over the plain and the measured flap, flap of their wings makes you drowsy. It is hot. An hour passes, then another. Still there is nothing but the boundless steppelands and the same far-away mound. Your coachman tells some long, pointless tale, with many a sideways jab of his whip, and a great calm comes over you. You don't want to think about the past. . . .

A troika was sent to fetch Vera Kardin. The coachman stowed her luggage and began adjusting the harness.

Vera looked about her. 'Nothing's changed,' she said. 'It's ten years since I was here, and I was only a child then. I remember old Boris coming to fetch me. I say, is he still alive?'

The coachman made no answer, but just gave her an angry look—so like a Ukrainian—and climbed on his box.

They had about twenty miles to go from the station and Vera yielded to the charm of the countryside, forgot the past and thought only of these free, open spaces. She was a healthy, intelligent, good-looking young woman of only twenty-three and the sweep of these broad horizons seemed to fill a gap in her life.

The great plain . . . the trotting horses, the sun climbing ever higher in the sky. Was the steppe ever so rich and blooming in June when she saw it as a child? There were flowering grasses—green, yellow, mauve and white—their scent mingling with that of the warm earth and there were some strange blue birds on the road.

Vera had long ago given up saying her prayers, but now she fought off her drowsiness and whispered, 'Lord, grant I may be happy here.'

She felt deliciously serene, as if she could have spent the rest of her days just driving along and looking at the open country.

Suddenly, quite unexpectedly, they came on a deep gully full of young oaks and alder, with a whiff of damp to show that there must be a stream at the bottom. On the near side a covey of partridges whirred into the air from the very lip of the gully. Vera remembered going for evening walks to this gully, so the house must be near. And sure enough poplars and a barn came into sight some way off, with black smoke on one side where old straw was being burnt. And look— Aunt Dasha was coming out to meet her, waving a handkerchief, and Grandfather was on the terrace.

How absolutely marvellous.

'Darling! Darling!' her aunt screeched hysterically. 'Welcome to the lady of the manor! Well, that's what you are, really—you're our little princess! All we have is yours. My darling, my pretty one, I'm not your aunt, I'm your obedient slave!'

Vera had no relatives except her grandfather and aunt, for her mother had long been dead and her father, an engineer, had died three months ago in Kazan on his way back from Siberia. Grandfather had a large white beard. He was fat, red, short of breath and walked with his stomach stuck out, leaning on a stick. Her aunt, a lady of some forty-two years in a fashionable dress with wide sleeves, tightly laced in at the waist, obviously did her best to look young and attractive. She walked with tiny steps, her back quivering.

'You're going to like us, aren't you?' she said, embracing Vera. 'I'm sure you're not standoffish.'

At Grandfather's wish they said thanksgiving prayers, then had a leisurely dinner. So Vera's new life began. They gave her the best room, where they had put all the carpets in the house and lots of flowers. When she lay down that night in her cosy, wide, soft bed, snuggling under a silk coverlet with a musty smell as though it had not been used for some time, she was so happy that she burst out laughing. Aunt Dasha came in for a moment to wish her good night.

'Well, here you are, thank goodness,' she said, sitting on the bed. 'We're doing very nicely, as you see, and things could hardly be better. Only your Grandpa is so poorly. He's in a terribly bad way, what with his asthma, and now his memory's going. And he was such a fine, strong man—remember? Oh, he was someone to be reckoned with. . . . If a servant so much as put a foot wrong in the old days, he'd be on his feet with his "Flog him! Twenty-five of the best!" But now he's quietened down and you can't get a word out of him. But then times have changed, dear, you mustn't beat the servants nowadays. There's a lot of sense in that, of course, but you can't let them be too slack either.'

'Are they still beaten, Aunt?' Vera asked.

'Our manager sometimes does it, but I don't. Let them be, say I. And your Grandpa sometimes lashes out with his stick for old time's sake, but you can't call that beating.'

Aunt Dasha yawned and made the sign of the cross over her mouth and then over her right ear.

'Isn't it a bit dull living here?' asked Vera.

'I don't know what to say. There are no more country squires about, they've all gone, but they've been putting up factories here there and everywhere, dear, and there are plenty of these engineers, doctors, miners and that sort. We have shows and concerts of course, but the great thing round here is cards. And we have visitors. Dr. Neshchapov from the factory often calls—such a handsome, attractive man! He's fallen in love with your photograph. So I've quite made up my mind. "That's Vera's future settled," I thought. He's young, good-looking, well-off—in fact highly eligible. And then you're a wonderful catch yourself, dear. We're a good family. The estate's mortgaged, true, but what of it? It's in good order, hasn't been neglected. Part of it's mine, but it'll all come to you. I'm yours to command. And your father —my brother that was—left fifteen thousand. . . . Anyway, I see you can hardly keep your eyes open. Sleep well, child.'

Next day Vera spent some time wandering round the grounds. The garden, old and unattractive with no paths, was awkwardly laid out on a slope and was utterly neglected—they must have thought it not worth bothering about. There were lots of grass-snakes. Hoopoes flew about under the trees, calling as if to jog someone's memory. Down below was a river overgrown with tall reeds and beyond the river, a few hundred yards from the bank, was the village. Passing from the garden into open country, Vera looked into the distance and thought of her new life in the old home. What did the future hold? That was what she wanted to know. This sweeping vista and the glorious stillness of the steppe seemed to say that she would soon be happy—perhaps already was. To be a healthy, educated young woman living in her own country house—wasn't that happiness?

Lots of people would say that it was. Yet the boundless plain, so monotonous, so empty, frightened her. This quiet, green monster sometimes looked as if it would swallow up her life without trace.

She was young, pretty, full of life. She had been to boarding-school, learnt to talk three languages, read a lot, and travelled with her father. But where was it all leading? To settling down on a farm in the depths of the country? Strolling from garden to fields and back again, day in, day out, for want of anything better to do? And then sitting at home listening to Grandfather breathing? Surely not! But what should she do? Where could she go? At a loss for an answer, she felt, as she made her way home, that she had little chance of finding happiness in a place that was more interesting to drive to from the station than to live in.

Dr. Neshchapov drove over from the factory. Though a doctor, he had bought shares in the factory about three years earlier and become a director. He still practised, but no longer thought of medicine as his main job. He was pale and well built with dark hair and wore a white waistcoat. But what really went on in his mind? What were his true feelings? It was hard to decide. He kissed Aunt Dasha's hand by way of greeting and was forever jumping up to give someone a chair or let them pass. He was always very solemn and silent, and when he opened his mouth you somehow never quite caught the first few words, though he spoke correctly and audibly.

'Do you by any chance play the piano?' he asked Vera and suddenly jumped up as she dropped a handkerchief.

He stayed from noon till midnight, hardly speaking, and Vera did not take to him at all. She thought his white waistcoat quite wrong for the country. His refined politeness, his manner, his pale, solemn face with its dark eyebrows—all this was a bit too much of a good thing. She wondered why he said so little. Was he just not very bright? Could that be it?

'Well, what do you think?' asked her aunt cheerfully after he had gone. 'Charming, isn't he?'

II

Aunt Dasha ran the place. Tightly laced, bracelets jingling on both arms, she went to kitchen, barn or cattleyard with short steps and quivering back. For some reason she always put on pince-nez to talk to her manager or the peasants.

Grandfather always stayed put and played patience or dozed. He ate fantastic quantities of dinner and supper. Today's dishes, yesterday's, last Sunday's cold pie, salt meat meant for the servants—they served him up the lot. He wolfed it all down, and dinner had such an effect on Vera that afterwards, seeing anyone driving sheep or carting flour from the mill, she would think, 'That'll end up inside Grandpa'. Engrossed in his food or his game of patience, he barely spoke, but sometimes at dinner a glance at Vera moved him deeply.

'My only granddaughter!' he would say tenderly, tears shining in his eyes. 'Vera dear!'

Or his face would suddenly flush crimson as his neck swelled and he glared at a servant.

'Where's the horse-radish?' he would ask, banging his stick.

He never left the house in winter, but in summer sometimes went into the fields to look at the oats and grass. When he came back he would brandish his stick and say what a mess things had got into since he last went out.

'Your grandpa's in a bad mood,' whispered Aunt Dasha. 'Ah well, it means nothing now. But once he was a holy terror with his "Flog him! Twenty-five of the best!" '

Vera's aunt complained that everyone was bone idle and hardly lifted a finger, so the estate produced no income. There was certainly no serious farming. They ploughed and sowed a bit from force of habit, though no one really did anything—they just lazed about. Yet all day long people were coming and going, counting things, and generally bestirring themselves. From five in the morning the house buzzed with a never-ending 'serve this', 'bring that' or 'go and fetch the other' and by evening the servants were almost dead on their feet. Aunt Dasha changed her cooks and housemaids weekly. Some she dismissed for immorality, others said they had had quite enough and gave their notice. No one from the local village would work there, so they had to take on strangers.

One local girl called Alyona did live in, but she only stayed because she kept a whole family of old folk and children at home on her wages. This Alyona, a small, pale, rather silly girl, was at it all day, tidying rooms, serving at table, making up stoves, sewing and laundering clothes, but all she ever seemed to do was bustle about clattering her boots and getting in everyone's way. Scared of being given notice and sent home, she was always dropping crockery, and had her wages docked for what she broke. Then her mother and grandmother used to come and make abject appeals to Aunt Dasha.

Once a week, sometimes more often, there were guests. Aunt used to come into Vera's room.

'Do go and sit with the visitors,' she would say, 'or else they'll think you're stuck up.'

Vera would join the guests and have long games of cards or play the piano while they danced. Very gay and out of breath from dancing, Aunt would come up to her and whisper. 'Do be a bit nicer to Marya Nikiforovna.'

On the sixth of December, Saint Nicholas's Day, a whole horde of visitors descended in a body, about thirty of them. They played cards till quite late and many stayed the night. Next morning they sat down to cards again, then lunched, after which Vera went to her room for a rest from the talk and tobacco smoke, but found guests there too and felt so frantic that she was ready to weep. In the evening when they were all about to leave, she was so glad to see the back of them that she said they really should stay a bit longer.

The guests were a strain and a nuisance. Yet nearly every evening she felt that she must get out of the house as darkness fell, and would go visiting at the factory or at some neighbouring landowner's. That meant cards, dances, party games and suppers.

Young men—factory or mine officials—sometimes sang Ukrainian songs, and rather well at that. Their singing made one sad. Or everyone forgathered in one room and told tales in the dusk about mines, treasures buried long ago in the steppe and the Tomb of Saur.

Talking late at night, they sometimes heard a cry of 'He-e-elp!' That would be a drunk or someone being robbed in the near-by mines. Or the wind howled in the stoves. Or shutters banged and a little later church bells gave warning that a blizzard was getting up.

The most interesting woman at all these parties, picnics and dinners was invariably Aunt Dasha, the most interesting man—Dr. Neshchapov. Not much reading was done at these factories and country houses and the only music they played was marches and polkas. The young people were forever arguing heatedly about things that they did not understand and the effect was rather uncouth. They argued loud and heatedly, but curiously enough Vera had never met people who were so casual and indifferent. They seemed to have no country, no religion and no interest in public affairs. When they spoke of literature or aired some abstract problem, Neshchapov's face showed utter indifference and you could tell that it was many a long year since he had read—or wanted to read—anything. Solemn, blank-looking, like a badly painted portrait in his inevitable white waistcoat, he was silent and enigmatic as ever. The women and girls found him attractive. Delighted by his manners, they envied Vera because he was clearly so much taken with her.

Leaving for home, Vera was always miserable and swore that she would stay at home another time. But a day passed, another evening arrived and off she would rush to the factory again. So it went on almost all winter.

She ordered books and magazines and read them in her room. She read in bed at night too. When the corridor clock struck two or three and her head ached from reading, she sat up in bed thinking. What should she do and where could she go? The question nagged at her, confound it. She had had plenty of answers for a long time—but no real solution.

Serving the peasants, alleviating their sufferings, educating them—what a fine, noble, glorious thing that must be! But Vera did not know any peasants. How could she make contact? She had nothing in common with them and they bored her. She could not stand the stink of their huts, the swearing in their taverns, their unwashed children or their women talking about their illnesses. Plodding half-frozen through snowdrifts, then sitting in a stuffy hut teaching children whom you dislike—why, better be dead! And teaching village children while Aunt Dasha was making money from village inns and fining the peasants—a nice farce that would be!

There was all this talk about schools, village libraries and mass education, but if these engineers, factory officials and ladies of her acquaintance were not all hypocrites, if they truly believed in education, they would not pay teachers fifteen roubles a month as they did now, which came pretty near to starving them to death. These schools and all this talk about ignorance were only meant to lull their consciences because they were ashamed to own fifteen or twenty-five thousand acres and not give a damn for the peasants.

Take Dr. Neshchapov. The ladies said how kind of him it was to build a school at the factory. It was quite true that he had built a school —for about eight hundred roubles out of old stones left over from building the factory, and at the opening everyone had sung 'For he's a Jolly Good Fellow'. But you catch him giving up his shares! Not likely! It never even crossed his mind, to be sure, that peasants were men like himself and that they too needed university education, not just these wretched factory schools.

Vera was annoyed with herself and everyone else. She would take up her book again and try to read, but a little later would sit down and think again. Should she become a doctor? But that meant taking an examination in Latin—and besides, corpses and diseases utterly disgusted her. How pleasant to be a mechanic, judge, steamship captain or scholar—something that brought your whole strength, physical and moral, into play, tired you out and made you sleep soundly at night. Was there nothing she could give her life to—nothing to make her an interesting person, liked by other interesting people, able to love and have a real family of her own?

But what should she do? Where could she start?

One Sunday in Lent her aunt came into her room early in the morning to borrow an umbrella. Vera was sitting up in bed, clutching her head and thinking.

'You ought to go to church, dear,' said her aunt. 'Otherwise people will think you don't believe in God.'

Vera made no answer.

'You're bored, you poor dear, I can see that,' said her aunt, dropping on her knees by the bed. She adored Vera. 'You are, aren't you? Admit it.'

'Terribly.'

'My lovely, darling little princess, your wish is my command. It's your own good—your happiness—I want.... Tell me, why won't you marry Neshchapov? What more could you ask, child? I'm sorry, but we mustn't be so fussy, dear—beggars can't be choosers, you know. ... Time's running on and we're not sweet seventeen any more.... This makes no sense to me. He loves you, adores you!'

'Oh really! How am I supposed to know?' Vera was annoyed. 'He hasn't said anything—he hardly opens his mouth.'

'He's shy, dear.... Perhaps he thinks you'll turn him down.'

Her aunt went away and Vera stood in the middle of her room, not knowing whether to dress or lie down again. There was her loathsome bed and if she looked through the window she saw bare boughs, grey snow, loathsome jackdaws, pigs that would end up inside Grandpa....

'Marriage!' she thought. 'It's an idea.'

III

For two days Aunt went round with a tear-stained, heavily powdered face and kept sighing and looking at the icon at dinner, but what the

trouble was no one could tell. Then she made up her mind and went
into Vera's room.

'By the way, child,' she said off-handedly. 'We've an interest payment
due at the bank, but our tenant's behind with his rent. Can I pay out
of the fifteen thousand your father left you?'

During the rest of the day Aunt was making cherry jam in the
orchard. Red-cheeked from the heat, Alyona kept dashing between
garden, house and cellar. Aunt was always terribly solemn about
her jam-making, and looked like a sort of priestess. She wore short
sleeves, exposing her small, firm, tyrannical arms, and servants ran
about non-stop, helping to make jam that none of them would eat.
It was always a painful experience. . . .

The garden smelt of hot cherries. The sun had gone down and they
had taken the brazier away, but a pleasant, sweetish smell still hung
in the air. Vera sat on a bench, watching the new odd-job-man, a
young soldier who was working his way across country. He was laying
paths to her orders—cutting turf with a spade and tossing it in a wheelbarrow.

'Where were you stationed?' Vera asked him.

'In Berdyansk.'

'Where are you making for now? Home?'

'No miss,' the labourer answered. 'I haven't got a home.'

'Well, where were you born? Where did you grow up?'

'In Oryol Province. Before I was in the army I lived with my
mother, at my stepfather's place. My mother kept house and they
thought a lot of her and gave me my board and lodging. But while I
was away in the army I had a letter saying my mother was dead. . . .
I don't feel like going home any more somehow. Being as it's not
my own father, the house isn't really home.'

'Is your real father dead?'

'I don't rightly know, miss, being illegitimate.'

Just then Aunt appeared at a window.

'Il ne faut pas parler aux gens . . .' she said and turned to the soldier.
'Go into the kitchen, my man. You can tell them about it there.'

Then, like yesterday and every other day, came supper, reading,
the sleepless night and the thoughts that went on and on, always about
the same thing. At three o'clock the sun began to rise and Alyona
was already busy in the corridor, but Vera still could not sleep and tried
to read. She heard the squeak of the wheelbarrow as the new man came
into the garden.

Vera sat with her book by the open window, dozing and watching the soldier make paths for her, and this absorbed her. The paths were smooth, level bands and she enjoyed thinking what they would look like when sprinkled with yellow sand.

Just after five o'clock she saw Aunt go out of the house in a pink dressing-gown, with her hair in curlers. She stood on the porch for a minute or two in silence, then spoke to the soldier.

'Take your papers and go about your business,' she said. 'I'm not having anyone round here who's illegitimate.'

Vera felt depressed and angry. A hard lump seemed to heave inside her chest. She was furious. She hated Aunty—in fact she was sick and tired of Aunty.

But what could she do? Butt in when her aunt was talking? Give her a piece of her mind? But what good would that be? Suppose she tackled her aunt, pushed her out of the way, made her harmless? Suppose she stopped Grandfather hitting out with his stick? What good would it all do? It would be like killing a single mouse or snake in the boundless plains. The vast expanses, the long winters, the monotony and tedium made you feel so helpless. There seemed to be no way out. Why do anything when nothing does any good?

Alyona came in, bowed to Vera and began taking away the arm-chairs to beat the dust out of them.

'A fine time you've chosen to clean my room!' said Vera, annoyed. 'Go away!'

Alyona was flabbergasted. Too scared to know what was wanted of her, she began rapidly tidying up the top of the chest of drawers.

'Clear out, I tell you!' shouted Vera, shivering. She had never been so depressed in all her life. 'Get out!'

Alyona gave a sort of moan that might have come from a bird, and dropped a gold watch on the carpet.

'Clear out!' Vera shouted like one possessed, jumping up and shaking all over. 'Get rid of her! I'm sick to death of her!' she went on, rushing down the corridor after Alyona and stamping her feet. 'Away with her! Beat her! Flog her!'

Then she suddenly came to her senses. Just as she was, not having washed or done her hair, she rushed headlong out of doors in her dressing-gown and slippers, ran to the gully that she knew so well, and hid among the thistles where she could be out of everyone's way. She lay quite still on the grass, not crying, not particularly put out, but just staring up at the sky without blinking, reflecting coldly and precisely. As long as she lived she would never forget what had happened, never forgive herself.

'This has got to stop, it really has,' she thought. 'If I don't pull myself together it'll go on for ever. . . . It must stop.'

At noon Dr. Neshchapov drove through the gully to the house. Seeing him, she quickly decided to make a fresh start—she would force herself to it. This resolve calmed her. She watched the doctor go past, a fine manly figure, and tried to sugar the bitter pill of her decision.

'He's a fine man . . . ' she said. 'We'll manage somehow.'

She went back home. As she was dressing, Aunt Dasha came into the room.

'Alyona annoyed you, dear,' she said, 'so I sent her back to the village. Her mother's given her a good hiding and she came up here crying. . . .'

'Look, Aunt,' said Vera hurriedly. 'I will marry Dr. Neshchapov. But you talk to him because I can't. . . .'

She went back to the fields. Walking off at random, she decided that after she was married she would run her household, dispense medicine, teach and behave just like every other woman of her circle. As for her perpetual discontent with herself and others—the overwhelming mass of blunders that loom before you the moment you think of your past life—why, she would look on all that as her true life, the life for which she had been chosen. She would expect nothing better.

Could one, after all, hope for more?

Music, dreams, wonderful scenery are one thing, but ordinary living is another story altogether. Happiness and truth have nothing to do with ordinary life, that's clear enough.

Better not live at all—better be at one with these glorious plains, boundless and indifferent as eternity, with their flowers, burial-mounds and far horizons. Then everything would be splendid.

A month later Vera was living at the factory.

A CASE HISTORY

A TELEGRAM arrived for the Professor of Medicine from a textile mill—Lyalikov's—urgently requesting his presence. A girl was ill: daughter of some Mrs. Lyalikov, who seemed to be the mill-owner—that was all the long, ineptly framed message conveyed. The professor did not go himself, but sent one of his house-surgeons, Korolyov, instead.

Korolyov had to travel two stations down the line from Moscow, then drive three miles. He was fetched from the station in a three-horse carriage by a coachman sporting a peacock feather in his hat, whose answer to all questions was a loud regimental 'Yessir!' or 'No sir!'. It was Saturday evening, the sun was setting. Trooping from works to station, mill-hands bowed their heads to the horses pulling Korolyov's carriage. The evening, the country houses and cottages on each side, the birches . . . they all enchanted him. The whole atmosphere was so peaceful, as if fields, woodlands and sun were about to join the workers in their Saturday evening's rest and relaxation—in their prayers too, perhaps.

He had been born and grown up in Moscow, he knew nothing of country life, he had never taken an interest in factories, never visited them. But he had read about such things, he had been entertained by industrialists and had talked to them. Whenever he saw a factory—near by or afar—he always thought: how quiet and peaceful the façade, but how different the reality must be: the owners' crass boorishness and brute selfishness, the workers' unhealthy drudgery . . . the fights, the vodka, the vermin. Now, too, as the workers humbly and nervously made way for his carriage, he seemed to sense squalor, drunkenness, tension and bewilderment in faces, caps and gait.

They drove through the mill entrance. There was a glimpse of workers' cottages on both sides, of women's faces, of washing and blankets on the porches.

'Out of my way!' yelled the coachman, not slackening speed.

Now came a spacious area bare of grass. On it stood five vast chimneyed mill-sheds, some distance apart from each other. There were warehouses and barracks too, all covered with a film of grey dust. Here and there, like desert oases, were the wretched little gardens and the green or red roofs of the houses where the management lived.

The coachman pulled up his horses sharply, and the carriage halted at a house with a new coat of grey paint. Here was a small front garden with dusty lilac and a reek of paint on the yellow porch.

'Please come in, Doctor,' said female voices in the lobby and hall. There was some sighing and whispering. 'Come in, we've waited so long—oh, what a to-do! This way, please.'

Mrs. Lyalikov, a stout, elderly person in a black silk dress with modish sleeves—but homely and uneducated, from the look of her—gazed anxiously at the doctor, hesitating, not venturing to shake hands. Beside her stood a short-haired, emaciated, middle-aged, pince-nez-wearing creature in a brightly patterned blouse. The servants called her Miss Christine, and Korolyov put her down as the governess. It was as the most educated person in the house, probably, that she had been assigned to greet and receive the doctor—anyway, she was in a great hurry to rehearse the causes of the disease in niggling minor detail. Who the patient was, though, what this was all about . . . that she didn't say.

Doctor and governess sat talking while the mistress of the house stood motionless by the door, waiting. From what was said Korolyov learnt that it was a girl of twenty—Liza, Mrs. Lyalikov's only daughter and heiress—who was ill. She had been unwell for some time, she had been under various doctors, and during the entire previous night she had suffered heart palpitations so acute that no one in the house had slept—they had feared for her life.

'She's always been poorly since she was little, as you might say,' explained Miss Christine in a sing-song voice, now and then wiping her lips with her hand. 'The doctors call it nerves. But if you ask me it may be the scrofula she had as a child—drove it right inside her, them doctors did.'

They went to see the patient. Fully grown, large, well-built, but plain and like her mother—the same small eyes, the same wide, outsize lower jaw—hair uncombed, blankets up to her chin . . . she first struck Korolyov as a poor, miserable creature sheltered and cherished here out of pity. It was hard to see her as the future owner of five huge mills.

'Well, here we are,' began Korolyov. 'We've come to make you well. Good evening.'

He gave his name, took her hand: her large, cold, ungainly hand.

She sat up—long used to doctors, obviously, not caring that her shoulders and chest were uncovered—and let him examine her.

'It's palpitations,' she said. 'I felt terrible all night, nearly died of fright. Do give me something to take.'

'Yes, yes, don't worry.'

Korolyov examined her and shrugged his shoulders.

'There's nothing wrong with the heart,' he said. 'Everything's fine —no cause for worry. Your nerves must have been playing up a bit, but that's nothing. The attack must have ended, so you lie down and get some sleep.'

Then a lamp was brought into the bedroom. The sick girl squinted in the light, suddenly clutched her head in her hands—and burst out sobbing. The impression of a miserable, ungainly creature suddenly vanished, and Korolyov no longer noticed the small eyes and the out-size lower jaw. He saw a gentle, suffering look so wise, so moving that she seemed all feminine grace and charm—he wanted to soothe her, now, with a few simple, kind words: not with medicines or advice. The mother clasped her daughter's head and clutched her to herself. What grief, what despair was in the old lady's face! Mother had reared and nurtured daughter, no expense spared. She had sacrificed every-thing to have the girl taught French, dancing, music. She had engaged a dozen teachers and all the best doctors, she kept a governess. And now she couldn't understand: why all the tears, whence all the anguish? She couldn't understand, she was baffled, and she wore a guilty, anxious, desperate look. Was there something else—something crucial —that she had omitted? Had she left something undone? Was there someone or other, some unknown, whose services she had failed to enlist?

'You're crying again, Liza,' she said, clasping her daughter. 'My own dearest little darling, tell me what's the matter. Tell me, for pity's sake.'

Both wept bitterly.

Korolyov sat on the edge of the bed and took Liza's hand. 'There, there, don't cry,' he said kindly. 'There's nothing on earth worth all those tears, now, is there? So don't let's cry, then. No need to——'

The thought struck him that it was 'time she got married'.

'Our works doctor's been giving her potassium bromide,' said the governess. 'But it only makes her worse, I notice. If it's heart trouble, then it's my opinion she should have those drops—what are they called? Convallamarin, or something?'

Out came all the different details all over again. She interrupted

Korolyov, she wouldn't let him get a word in edgeways. And she wore a long-suffering expression which seemed to imply that she, as the most educated individual in the house, needs must keep up a non-stop, exclusively medical conversation with the doctor.

Korolyov found this a bore.

'I don't see anything to worry about,' said he, leaving the bedroom and addressing the mother. 'If the works doctor has been treating your daughter, let him carry on. The treatment's been all right so far, I see no need to change doctors. There's no point, anyway—it's quite a common ailment, nothing serious.'

He spoke slowly, putting on his gloves, while Mrs. Lyalikov stood motionless and looked at him with tear-filled eyes.

'I have half an hour to catch the ten o'clock train,' he said. 'I hope I shan't miss it.'

'Can't you stay with us?' she asked, and tears again flowed down her cheeks. 'I don't like troubling you, but do be so kind——. For God's sake,' she went on in a low voice, glancing round at the door, 'do stay the night here. She's all I have, my only daughter. She did scare me so last night, I can't get over it. For pity's sake don't leave us.'

He wanted to say that he had a lot to do in Moscow, that his family was expecting him home. To spend an entire evening and night in a strange house for no reason . . . it would be an ordeal. But he looked at her face, sighed—and silently removed his gloves.

All the lamps and candles had been lit for him in both drawing-rooms. He sat by the grand piano turning over the music, then scrutinized the portraits and other pictures on the walls. The paintings —in oils, gilt-framed—showed views of the Crimea, a small boat on a stormy sea and a Catholic monk with a wine-glass: dim, glib, uninspired stuff, all of it. As for the portraits, there wasn't a single handsome or attractive face among them—it was all broad cheek-bones, all startled eyes. Liza's father had a small forehead, a self-satisfied expression—and a baggy uniform which sat ill on his large, plebeian frame. He wore a medal and Red Cross badge on his chest. It was all in such poor taste: haphazard, mindless luxury as ill-fitting as that uniform. The gleaming floors irritated him, and so did the chandelier—they somehow suggested the merchant in the story, the one who always wore his medals in the bath.

There was a sound of whispering from the hall, and of someone softly snoring. Then, suddenly, certain noises—harsh, staccato, metallic —came from outdoors: noises such as Korolyov had never heard before and could not make out now. They aroused in him strange, unpleasant feelings.

'I don't think I'd live here for anything,' he thought, picking up the music again.

'Will you come and eat now, Doctor?' the governess called in a low voice.

He went in to the meal. There was a large table with quantities of food and wine—but only two for supper, himself and Miss Christine. She drank Madeira and ate greedily.

'We're very popular with the workers,' she said, eyeing him over her pince-nez. 'We have our own theatricals at the works every winter —with workers actually acting in them! They have their magic-lantern talks, such a lovely canteen, and all they could possibly want. They're devoted to us, and when they heard that Liza was worse they had prayers said for her. Ignorant folk, but they've got their feelings same as us.'

'You have no man about the house apparently,' said Korolyov.

'No. Mr. Lyalikov passed away eighteen months ago, and we were left on our own. That's how we live, us three. We spend summer here and winter in Moscow, in Polyanka Street. I've been with them over ten years—quite one of the family, I am.'

For supper sturgeon, chicken rissoles and stewed fruit were served. The wines were French . . . and expensive.

'Now, don't stand on ceremony, Doctor,' said Miss Christine, eating away, wiping her mouth with the back of her hand and obviously doing herself proud. 'Do help yourself.'

After supper the doctor was shown to the room where a bed had been made up for him. But he didn't feel like sleeping in this stuffy room smelling of paint. He put on his overcoat and went out.

It was cool outside, and there was already a glimmer in the sky. The five mills with their tall chimneys, the barracks, the warehouses . . . all showed up clearly in the damp air. All work had stopped because it was a Saturday night, and the windows were dark. In just one mill the furnace was still burning, two windows glowed blood-red and a flame occasionally issued from the chimney along with the smoke. Far from the works frogs croaked, a nightingale sang.

Looking at the mills, at the barracks where the workers slept, he again thought what he always thought when he saw factories. The workers had their theatricals, granted—their magic lanterns, their factory doctors, their various amenities. Yet those mill-hands he had seen on the road from the station this evening . . . they had looked exactly like the workers he had seen long ago as a boy, when there had been none of these theatricals and amenities. As a doctor accustomed to forming accurate diagnoses of incurable chronic ailments deriving from some unknown ultimate cause, he considered factories a mystery of comparably vague and intractable antecedents. As for improvements in the workers' lives, he didn't think them unnecessary, but compared them to the treatment of incurable diseases.

'It's all a misunderstanding, of course,' he thought, looking at the blood-red windows. 'Fifteen hundred or two thousand mill-hands work unceasingly in unhealthy conditions making cheap printed cotton. They live on the edge of starvation. Only occasionally do they sober up—and in the pub!—from this nightmare. A hundred people super- vise the work. They devote their whole lives to recording fines, shouting abuse and mistreating people. Only two or three individuals —the "bosses"—reap the benefits, though they do no work at all and despise cheap cotton. What *are* the benefits, though, how *do* they enjoy them? The Lyalikov woman and her daughter are unhappy—they look pathetic—and the only one to enjoy life to the full is this Miss Christine: an elderly, rather silly old maid with a pince-nez. So what does it all come down to? What are these five mills working for? To what end is cheap cotton sold in eastern markets? Just so that Miss Christine can eat her sturgeon and drink her Madeira!'

Suddenly strange sounds rang out, just like those which Korolyov had heard before supper. Near one of the sheds someone was hitting a metal sheet, but then immediately muffling the sound—thus creating short, harsh, blurred thudding noises. Then, after thirty seconds' silence, from another shed rang out a sound similarly staccato and disagreeable—but on a lower, deeper, clanging note. Eleven times. Evidently the watchmen were striking eleven o'clock.

From the third shed came a similar repeated sound on yet another note. Such noises came from all the sheds, and then from behind the barracks and the gates. These sounds in the quiet of the night . . . they seemed to proceed from that monster with the blood-red eyes, that devil who ruled everyone around here—bosses and workers alike— deceiving one and all.

Korolyov went out of the grounds into the fields.

'Who goes there?' someone shouted roughly by the gate.

'Just like prison,' he thought, and made no answer.

Here nightingales and frogs were more audible, one sensed the May night. The sound of a train came from the station. Drowsy cocks were crowing somewhere, but still the night was quiet, still the world slept peacefully. In a field not far from the mills stood the framework of a building with material for its construction stacked near by. Korolyov sat on the planks.

'Only the governess enjoys life here,' he continued his reflections. 'The mill works for her pleasure. That's an illusion, though—she's only a figurehead. The principal, the main beneficiary, is the devil.'

Considering the devil, in whom he did not believe, he looked back at the two windows where the fire glowed. Those blood-red eyes watching him . . . they did belong, he felt, to the devil, to that mysterious force which has forged the relations between weak and strong—a gross blunder now wholly irreparable. The strong are bound to make life miserable for the weak, that is a law of nature. But only in a newspaper article or textbook is that law intelligible and psychologically acceptable, whereas in the chaos of everyday life—in the tangle of trifles which go to make up human relations—it ceases to be a law, and becomes a paradox rendering both weak and strong equal victims of their mutual relations as they unwillingly submit to some mysterious controlling force unconnected with life and alien to man. Such were Korolyov's thoughts as he sat on the planks, gradually overcome by the feeling that his mysterious unknown force really was close at hand, really was watching him. Meanwhile the east was growing ever paler, and time was passing quickly. Against the grey background of the gloaming, in the absence of any living soul, the world seemed dead, while the five mill-sheds and their chimneys had a special look—unlike that of daytime. Completely forgetting that they contained steam engines, electricity and telephones, he somehow kept thinking about ancient lake-dwellings and the Stone Age. He sensed the presence of that primitive, mindless force.

Once again those blurred thuds were heard: twelve strokes. Then there was quiet, thirty seconds' quiet, followed by the deeper clanging note at the other end of the works.

'How revolting!' thought Korolyov.

From a third place a harsh, staccato, seemingly exasperated sound rang out on yet another note.

It took four minutes to strike twelve o'clock. Then things grew quiet, and once again he had the impression that everything around him was dead.

Korolyov sat on for a while before going back to the house, but it was still a long time before he went to bed. There was whispering in the adjoining rooms. The shuffling of slippers and the padding of bare feet were heard.

'Has she had another attack?' wondered Korolyov.

He went out to look at his patient. It was already quite light indoors. Piercing the morning mist, a feeble sunbeam quivered on the drawing-room wall and floor.

Liza's door was open. She was sitting in an arm-chair by the bed wrapped in a house-coat and shawl, with her hair loose. The blinds were drawn.

Korolyov asked how she was.

'All right, thank you.'

He felt her pulse, pushed back the hair which had fallen on her forehead.

'You can't sleep,' he said. 'There's wonderful weather outside—spring, nightingale song—but you sit brooding in the darkness.'

She listened, gazed into his face. Her eyes looked sad and wise, she obviously wanted to tell him something.

'Does this happen to you often?' he asked.

She moved her lips. 'Yes, I feel depressed almost every night.'

Then the watchmen began striking two o'clock outside. Hearing those blurred thuds, she shuddered, and he asked whether the banging bothered her.

'I don't know. Everything bothers me here, everything,' she answered, gathering her thoughts. 'Your voice sounds sympathetic, and from the moment I saw you I've somehow felt I could talk to you about things.'

'Talk then. Do.'

'I want to tell you what I think. I don't think I'm ill at all. Why am I worried and scared? Because it *has* to be, because it can't be helped. Even the healthiest man can't help worrying if there's a burglar, say, prowling under his window. I'm always seeing doctors,' she went on with a shy smile, looking down at her lap. 'I'm most grateful, of course, I don't disbelieve in medicine. But I don't so much want to talk to a doctor as to someone close to me: a friend to understand me and show me whether I'm right or wrong.'

'Have you no friends, then?' asked Korolyov.

'I'm lonely. I do have a mother whom I love, but I'm still lonely. That's the way things are. Lonely people read a lot, but they don't talk or hear much, and they find life mysterious. They're mystics, and often see the devil when he isn't there. Lermontov's Tamara was lonely, and she saw the devil.'

'Do you read a lot?'

'Yes. After all, I am free all day from morning till evening. I read by day, but at night my head's empty—only shadows instead of thoughts.'

'Do you see things at night?' Korolyov asked.

'No, but I feel them——'

She smiled again, raised her eyes to the doctor, and looked at him so sadly and wisely that he felt she trusted him, shared his outlook, and wanted to tell him what she really thought. But she said nothing, perhaps waiting for him to speak.

He knew what to say to her now. Clearly she should run away from her five mills and her million roubles, if she had that much money—run away from this devil, this watcher of the night. Clearly, too, she had the same ideas as he—and she was only waiting for someone she trusted to confirm them.

But he didn't know how to put it. What could he say? It is awkward asking a condemned man what he has been sentenced for, and it's the same with very rich people: it's awkward asking them what they want with all that money, why they manage it so badly, why they don't give it up—even when they see it causing their unhappiness. Even if you do get them talking about it, the talk is usually embarrassed, uncomfortable and tedious.

'What shall I say?' wondered Korolyov. 'Need I say anything, actually?'

So he said what he had to say indirectly and obliquely.

'You, as mill-owner and rich heiress are dissatisfied, you don't believe you have the right to such things. And now you can't sleep. Well, that's better of course than if you were complacent, slept soundly and thought all was for the best. Your insomnia is admirable—it's a good sign, anyway. Indeed, the talk we're having now . . . it would have been unthinkable for our parents. They didn't hold conversations in the middle of the night; they slept soundly—whereas we, our generation, sleep badly. We suffer, we talk a lot, and we keep worrying whether we're right or wrong. Now, for our children or grandchildren this problem of being right or wrong will have been solved. They'll see more clearly than we can. Life will be good in fifty years' time—it's a shame we shan't live to see it, though. It would be interesting to have a peep.'

'What will our children and grandchildren do?' asked Liza.

'I don't know. Very likely drop everything and run away.'

'But where will they run to?'

'Where to? Why, anywhere!' laughed Korolyov. 'There's no lack of horizons for a decent, intelligent man.'

He looked at his watch. 'I say, the sun is up. It's time you went to sleep. You undress and have a really good sleep. I'm very glad to have met you,' he went on, pressing her hand. 'You're a fine, interesting woman. Good night.'

He went to his room and to bed.

When the carriage was brought round in the morning, everyone came out on the porch to see him off. Liza wore a white dress as it was Sunday, and a flower in her hair. She looked pale and languid. She gazed at him sadly and wisely, as on the previous night, smiling and speaking with the same air of wanting to say something special, something vital, something for his ears only. Larks sang, church bells pealed, mill windows glinted merrily. As he drove through the grounds along the station road, Korolyov had forgotten workers, lake-dwellings and devil—he was thinking of the time, which may already be near, when all life will be as bright and joyful as this quiet Sunday morning. How pleasant, thought he, to drive in a fine carriage pulled by three horses, sunning oneself on such a fine spring morning.

ALL FRIENDS TOGETHER

(A Story)

ONE morning a letter arrived.

> Kuzminki, 7 June
>
> Dear Misha,
>
> You've quite forgotten us. Do come and visit us soon, we
> miss you. Come out today—we beg you, sir, on bended knee!
> Prince Charming, show yourself!
>
> Dying to see you,   TA and BA

The letter was from Tatyana Losev: 'Ta', as she had been called
when Podgorin was staying at Kuzminki ten or twelve years ago.

But who might Ba be?

Podgorin remembered long conversations, gay laughter, flirtations,
evening walks and a whole bevy of girls and young women who had
once lived at Kuzminki and near by. Then he remembered that frank,
lively, intelligent face with the freckles which so well set off the dark
auburn hair of . . . Barbara, Tatyana's friend. Barbara had taken a
medical degree and had a job at a factory somewhere out beyond Tula.
Now she was obviously staying at Kuzminki.

'Dear old Ba!' thought Podgorin, letting memories engulf him.
'Splendid girl!'

Tatyana, Barbara and he were of an age. But he had only been a
student then, and they marriageable girls who regarded him as a mere
boy. Now that he was a lawyer with greying hair they still treated
him as not quite grown up, still stressed how young he was, still said
he knew nothing of life.

He was very fond of them—but rather as figures of the past, he felt,
than as anything else. Of their present situation he knew very little: it
sounded all very mysterious and alien to him. Alien too was this short,
jocular letter, no doubt composed with much time and effort. When
Tatyana was writing it her husband Sergey must have been standing
behind her.

The estate of Kuzminki had come to her as part of her dowry only
six years ago, but had already been run into debt by this same Sergey.
Whenever a bank or mortgage payment fell due these days they would

ask Podgorin for legal advice. They had, moreover, twice asked him for a loan. Now too it was either advice or money they wanted from him, obviously.

Kuzminki had lost its old hold over him. It was so sad out there. The laughter, the bustle, the jolly, carefree faces, the trysts on quiet moonlit nights . . . these things were no more. Above all, they weren't as young as they had been. And it was only in retrospect, probably, that it all seemed so magical.

Besides Ta and Ba there had also been a Na: Tatyana's sister Nadya whom—half in jest, half seriously—they used to call his fiancée. He had watched her grow up, and they had reckoned on his marrying her. He had indeed been in love with her at one time, he had been going to propose. But she was twenty-three now and he still hadn't married her.

'Odd, how it has all turned out,' he thought as he re-read the letter with embarrassment. 'And I can't *not* go because they'd be offended.'

His failure to visit the Losevs recently . . . it weighed heavily on his conscience, and so, after pacing his room and brooding, he overcame his reluctance and decided to go and stay for a couple of days. His duty thus discharged, he could relax and feel free until next summer at least. As he made ready to leave for the Brest Station after lunch he told his servants that he would be back in three days.

From Moscow to Kuzminki was a two-hour train ride followed by a twenty-minute coach drive from the station. When he got out of the train Tatyana's wood came into view together with three tall, narrow summer cottages which Losev—who had taken up various business enterprises during the first years of his marriage—had started building but hadn't finished. He had been ruined by these cottages, by other money-making schemes and by his frequent trips to Moscow—what with lunching at the Slav Fair, dining at the Hermitage and ending up on Little Bronny Road or at the gipsy dive called Knacker's Yard.

He called this 'pushing the boat out'.

Podgorin drank a certain amount himself, quite a lot at times, and consorted with women indiscriminately—but coldly and sluggishly, without enjoyment, and he was quite disgusted when his associates went in for that sort of thing wholeheartedly. As for those who felt more relaxed at Knacker's Yard than in their own homes with respectable women . . . such men he neither understood nor liked. Anything the least bit smutty . . . it seemed to stick to them like burrs. He disliked Losev—he thought him a dull dog, utterly incompetent and lazy. Many were the times he'd found his company rather off-putting.

Sergey and Nadya met him just beyond the woods.

'Why have you been neglecting us, my dear chap?' asked Losev, kissing him thrice and then putting both arms round his waist. 'You don't love us any more, old pal.'

He had gross features, a fleshy nose, a thin, light brown beard. He combed his hair to one side, merchant fashion, to give himself that simple, oh-so-Russian look. He breathed straight in your face when he spoke and when he wasn't speaking he breathed heavily through his nose. His beefy frame, his air of excessive self-indulgence . . . they embarrassed him, and he kept puffing out his chest to ease his breathing —which gave him a haughty look. His sister-in-law Nadya seemed ethereal by comparison. She was very fair, pale and graceful with friendly eyes which seemed to caress one. Was she or was she not beautiful? Podgorin couldn't tell, having known her since childhood and taking her looks for granted. She wore a white, open-necked dress, and the view of that long, white, bare neck was new to him and not altogether nice.

'Tatyana and I have been expecting you since morning,' she said. 'Barbara's staying with us, and she's looking forward to seeing you too.'

She took his arm and abruptly laughed for no reason, giving a spontaneous cry of joy as if enchanted by some sudden thought. The fields of blooming rye so still in the quiet air, the sun-drenched woods . . . how lovely they were! But only now that she was walking beside Podgorin did Nadya seem to notice these things.

He told her that he would be staying for three days. 'I'm sorry, I couldn't get away from Moscow any sooner.'

'You've quite neglected us—very, very naughty of you!' was Sergey's good-humoured reproach. '*Jamais de ma vie!*' he suddenly added, clicking his fingers.

He had this trick of unexpectedly bringing out some utterly irrelevant exclamation with a snap of the fingers. He was for ever mimicking someone: if he rolled his eyes, nonchalantly tossed back his hair or struck a pathetic pose, the reason was that he had been to the theatre on the previous night, or had attended a banquet with speeches. Now he was walking like a gouty old man—taking short steps, not bending his knees: aping someone or other, no doubt.

'Tatyana couldn't believe you'd come, you know,' Nadya said.

'But Barbara and I felt sure you would—I somehow knew you'd
come by this train.'

'*Jamais de ma vie!*' repeated Sergey.

The ladies awaited them on the garden terrace. Ten years ago
Podgorin—then a poor student—had coached Nadya in mathematics
and history in exchange for his board and lodging, while Barbara (a
medical student at the time) had incidentally had some Latin lessons
from him. As for Tatyana, that strapping, good-looking girl had
thought only of love. Love and happiness . . . she was obsessed with
them, she craved them, she was for ever expecting to meet that future
husband who filled her dreams morning noon and night. Now
turned thirty, she was just as beautiful and striking as ever, in her loose
peignoir, with her plump white arms. Her thoughts were only of her
husband and her two little girls. She might be talking and smiling now,
her expression said, but her mind was really on other things: she was
still mounting guard over her love and over her rights to that love, she
still stood poised to pounce on any enemy who might want to remove
her husband and children. Hers was a strong love and she felt that it
was reciprocated, but jealousy and fear for her children tormented her
unceasingly and prevented her from being happy.

After a noisy reunion on the terrace everyone except Sergey went
to Tatyana's room. Lowered blinds kept out the sun, and the light was
so dim that all the roses in a large vase seemed of the same colour.
They sat Podgorin down in an old arm-chair by the window while
Nadya sat on a low stool at his feet. Besides the friendly reproaches,
the jokes and the laughter which he now heard, and which reminded
him so vividly of the past, there would—he knew—also be a disagreeable conversation about promissory notes and mortgages. There
was no escape, so he thought it might be best to have their business
talk now, without more ado, and get it over with—then go out into
the garden and the fresh air.

'Might we talk business first?' he asked. 'What's new here in Kuzminki? Anything rotten in the state of Denmark?'

'Kuzminki *is* in a rotten way,' Tatyana sadly sighed. 'Things are in
such a mess, dear me, they really are—they could hardly be worse.'
She paced the room in agitation. 'The estate's up for sale, the auction's
on the seventh of August, there are advertisements everywhere, and
prospective buyers come here and walk round the house staring.
Anyone has the right to come and look round my room these days.
Oh, it may be perfectly legal, but I find it deeply humiliating and

insulting. We're out of funds—*and* out of places to borrow them from. It's simply awful.'

She paused in the middle of the room, her voice trembling, tears starting from her eyes. 'I swear, I swear by everything most sacred, by my children's happiness, I can't live without Kuzminki. I was born here, it's my home, and if it's taken away from me I can't carry on, I shall die of despair.'

'I think you take too gloomy a view,' said Podgorin. 'It will be all right. Your husband will get a job, you'll find a new niche: live a new life.'

'How can you say such a thing!' shouted Tatyana, looking very beautiful and fierce. She was poised to pounce on that enemy who might try to remove her husband, children and home—as her face, her whole figure, expressed with particular force. 'New life, indeed! How can you say such a thing? Sergey has been making inquiries, and he's been promised a tax inspectorship somewhere out Ufa or Perm way. And I don't mind where I go. Let it be Siberia, even, I'm prepared to stay there ten, twenty years. But I must be sure of coming back to Kuzminki sooner or later. I can't live without Kuzminki, I can't, I shan't, I won't!'

She shouted, stamped her foot.

'You're a lawyer, Misha,' said Barbara. 'You know all the tricks, and it's your job to tell us what to do.'

There was only one fair and rational reply: that the situation was hopeless. But Podgorin could not bring himself to blurt it out.

'I must think about it,' he mumbled indecisively. 'I'll give it some thought.'

He was two different men. As a lawyer he'd had to handle some pretty nasty cases. In court, with clients, he behaved arrogantly and always expressed his opinion directly and harshly. He was used to somewhat crude jollifications with his cronies. But in the intimacy of his personal life, with people very close to him or old friends, he showed extraordinary delicacy, he was shy and sensitive, and he could never put things bluntly. A single tear, one sidelong glance, a lie—an ugly gesture, even . . . they were enough to make him flinch and cave in. And now that Nadezhda was sitting at his feet he disliked her bare neck. It put him off and even made him want to leave for home. A year ago he had chanced to run across Sergey at a certain Madame's premises in Bronny Road, and he was as embarrassed by Tatyana's presence, now, as if it was he who had been unfaithful to her. Besides this talk about Kuzminki put him in a very difficult position. He was used to having judges, juries—or simply some legal provision—settling all ticklish and unpleasant questions, and when faced with a problem for his personal decision he was lost.

'You're our friend, Misha, we all love you, you're like one of the family,' Tatyana went on. 'Now, I'll be perfectly frank with you: you're our only hope. Tell us what to do, for God's sake. Perhaps there's somewhere we could apply for help? Perhaps it's not too late to put the estate in Nadya's name, or Barbara's? What shall we do?'

'Save us, Misha, save us,' said Barbara, lighting a cigarette. 'You were always such a clever boy. You haven't really lived, you're not very experienced, but you do have your head screwed on. You'll help Tatyana, I know you will.'

'I must think—perhaps I'll come up with something.'

They went for a walk in the garden and then in the fields. Sergey came along too and took Podgorin's arm—kept leading him ahead, obviously intending to discuss something: probably the mess he was in. This walking and talking with Sergey were quite an ordeal too. Sergey kept embracing his guest—always the regulation three kisses—took Podgorin's arm, put his own arm round Podgorin's waist, breathed in his face. It was as if he had been smeared with a sweet glue which was liable to stick fast to you whenever he touched you. And that look about the eyes which showed that he wanted something out of Podgorin, that he was just going to ask Podgorin for it . . . it was downright depressing, as if the man was pointing a revolver at you.

The sun set, it was getting dark. Along the railway line green and red lights came on here and there.

Barbara paused, looked at the lights and recited.

> '*Through narrow cuttings, over bridges*
> *Past posts the line runs true and brave.*
> *Behold that splendid railway's verges:*
> *The Russian workers' common grave!*

How does it go on? Good Lord, I've forgotten!

> '*In sultry heat, in freezing winter*
> *We strained our sinews, bent our backs.*'

She declaimed with gusto in a magnificent contralto voice, her face flushing vividly, tears in her eyes. This was the old Barbara, the college girl. Hearing her reminded Podgorin of his own old student days when he had known a lot of good poetry by heart and had enjoyed reciting it.

> '*His back still hunched and never straightened,*
> *The navvy grimly holds his peace——*'

But Barbara remembered no more.

She fell silent, smiling weakly and feebly. The green and red signal lights seemed sad now that her recitation was over.

'Oh, I've forgotten it.'

But Podgorin did suddenly remember—it had somehow stuck in his memory from his student days—and he recited softly, under his breath.

> '*Enough our Russian worker suffered*
> *To build another railway line.*
> *Next will he build a mighty future:*
> *His own new highway broad and fine!*
> *The pity is——*'

'The pity is,' Barbara broke in, now remembering the words.

> '*The pity is that neither you nor I*
> *Will see that brave new world before we die.*'

She laughed and clapped him on the back.

They went home and sat down to supper. Sergey nonchalantly tucked a corner of his napkin into his collar in imitation of someone or other.

'Let's have a drink,' he said, pouring vodka for himself and Podgorin. 'At college in the old days we could hold our liquor, we had the gift of the gab, *and* we got things done. I drink your health, old pal. Now, why don't *you* drink to a silly old idealist, coupled with the wish that he may die an idealist. Can the leopard change his spots?'

All through supper Tatyana was casting tender, jealous glances at her husband, afraid of his eating or drinking something which might disagree with him. He had been spoilt by women, exhausted by them, she felt—which attracted her, but also caused her pain. Barbara and Nadya had a soft spot for him too, their worried looks betraying the fear that he might suddenly make off and leave them. When he made to pour himself a second glass of vodka Barbara's expression grew peeved.

'You're poisoning yourself, Sergey,' she said. 'You're a highly-strung, sensitive person, and you might easily become an alcoholic. Tell them to remove the vodka, Tatyana.'

Sergey was a great ladies' man on the whole. They liked his height, his build, his strong features, his idleness, his misfortunes. His extravagances were only due to kindness, said they—he was impractical because he was an idealist, he was honest, he had integrity. If he owned nothing and couldn't find a proper job, that was because he couldn't truckle to people and circumstances. Such great faith did they have in him, idolizing him, spoiling him with their adoration . . . he even began thinking that he *was* idealistic, impractical and the soul of decency and integrity: head and shoulders above these very women, in fact.

'Now, why don't you say something nice about the children?' asked Tatyana, looking lovingly at her two little girls—healthy, sleek and resembling cream buns—as she piled their bowls with rice. 'Just look at them, now! All mothers dote on their children, it's said. But I'm quite unbiased, believe me, and my little girls are outstanding. Especially the elder.'

Podgorin smiled at her and the little girls while wondering how a healthy and rather intelligent young woman—so essentially large and complex an organism—could lavish her entire energy and vital forces on a labour as trivial and devoid of complexity as managing a home which was perfectly well managed already.

'There may be some reason for it,' thought he. 'But how dull and dreary it all is!'

> *'Before he'd time to turn a hair*
> *He'd been knocked over by a bear,'*

said Sergey, snapping his fingers.

They finished supper. Tatyana and Barbara sat Podgorin down on the drawing-room sofa and began a low-voiced discussion: business again.

'We must rescue Sergey, it's our moral duty,' said Barbara. 'He has his weaknesses, he's not provident—doesn't put by for a rainy day—but that's because he's so kind and generous. He's just a child at heart. Present him with a million roubles, and none of it would be left in a month, he'd give it all away.'

'It's true, it really is,' said Tatyana, tears streaming down her cheeks. 'I've had an awful lot to put up with from him, but he is a wonderful person, there's no denying it.'

Then Tatyana and Barbara were both sufficiently cruel, in a small way, to reproach Podgorin by saying that his generation was 'quite different, Misha'.

Why this generation stuff, wondered Podgorin—after all, Losev was only six years older than he, no more.

'Life isn't easy,' sighed Barbara. 'One's always threatened with losing something. Either they want to take your estate, or someone dear to you falls ill and you fear for their life. So it goes on, day in day out. But what can we do, my dears? We must submit to a Higher Will without complaining, we must remember that nothing in this world is accidental, but that everything has its own ultimate purpose. You haven't really lived, Misha, you haven't suffered much, and you'll laugh at me. All right—laugh, but I'll say it all the same. During my acutest periods of anxiety I have had several experiences of second sight. This has quite transformed my consciousness, and I now know that nothing is contingent—that everything in life is necessary.'

How different she was, this Barbara . . . grey-haired now, corseted, in her modish dress with its puffed sleeves . . . Barbara twisting her cigarette in her long, thin, nervously twitching fingers . . . Barbara so prone to mysticism . . . Barbara of the flat, monotonous voice—how different she was from Barbara the medical student, that jolly, merry, hearty, venturesome red-head!

'What ever became of all that?' wondered Podgorin, bored with her chatter.

'Sing us something, Ba,' he asked, to cut short this talk of second sight. 'You used to sing so beautifully.'

'That's all ancient history, Misha.'

'Then recite some more Nekrasov.'

'I've forgotten all that. Those quotations just now . . . I just remembered them by accident.'

Despite that corset and those puffed sleeves she was obviously not well off, and had a pretty thin time of it out at that factory beyond Tula. Obviously, too, she had been overworking. Hard, grinding toil, perpetual worry about other people and interfering in their affairs . . . it had exhausted her, aged her. Looking at that sad face, which had already lost its bloom, Podgorin reflected that *she* was the one who really needed help: not Kuzminki and this Sergey whom she was making such a fuss about.

Her college education, her career as a doctor . . . they did not seem to have affected the woman in her. Like Tatyana she adored weddings, births, christenings, endless chat about children. She liked reading thrillers with happy endings and in newspapers she only read the bits about fires, floods and public ceremonies. She was very keen for

Podgorin to propose to Nadya—were it to happen she would burst into tears of ecstasy.

Whether accidentally or through Barbara's contrivance, Podgorin now found himself alone with Nadya. But the mere suspicion that he was under observation, that something was expected of him . . . it constrained him, cramped his style. In Nadya's presence he felt as if the two of them were shut up in a cage together.

'Let's go into the garden,' said she.

They went off to the garden: he disgruntled and annoyed, not knowing what to talk about, and she delighted, proud to be with him, obviously pleased that he was staying on another three days—possessed too, perhaps, by delicious fancies and hopes. Was she in love with him? That he didn't know. But that she was fond of him he did know—that she had long been attached to him, that she still looked on him as her teacher, and that she was now passing through the same emotional phase as her sister Tatyana before her: she was obsessed, that is, with love, with marrying as soon as possible, with having a husband, children, her own little place. She still retained that capacity for friendship which is so intense in children. Could it be that her feelings for Podgorin were only those of respect and friendliness—that she was not in love with him so much as with those dreams of a husband and children?

'It's getting dark,' he said.

'Yes, the moon rises late now.'

As they walked they kept to one path near the house. Podgorin didn't want to go far into the garden where it was dark, and where he would have to take her by the arm and be very close to her. Shadows moved on the terrace: Tatyana and Barbara watching him, he felt.

'I must ask your advice.' Nadya halted. 'If Kuzminki's sold Sergey will go away and get a job, and our lives are bound to change completely. I shan't stay on with Tatyana—we shall separate because I don't want to be a burden on the family. I must work. I'll get a job in Moscow and earn some money to help Tatyana and her husband. You will advise me, won't you?'

Knowing nothing at all about it, she was yet inspired by the idea of an independent working life, she was making plans for the future—it was written all over her face. Working, helping others . . . she thought it all so wonderfully romantic. Seeing her pale face and dark brows close to him, he remembered what a keen, intelligent, promising pupil she had been—remembered how he had enjoyed coaching her. She was no longer just a young lady looking for a husband, probably, but a decent, intelligent, exceptionally kind, tender, soft-hearted girl who could be moulded, like wax, to one's wishes. Given a proper environment, what an admirable woman she might become!

'Now, why *don't* I marry her, actually?' wondered Podgorin, but at once rather took fright at the idea and made for the house. Tatyana was sitting at the grand piano in the drawing-room. Her playing brought back vivid memories of the time when playing, singing and dancing had gone on until late at night in this same drawing-room with the windows open and the birds also singing away in the garden and by the river. Podgorin cheered up, became exuberant, danced with Nadya and Barbara, and then sang. Hampered by a corn on his foot, he asked if he could wear Sergey's slippers. And, oddly enough, he felt at home—quite one of the family—in those slippers: 'a typical brother-in-law' flashed through his mind. He became even cheerier. Looking at him, everyone else came to life and brightened up as if rejuvenated. Their faces glowed with hope: Kuzminki was saved! It was all so simple, wasn't it? They only needed to devise some scheme, rummage around in law books, or have Nadya marry Podgorin.

That affair was obviously prospering. Nadya—pink, happy, eyes filled with tears in anticipation of excitement—twirled as she danced. Her white dress billowed, showing her pretty little legs in flesh-coloured stockings.

Barbara was delighted and took Podgorin's arm. 'Don't run away from your happiness, Misha,' she said quietly, with a meaningful expression. 'Just take it when it's offered—otherwise you'll be chasing after it when it's too late to catch it.'

Podgorin wanted to give an undertaking, confirm her hopes. By now he himself believed that Kuzminki was saved: there was nothing to it!

'Thou sha-alt be the quee-een of all the world,' he sang, striking a pose. But then he suddenly realized that there was nothing, absolutely nothing, that he could do for these people—so he stopped singing, looking guilty.

Then he sat silently in a corner, tucking under him those feet shod in someone else's slippers.

The others realized from the way he looked that nothing could be done. They too fell silent. The piano was closed. Everyone noticed that it was late—time for bed—and Tatyana extinguished the big lamp in the drawing-room.

They had made up a bed for Podgorin in the same little hut in the grounds where he used to sleep in the old days. Sergey went along to say good night, holding a candle high above his head, though the moon had risen and it was already bright. They went down a path flanked by lilac bushes, gravel crunching underfoot.

'Before he'd time to turn a hair
He'd been knocked over by a bear,'

said Sergey.

Podgorin felt as if he'd heard these lines a thousand times. He was sick of them!

When they reached the hut Sergey produced a bottle and two glasses from his loose-fitting jacket and put them on the table.

'Cognac,' said he. 'Double Zero brand. One can't drink in the house with Barbara around because she only starts nagging about alcoholism. But here we're free. A fine cognac, this!'

They sat down, and the cognac was indeed good.

'Let's have a proper drink tonight,' went on Sergey, chewing on a lemon. 'I've always been rather one of the boys, myself, and I do like pushing the boat out now and then. Matter of necessity!'

But there was still that look about his eyes which said that he needed something from Podgorin and was just about to ask for it.

'Drink up, old boy,' he sighed. 'Things are pretty tough, I can tell you. It's all up with chaps like me—us individualists. We're finished. Idealism's out of fashion these days. It's money that talks nowadays, and if you don't want to be kicked aside you must fall down and worship Mammon. But that I can't do—I'm a sight too squeamish!'

'When's the auction?' Podgorin asked, to change the subject.

'Seventh of August. But I have no hope of saving Kuzminki, old boy. Those arrears are colossal, and the estate brings in nothing: it's losses, losses, losses every year. The game's not worth the candle. Tatyana's upset of course—it *is* her family home—but I'm not all that sorry, quite frankly. I'm not cut out for the country. Give me a large, bustling city! Conflict . . . there's my element!'

He went on, still dodging the issue, while watching Podgorin keenly as if waiting his chance. Then, suddenly, Podgorin saw those eyes near to him and felt the man's breath on his face.

'Come to my rescue, dear old boy!' gasped Sergey. 'Lend me two hundred roubles, I beg you.'

Podgorin wanted to say that he was short of money himself. It seemed better to give those two hundred roubles to some poor man, or just lose them at cards, even. But he was terribly embarrassed. Feeling trapped in this small room with the one candle, desiring a swift escape from that breath, from those soft arms round his waist—which already seemed glued to his person—he hastily rummaged in his pockets for his note-case.

'There you are,' he mumbled, taking out a hundred roubles. 'You can have the rest later, I have no more on me. As you see, I can't refuse.' He was annoyed and beginning to lose his temper. 'I'm an insufferably feeble character. But please let me have it back sometime because I'm hard up myself.'

'Grateful, grateful indeed, old chap.'

'And for God's sake stop fancying yourself an idealist. You're as much an idealist as I am a turkey-cock. You're just a frivolous, idle person, that's all.'

Sergey sighed deeply and sat on the sofa.

'You're angry, dear old boy,' he said. 'Oh, if you did but know what I have to put up with! I'm having a hellish time. Now, it's not myself I'm sorry for, dear old boy—it's the wife and kids, believe you me. If it wasn't for the wife and kids I'd have ended it all long ago.'

His shoulders and head suddenly shook and he burst out sobbing.

'This is the last straw,' said Podgorin, agitatedly pacing the room and feeling exasperated.

'Look here, what am I to do about someone who first behaves like a scoundrel and then bursts into tears? Your tears disarm me, I can say nothing to you. You sob, therefore you are right.'

'*Me* behave like a scoundrel!' said Sergey, standing up and staring at Podgorin with amazement. 'How can you say such a thing, dear old boy? Me behave like a scoundrel! Oh, how little you know me, how little you understand me!'

'All right then, I don't understand you, but please stop blubbering. It's revolting.'

'Oh, how little you know me!' repeated Sergey in all sincerity. 'How little indeed!'

'Just look at yourself in the mirror,' Podgorin went on. 'You're getting on in life, you'll soon be old, and it's high time to pull yourself together and take stock of who you are and what you are. Your whole life has been one long round of idleness, affectations, posturings and futile, childish chit-chat. I wonder it doesn't nauseate you. Aren't you sick of it all? Oh, you *do* depress one so! And you *are* such a stupefying bore!'

This said, Podgorin left the hut and slammed the door. It was just about the first time in his life that he had ever been sincere and said what he meant.

Soon afterwards he was regretting his brusqueness. What was the good of talking seriously or arguing with a congenital liar, guzzler and toper who spent large quantities of other people's money while remaining convinced that he was an idealist and a martyr? The problem here was either sheer stupidity or ingrained bad habits corroding his organism like an incurable disease. Indignation, severe reprimands . . . they were useless here, anyway. It would have been better to laugh at him. One good sneer would do more than ten sermons!

'Better still, pay no attention,' thought Podgorin. 'And above all don't lend him money.'

Soon afterwards he had forgotten both Sergey and his hundred roubles. It was a quiet, melancholy night, very bright. When Podgorin gazed at the sky on moonlit nights he always felt as if only he and the moon were awake, and that everything else was asleep or dozing. He forgot all about people and money. A calm, peaceful mood gradually came over him. He felt alone in the world and his footsteps had a melancholy sound in the silence of the night.

The garden was enclosed by a white stone wall. On the right-hand corner of the side facing open country was a tower built long ago in the days of serfdom. The lower part was of stone, while the top was wooden—consisting of a platform, a conical roof and a tall spire with a black weathercock on it. Below were two gates giving access from garden to fields. A staircase led up to the platform and creaked underfoot. Some broken old arm-chairs dumped under the stairs were now bathed in moonlight filtering through the gate. With their crooked legs sticking up, those chairs seemed to have become alive at nightfall and to be lying in wait for someone here in the silence.

Podgorin climbed the stairs to the platform and sat down. Just beyond the fence were a ditch and bank marking the boundary of the estate, and beyond that were broad moonlit fields. Podgorin knew that there was a wood directly opposite, about two miles from the grounds, and thought he could descry a dark strip in the distance. Quails and landrails were calling. Now and then the cry of a cuckoo, also suffering from insomnia, was borne from the direction of the wood.

There was a sound of footsteps: someone walking in the garden and coming towards the tower.

A dog barked.

'Beetle! Come back, Beetle,' a woman's voice softly called.

Someone was heard entering the tower below, after which a black dog—an old friend of Podgorin's—appeared on the bank. It paused and looked up towards where Podgorin was sitting, wagging its tail affectionately. A little later a ghostly white figure arose from the black ditch and also paused on the bank. It was Nadya.

'What can you see there?' she asked the dog, and looked up.

She couldn't see Podgorin but evidently sensed his presence because she smiled, and her pale, moonlit face looked happy. The tower's black shadow running along the ground far into the field, the still, white figure with the beatific smile on the pale face, the black dog and the shadows of them both . . . it was all so dream-like.

'There *is* somebody there,' said Nadya softly.

She stood and waited for him to come down or call her: to declare his love at last and make them both happy on this calm, lovely night. White, pale, slim, lovely indeed in the moonlight, she awaited his caress. Her perennial dreams of happiness and love . . . they had wearied her. No longer could she hide her feelings. Her whole figure, her brilliant eyes, her fixed and blissful smile . . . all betrayed her secret thoughts. He felt awkward huddled there in the silence. Should he speak? Should he turn it all into the usual joke? Hold his peace? He didn't know, and he felt aggrieved. All he could think of was that here, in this garden, on this moonlit night, close to this beautiful, love-lorn, wistful girl, his emotions were as uninvolved as on Little Bronny Road. Just as dead for him—evidently—was this poetic vision, as that prosaic squalor. They meant nothing to him now, did these assignations on moonlit nights, these slim-waisted white figures, these mysterious shadows, towers, country houses, these types like Sergey and other types like himself—this Podgorin with his apathy, his boredom, his perpetual bad temper, his inability to adapt to real life, his incapacity for making the most of it, his tiresome, obsessive craving for what did not, what never could, exist on earth. Now that he was up here in the tower he would have preferred a good firework display, a moonlight procession, or Barbara reciting Nekrasov's 'Railway' again. He would rather have seen another woman on that bank instead of Nadya standing there: one who might tell him of something fresh and original unconnected with love and happiness, or who—had she indeed spoken of love—would have summoned him to those new, lofty, rational modes of existence such as we shall perhaps live to see one day and already sometimes anticipate.

'There's no one there,' said Nadya.

After waiting a little longer she set off slowly towards the wood, bowing her head. The dog ran ahead. For some time Podgorin saw her as a white shape.

'Odd, how it has all turned out,' he reflected again as he returned to the hut. What he would say to Sergey and Tatyana tomorrow he had no idea. How would he behave towards Nadya? And what about the day after that? The prospect was embarrassing, frightening, boring. How was he to fill the three interminable days which he had promised to spend here? He remembered the talk about second sight and Sergey's 'before he'd time to turn a hair he'd been knocked over by a bear'. He remembered that he would have to humour Tatyana by smiling at those sleek, tubby little girls on the morrow. So he decided to leave.

At half past five in the morning Sergey appeared on the terrace of the big house wearing a Bokhara dressing-gown and a tasselled fez. Losing no time, Podgorin went up to him and started saying good-bye.

'I must be in Moscow by ten,' he said, averting his eyes. 'I have an appointment with some solicitors—it had entirely slipped my mind. Please don't detain me. When the others get up tell them I apologize, I'm most frightfully sorry——'

He did not hear Sergey's reply as he hurried away, casting glances at the manor windows and fearful of the ladies waking up and trying to stop him leaving. He was ashamed of being so neurotic. This was, he felt, his last visit to Kuzminki—never would he go there again. As he drove off he cast several backward glances at the hut in which he had spent so many happy days. But he merely felt indifferent: not sad.

When he reached home the first thing he saw on the table was yesterday's letter.

Dear Misha,
    You've quite forgotten us. Do come and visit us soon——

For some reason he remembered Nadya twirling in the dance, with her dress billowing and showing her legs in those flesh-coloured stockings.

Ten minutes later he was working at his desk. Kuzminki had been forgotten.

THE BISHOP

I

IT was the eve of Palm Sunday service at the Old Convent of St. Peter. When they started handing out the palm leaves it was nearly ten o'clock, lights had dimmed, wicks needed snuffing, everything was blurred and the congregation swayed like a sea in the gloomy church. To Bishop Peter, who had been unwell for three days, all these faces—old and young, male and female—appeared alike: coming up for their palms, they all had that same look about the eyes. He could not see the doors for haze, and the congregation kept moving—never-ending, it seemed. A women's choir sang, a nun was reading the lesson.

It was so hot, so stuffy. The service seemed interminable, and his lordship was tired. He was breathing heavily—panting—his throat was parched, his shoulders ached with fatigue, his legs trembled. He was upset, too, by the occasional shrieks of some religious maniac in the gallery. Then, suddenly, as if dreaming or delirious, he thought he saw his mother whom he had not set eyes on for nine years—or an old lady resembling his mother—approach him in the congregation, take her palm and move away, gazing at him with a bright, radiant, kindly smile until lost in the crowd. Tears began trickling down his face, he knew not why. He felt serene and all was well, but he stared at the choir on his left where the lesson was being read and where he could no longer see who was who in the gloaming—and wept. Tears glittered on his face and beard. Then someone near him also started crying, followed by someone else a little further off, and then by more and more people until the whole church was gradually filled with this quiet weeping. But about five minutes later the nuns' choir was singing, the crying had stopped, everything was back to normal.

The service ended soon afterwards. As the Bishop climbed into his carriage to go home a melodious, rich, merry clang of heavy bells flooded the moonlit convent garden. White walls, white crosses on graves, white birches, black shadows, the moon far away in the sky directly over the convent . . . all seemed to be living a life of their own —a life incomprehensible yet close to man's. It was early April with the seasonal chill which follows a warm day, there was a touch of frost and a breath of spring in the soft, cold air. The road from convent to city was sandy, and they had to keep their horses to a walk. In the moonlight, bright and serene, churchgoers were trudging through the sand on both sides of the carriage. All were silent, plunged in thought. So congenial, fresh and intimate was this ambience—trees, sky and moon too—that one found oneself hoping it would never change.

The carriage reached town at last and rumbled down the main street. The shops were shut, except that at Yerakin's—the millionaire merchant's—the electric lighting was being tested, and flickered violently while a crowd stood around. Then came a series of wide, dark, deserted streets followed on the far side of town by a metalled road (built by the local authority), open fields, fragrant pines. Suddenly a white castellated wall arose before his eyes and behind it a tall bell-tower bathed in moonlight with a cluster of five large, glittering onion-domes. It was the Monastery of the Almighty, where Bishop Peter lived. Here too, high above the monastery, rode that same calm, dreaming moon. The carriage drove in at the gate, crunching on sand. Here and there black monkish figures flitted through the moonlight, footsteps echoed on flagstones.

'Your mother called while you were out, my lord,' said the lay brother as the Bishop was entering his quarters.

'My mother? When did she arrive?'

'Before the service—she asked where you were, then went to the convent.'

'So it *was* her I saw in church just now—good heavens!' The Bishop laughed happily.

'She asked me to tell your lordship that she'll be here tomorrow, the lay brother continued. 'She has a little girl with her—her grand-daughter, I suppose. They're staying at Ovsyannikov's inn.'

'What time is it now?'

'Just after eleven.'

'Oh, what a pity.'

The Bishop sat for a while in his parlour, meditating and somehow not believing that the hour was so late. His arms and legs ached, the back of his neck hurt, he felt hot and uncomfortable. After resting he went to his bedroom, where he also sat for a while, still thinking of his mother. He heard the lay brother going away, and a monk—Father Sisoy—coughing in the next room. The monastery clock struck the quarter.

The Bishop changed and began saying his bed-time prayers. While carefully reciting the old familiar words he thought about his mother. She had had nine children and about forty grandchildren. She had once lived with her husband, a deacon, in a poor village: lived there for most of her life, between the ages of seventeen and sixty. The Bishop remembered her from early childhood—from the age of three, almost—and how he had loved her! Dear, precious, unforgettable childhood, that time now vanished and gone beyond recall . . . why does it always seem brighter, richer, more carefree than it actually was? When he had been ill in childhood or youth . . . how tender, how solicitous his mother had been! By now his prayers were mingled with memories which blazed up like flames, ever more radiantly, and his prayers did not stop him thinking about his mother.

His prayers finished, he undressed and lay down. No sooner had darkness closed around him than he had a vision of his father—now dead—his mother, his native village of Lesopolye.

Wheels creaking, sheep bleating, church bells pealing on bright summer mornings, gipsies at the window . . . how delightful to think of these things. He remembered the Lesopolye priest, Father Simeon: that meek, mild, good-natured man—short and lean, but with an enormously tall theological student son who had a thundering bass voice. Losing his temper with a cook, once, the son had called her 'thou ass of Jehudiel', hearing which Father Simeon had gone very quiet—ashamed that he could remember no such ass in the Bible. His successor at Lesopolye had been Father Demyan: a heavy drinker who sometimes reached the point of seeing green serpents and was even nicknamed Old Snake-Eye. The Lesopolye schoolmaster had been a Matthew Nikolayevich: a former divinity student—kind, rather intelligent, also a drunkard. He never beat his pupils, but for some reason always had a birch hanging on the wall with a notice under it in 'Latin' gibberish: BETULA KINDERBALSAMICA SECUTA. He had a shaggy black dog called Syntax.

The bishop laughed. Five miles from Lesopolye was another village, Obnino, with a miracle-working icon which was carried in procession round the neighbouring villages every summer while bells rang all day —first in one village, then in another. To the Bishop ('Young Paul' at the time) the very air had seemed vibrant with rapture, and he had followed that icon—bare-headed and barefoot, blissfully happy with his innocent faith and his innocent smile. At Obnino, he now recalled, there had always been a large congregation, and Father Alexis—the

local priest—had saved time in church by getting his deaf nephew
Ilarion to recite the notices and the inscriptions attached to communion loaves: all about prayers 'for the health of' and 'for the soul
of' various people. Ilarion did it, receiving the occasional five or ten
copecks for these services, and only when he was grey and balding—
only when life had passed him by—did he suddenly notice one day a
paper with the words ILARION IS A FOOL written on it. Young Paul
had been backward until the age of fifteen or more, and had done so
badly at his church school that they had even thought of taking him
away and placing him in a shop. When fetching letters once from
Obnino post-office, he had directed a prolonged stare at the clerks, and
had then asked them to 'permit me to enquire' how they received
their salary: was it monthly or daily?

The Bishop crossed himself, turning over so that he could stop
thinking and go to sleep. Remembering that his mother had come to
see him, he gave a laugh.

The moon shone in at the window, the floor gleamed and shadows
lay across it. A cricket chirped. On the other side of the wall, in the
next room, Father Sisoy was snoring. There was a forlorn, bereaved
note—something of the homeless wanderer, even—in the old boy's
snores. Sisoy had once looked after a diocesan bishop, and was now
known as the 'Father Ex-Housekeeper'. He was seventy years old and
lived in a monastery ten miles from the city—but stayed in town too
when convenient. Three days ago he had called at the Monastery of
the Almighty, and the Bishop had put him up in his own quarters so
that they could discuss business and certain local arrangements at their
leisure.

The bell rang for a service at half past one. Father Sisoy was heard to
cough and mumble discontentedly, after which he got up and paced
the rooms barefoot. The Bishop called him by name, whereupon
Sisoy went to his own room, but appeared a little later in his boots,
carrying a candle. He wore cassock over his underclothes and a faded
old skull-cap.

'I can't sleep,' said the Bishop, sitting up. 'I must be unwell. But just
what the matter is I don't know. I feel so hot.'

'You must have caught cold, my lord. You need rubbing down with
candle grease.'

Sisoy stood there for a moment. 'Lord, forgive me, miserable
sinner.' He yawned and added that 'they had the electricity on at
Yerakin's just now—I don't hold with it, I don't.'

Father Sisoy was old, wizened, bent, always discontented. He had angry, bulging eyes like a crab's.

'I don't hold with it, confound it, that I don't,' he repeated as he went out.

II

On the next day, Palm Sunday, the Bishop took morning service in the cathedral, then visited the diocesan bishop and an old lady—wife of some general—who was very ill, and finally returned home. At about half past one he was entertaining some very special guests to lunch: his old mother and his little eight-year-old niece Katya. Throughout lunch the spring sun shone through the windows which looked on the yard, sparkling merrily on the white tablecloth and in Katya's red hair. Through the double frames rooks were heard cawing in the garden, starlings chattered.

'Nine years it is since we met,' said the old lady. 'But then I saw you in the convent yesterday, and—goodness me, you haven't changed a bit except that you're thinner and your beard's longer, Blessed Virgin, Mother of God! Yesterday at the service no one could help crying, and when I looked at you I suddenly started crying myself, I don't know why. It's the Lord's will.'

Fondly though she spoke she was clearly ill at ease, apparently wondering how intimately she should address him, and whether she might laugh or not. She seemed to feel herself more the deacon's widow than the bishop's mother, while Katya stared unblinking at her right reverend uncle as if trying to guess what manner of a man this was. Her hair sprouted up like a halo from her comb and velvet ribbon, she had a turned-up nose and an artful look. She had broken a glass before lunch, and her grandmother was now moving the tumblers and wineglasses away from her as she spoke. Listening to his mother, the Bishop remembered her long, long ago taking him with his brothers and sisters to see some supposedly rich relatives. She had been busy with her children then. Now it was her grandchildren, and so she had brought this Katya.

'Your sister Barbara has four children,' she explained. 'And Katya here's the eldest. Now, Father Ivan—your brother-in-law—fell ill, Lord knows why, and died three days before Assumption. And now she's real hard up, is poor Barbara.'

The Bishop asked after Nikanor, his eldest brother.

'He's all right, thank God. He hasn't much, but it's enough to live

on, praise be. The thing is, though, his son Nicholas—my grandson—
decided against a church career. He's at college, studying to be a
doctor. That's better, thinks he, and who knows? 'Tis the Lord's
will.'

'Nicholas cuts up dead bodies,' put in Katya, spilling water on her
lap.

'Sit still, child,' the grandmother remarked serenely, taking the
glass from her hands. 'Say a prayer as you eat.'

'It's so long since we met,' said the Bishop, fondly stroking his
mother's arm and shoulder. 'I missed you when I was abroad, Mother,
I really did.'

His mother said that she 'thanked him kindly'.

'Some evenings you'd be sitting on your own by an open window
when a band would strike up—and you'd suddenly want to be back in
Russia. You'd feel you'd give anything to go home and see your
mother——'

His mother beamed, but at once pulled a serious face and repeated
that she 'thanked him kindly'.

Then his mood changed rather abruptly. Looking at his mother, he
was baffled—why this nervous, deferential expression and tone of
voice? What was the point? It didn't seem like her. He felt depressed
and annoyed. Besides, he also had a headache like yesterday's and a
gnawing pain in his legs. The fish seemed tasteless and unappetizing,
he felt thirsty all the time.

After the meal two rich ladies, estate-owners, arrived and sat for
an hour and a half in silence with long faces. The Father Superior—
taciturn and a trifle deaf—came on some errand. Then the bell rang
for evensong, the sun sank behind the woods, and the day was done.
The Bishop came back from church, hastily prayed, went to bed and
covered himself up warmly.

That lunch-time fish had left a disagreeable aftertaste, the moonlight
disturbed him, and then he heard voices. Father Sisoy was discussing
politics in a near-by room, probably the parlour.

'The Japanese are at war now. Fighting, they are. The Japanese are
like the Montenegrins, missus. Belong to the same tribe, they do,
they were under Turkish rule together.'

Then the Bishop's mother was heard to speak. 'So, having said our
prayers, like, er, and had a cup of tea, we went to see Father Yegor at
Novokhatnoye er——'

From all this 'having had a cup' and 'having drunk a pot' stuff you'd have thought she'd never done anything in life but drink tea. Slowly and apathetically the Bishop recalled his theological school and college. He had taught Greek at that school—by then he could no longer read without glasses. Then he had become a monk and second master, then he had taken his doctor's degree. He had been made headmaster and Father Superior at the age of thirty-two, and life had been so easy and pleasant: looked as if it would go on and on like that for ever and ever. But then he had fallen ill, he had lost a lot of weight, he had nearly gone blind—and had had to drop everything and go abroad on doctors' orders.

'Then what?' asked Sisoy in the next room.

'Then we had tea,' answered the Bishop's mother.

'Father, you have a green beard,' Katya suddenly said with a surprised laugh.

Remembering that grey-haired Father Sisoy's beard really did have a greenish tinge, the Bishop laughed.

'The girl's a thorough pest, Lord help us,' said Sisoy loudly and angrily. 'She's so spoilt! You sit still!'

The Bishop remembered the completely new white church where he had held services when living abroad, remembered the roar of that warm sea. He had had an apartment of five high, airy rooms with a new desk in the study and a library. He had read and written a great deal. He remembered being homesick for Russia, remembered the blind beggar-woman singing of love and playing a guitar under his window every day—listening to her had always reminded him of the past, somehow. Then eight years had passed, he had been recalled to Russia. Now he was a suffragan bishop, and his entire previous life had vanished into some distant mist, as if it had all been a dream.

Entering the bedroom with a candle, Father Sisoy gave a surprised exclamation. 'Asleep, already, my lord?'

'What is it?'

'Why it's still early—ten or even earlier. I've just bought a candle, I wanted to rub you over with grease.'

'I have a temperature.' The Bishop sat up. 'We really should do something, my head's bad——'

Sisoy took the Bishop's shirt off and began rubbing his chest and back with candle grease.

'There, there,' he said. 'Lord bless us! There, there. I went into town today and visited that Father what's-his-name—Sidonsky—had tea with him. I don't hold with him, Lord love us, that I don't.'

III

The diocesan bishop—old, very stout and rheumaticky or gouty—had been bedridden for the last month. Bishop Peter visited him almost daily, and saw the people who came to ask the other's help. But now that he was unwell himself he was struck by the triviality and futility of all their tearful applications. Their ignorance and nervousness riled him. All this pettiness and pointlessness . . . the sheer weight of it got him down. He felt that he could understand the diocesan bishop: author of a *Studies in Free Will* in youth, but now apparently submerged in trifles, having forgotten everything and never thinking about God. Bishop Peter must have lost touch with Russian life while he was abroad. It wasn't easy for him now, what with the peasants seeming so rough and the ladies who sought his help so tiresomely stupid—while theological students and their teachers were ill-educated and at times barbarous. As for the documents coming and going, they were reckoned by their tens of thousands! And what documents! The higher clergy of the entire diocese were accustomed to award conduct marks to their juniors of whatever age—to wives and children, even—just as if they were school-children, all of which had to be discussed, perused and solemnly reported in documentary form. Never, never was there a single free minute: it was nervous tension all day long for Bishop Peter, who could relax only when he was in church.

Nor could he inure himself to the terror which, through no wish of his own, he inspired in others despite his meek and modest demeanour. Everyone in the county seemed small, frightened and guilty when he looked at them. Everyone—even older, senior clerics—wilted in his presence, they all prostrated themselves before him. So scared had one of his recent petitioners been (an old woman, wife of a country priest) that she had gone away empty-handed without uttering a single word. Meanwhile the Bishop—who could never bring himself to disparage anyone in his sermons, who felt too sorry for people to reproach them—was raging and losing his temper with those who consulted him, and throwing their applications on the floor. Not once since he had come to this place had anyone spoken to him sincerely and simply, as one human being to another. Even his old mother seemed to have changed, indeed she did. Why, he wondered, did she chatter away non-stop and laugh so much when she was with Sisoy, whereas with her own son she was so solemn, so tongue-tied, so embarrassed—which didn't suit her at all? The only person to behave freely and speak his mind in the Bishop's presence *was* old Sisoy, whose whole life had been spent attending bishops, and who had outlasted eleven of them—which was why his lordship felt at ease with him, difficult and cantankerous though the old boy assuredly was.

After Tuesday morning's service the Bishop went to the palace to deal with his appointments, which was all very upsetting and annoying, after which he went home. Again he felt unwell, again he wanted to go to bed. But hardly had he reached his room before he was informed that Yerakin—a young businessman and contributor to charities —had arrived on a most urgent errand. There was no question of not seeing him. Yerakin stayed for about an hour talking very loudly, practically shouting, so that it was hard to make out what he said.

'God grant something-or-other,' he said as he left. 'Oh, most emphatically! Depending on the circumstances, my lord. Wishing you something-or-other.'

Then came the Mother Superior of a distant convent. After she had left the bells rang for evensong, and he had to go to church.

That evening the monks' singing was tuneful and inspired. A black-bearded young priest was officiating. Hearing about the bridegroom who cometh at midnight and the mansion richly adorned, the Bishop felt neither grief nor repentance but spiritual calm and serenity as his thoughts floated back to the distant past, to his childhood and youth when that same bridegroom and mansion had also been hymned. That past now seemed vivid, wonderful and joyful. Not that it had really been anything of the sort, probably. In the next world, in the life to come, we shall perhaps recall the distant past and our present life with just such a feeling. Who knows? Tears coursed down the Bishop's face as he sat in the darkness of the chancel. He had achieved everything possible for a man in his position, he reflected. He had kept his faith. And yet not all was clear to him—something was missing. He didn't want to die. He still felt the lack of some crucial element which he had once vaguely imagined, and he was still disturbed at this very moment by that same hope for the future which had been his in boyhood, at college and abroad. Listening to the singing, he thought how good it was today: very good indeed.

IV

On Maundy Thursday he took morning service in the cathedral. As the congregation dispersed afterwards the weather was sunny, warm and cheerful, with water gurgling in ditches and ceaseless lark-song, sweet and restful, wafting over from the fields beyond the city. Newly burgeoning trees smiled their welcome, and above them a fathomless expanse of blue sky soared off into the unknown.

Arriving home, Bishop Peter had tea, changed, went to bed and told the lay brother to close the shutters. The bedroom grew dim. How tired he was, though, how his legs and back did ache with that dull, cold pain, and what a ringing there was in his ears! He felt as if he hadn't slept for a long time, felt himself prevented from sleeping by some trifle which glimmered in his brain as soon as his eyes were shut. Through the walls of adjoining rooms he heard voices, and the chink of glasses and tea-spoons—just like yesterday.

His mother was telling Father Sisoy some jolly tale with lots of little jokes while he responded sullenly and discontentedly with a 'confound them!', a 'not likely!' or a 'no fear!' Again the Bishop was annoyed, and then hurt, that the old lady could behave so normally and naturally with strangers—yet remained so nervous and tongue-tied with her own son, always saying the wrong thing, and even seeking a pretext all this time (or so he felt) to stand up in his presence because she was too shy to sit down. And what of his father? Had the old man still been alive he would probably have been unable to utter one word in his son's presence.

In the next room something fell on the floor and broke. Katya must have dropped a cup or saucer because Father Sisoy suddenly spat, announcing angrily that the girl was a thorough pest. 'Lord forgive me, miserable sinner, we'll soon have nothing left!'

Then all was quiet except for noises outside. When the Bishop opened his eyes he saw Katya in his room. She stood stock still, looking at him with that red hair sprouting as usual out of her comb like a halo.

'Is it you, Katya?' he asked. 'Who keeps opening and closing that door downstairs?'

'I can't hear it,' answered Katya, listening.

'There—someone just went through.'

'But it was your stomach rumbling, Uncle.'

He laughed and stroked her hair.

'So Cousin Nicholas cuts up dead bodies, does he?' he asked after a pause.

'Yes. He's a medical student.'

'Is he nice?'

'Yes, he's all right. But he doesn't half drink vodka!'

'What did your father die of?'

'Daddy was weak and ever so thin, and then suddenly he had a bad throat. I fell ill too, and so did my brother Theo—we all had bad throats. Then Daddy died, but we got better, Uncle.'

Her chin quivered. Tears filled her eyes and crawled down her cheeks.

'My lord,' said she in a thin little voice, now weeping bitterly. 'Mummy and I are so miserable, Uncle. Do give us a bit of money— please, Uncle darling.'

He wept as well. For some time he was too upset to say a word. Then he stroked her head, touched her shoulder.

'All right, all right, little girl. Soon it will be Easter Sunday and we'll have a talk. I will help you, certainly——'

His mother came in quietly and nervously, faced the icon and said a prayer. Noticing that he was still awake, she asked if he would 'like a drop of soup'.

'No thank you. I'm not hungry.'

'You seem unwell now I look at you. I'm not surprised, though. On the go all day long—goodness me, a sorry sight you are! Well, Easter isn't far off and then you can have a rest, God willing, and we'll talk. I won't bother you with my chatter now. Come on, Katya, let the Bishop sleep.'

He remembered her addressing some church dignitary just like this— long, long ago during his boyhood—with that same mixture of jocularity and respect.

The unusually kind look in her eyes and the nervous, anxious glance which she flashed as she left the room . . . these were the only indications that this *was* his mother. He closed his eyes and seemed to be sleeping, but twice heard the striking of the hours, heard Father Sisoy coughing behind the wall. His mother came in again and watched him nervously for a minute. He heard some coach or carriage drive up to the porch. Suddenly there was a knock, the door banged, and the lay brother came into the bedroom shouting 'your lordship'.

'What is it?'

'Your carriage is waiting. Time for evening service.'

'What time *is* it then?'

'A quarter past seven.'

He dressed and drove to the cathedral where he had to stand motion-less in the centre during all twelve lessons from the gospels. The first of these—the longest and most beautiful—he read himself. A buoyant, vigorous mood came over him. That first reading ('Now is the Son of Man glorified') he knew by heart. Reciting it, he occasionally raised his eyes, he saw a sea of lights around him and he heard the sputter of candles, but the congregation remained invisible as before. It was, he felt, that self-same congregation which he had seen as a boy and youth, and it would remain unchanged year after year—for how long God alone knew.

His father had been a deacon, his grandfather a priest, his great-grandfather a deacon. His entire family had quite possibly belonged to the clergy since Christianity had first come to Russia. His love of church services, of the priesthood, of ringing bells was innate, deep, ineradicable. In church—especially when he himself was officiating—he always felt active, cheerful and happy, which was just how he felt now. But after the reading of the eighth lesson he felt that his voice was failing, he could not even hear himself cough, a splitting headache came on. He began to worry—feared he might be about to fall down. Yes, his legs had grown completely numb, gradually losing all sensation. How he stayed upright and kept his feet—why he didn't just fall down—he could not tell.

The service finished at a quarter to twelve. Arriving home, the Bishop undressed and went to bed at once without even saying his prayers. He could not speak, he felt that he had lost the use of his legs. As he was pulling the blanket over him he suddenly felt an urge—an absolute craving—to go abroad. He was ready to sacrifice life itself just to be spared the sight of those wretched cheap shutters and low ceilings, to escape this oppressive monastic smell. If only there was one single person that he could talk to, open his heart to!

For some time he heard footsteps in the next room, but whose they might be he simply could not recall. Then the door opened at last, and in came Sisoy with a candle and tea-cup.

'Already in bed, my lord? It's me—come to rub you down with vodka and vinegar. Very good for you it is if you rub it in well, Lord love us. There, there. I've just been in our monastery, but I don't hold with it, like. I'm leaving tomorrow, Bishop. I want no more of it, Lord love us! There, there.'

Sisoy could never stay long in one place, and he felt as if he'd already spent a whole year at the Monastery of the Almighty. It was hard, indeed, to figure him out from the way he talked. Where was his home? Did he love anyone or anything? Did he believe in God?

He had no idea himself why he was a monk, he gave it no thought—
and as for the time when he had taken his vows, his mind was a blank.
It was as if he had simply been born a monk.

'I'm going tomorrow, confound it all!' said Sisoy.

'I'd like to talk to you, but I never seem to manage it.' The Bishop
spoke softly, with great effort. 'I don't know anyone or anything here,
you see.'

'I'll stay till Sunday if you like. So be it. I want no more of it,
confound them!'

'Why am I a bishop?' the Bishop went on quietly. 'I should have been
a village priest, a sexton or an ordinary monk. It all seems to—to
crush me.'

'Eh? Lord love us! There, there! Now, you have a good sleep, my
lord. Goodness gracious, whatever next? Good night to you.'

The Bishop did not sleep all that night. In the morning, at about
eight o'clock, he had an intestinal haemorrhage. The lay brother was
terrified. He rushed off: first to the Father Superior, and then to the
monastery doctor, Ivan Andreyevich, who lived in town. The doctor—
a stout old man with a long white beard—examined the Bishop at
length, shaking his head and frowning. Did his lordship realize that
this was 'typhoid fever, you know'?

Within about an hour the effect of the haemorrhage had been to
make the Bishop thin, pale and hunched. His face was wizened, his
eyes enormous. He seemed aged and shrunk. He felt thinner, feebler
and more insignificant, now, than everyone else—felt that all his past
had escaped him to some infinitely remote place beyond all chance of
repetition or continuation.

'And a very good thing too,' he thought.

His old mother arrived. Seeing his wizened face and big eyes she
took fright, fell on her knees beside the bed and began kissing his
face, shoulders and hands. She too rather felt that he was thinner,
feebler and more insignificant than everyone else, she forgot that he
was a bishop and she kissed him like a dearly loved child.

'Paul darling,' she said. 'My darling little son. What's happened to
you? Answer me, Paul.'

Katya stood near by—pale, stern, not understanding. What was the
matter with Uncle? Why did Grandmother look so unhappy, why
was she saying such moving, sad words? But the Bishop was past
speech, he could take nothing in. He just felt as if he was an ordinary
simple man walking quickly and cheerfully through a field and

thumping his walking-stick under a broad, sun-drenched sky. Now he was free as a bird, now he could go where he liked.

'Paul, answer me, son,' said the old lady. 'What's the matter, darling?'

'Don't bother the Bishop.' Sisoy went angrily through the room. 'Let him sleep. There's nothing to be done, no point——'

Three doctors arrived, consulted, went away. The day seemed to go on and on and on, and was followed by a night no less interminable. Just before dawn on Saturday the lay brother went to the old lady as she lay on a sofa in the parlour, and invited her to step into the bedroom because the Bishop had gone to his fathers.

The next day was Easter Sunday. There were forty-two churches in the city, and six religious houses. The clangorous, joyful, ceaseless pealing of bells haunted and stirred the spring air above the buildings from morn to eve. Birds sang. The sun was bright. The large market square was all a-bustle. Swings swung, hurdy-gurdies played, an accordion squealed, drunken shouts echoed. In the afternoon there was buggy-riding up and down the main street. It was all great fun, in other words, everything was all right—just as it had been all right last year and would probably go on being all right in years to come.

A month later a new suffragan bishop was appointed. No one remembered Bishop Peter any more. They forgot him altogether except for the old lady—the deceased's mother—who went to live with her deacon son-in-law in a remote provincial town. Going out of an evening to fetch her cow from the meadow, and meeting other women there, she would talk about her children and grandchildren, and about her son who had been a bishop. She spoke nervously, afraid of being disbelieved.

Nor did everyone believe her, actually.

A MARRIAGEABLE GIRL

I

It was ten o'clock in the evening and a full moon shone above the garden. At the Shumins' home a prayer meeting—arranged by the grandmother—had just ended. Nadya had gone into the garden for a minute. She could see them laying the dining-room table for supper while Grandmother bustled about, resplendent in her silk dress. Father Andrew, a canon from the cathedral, was talking to Nadya's mother Nina, who somehow looked very young when seen through the window in the evening light. Father Andrew's son—himself an Andrew—stood by listening attentively.

All was quiet and cool in the garden. Tranquil black shadows lay across the ground, while far, far away—out of town, no doubt—frogs croaked. May, lovely May, was in the air. Nadya could breathe freely, and liked to fancy that there was another place—beneath the sky, above the trees, far beyond town, in fields and woods—where springtime had generated a secret life of its own: a life wonderful, rich and hallowed . . . a life beyond the understanding of weak, sinful man. She felt rather like crying.

Nadya was twenty-three, had longed to be married since she was sixteen, and was engaged at last to this Andrew who could be seen through the window: Father Andrew's son. Though she liked him, and though their wedding was to be on the seventh of July, yet there was no joy in her heart, she was sleeping badly and her spirits were low.

Through the open window came the sound of people scurrying and clattering knives in the kitchen, which was in the basement. A door banged on its block and pulley. There was a smell of roast turkey and pickled cherries. Such, it rather looked, was to be the pattern of her life from now on for ever and ever without end.

Then someone came out of the house and stood on the steps. This was Alexander Timofeyevich—Sasha for short. He was staying with them, having arrived from Moscow about ten days earlier. At one time long ago a distant relative of Grandmother's—an impoverished widowed gentlewoman, small, thin and ailing—had been in the habit of visiting her and receiving assistance. Sasha was her son. He was said to be an excellent artist, goodness knows why, and on his mother's death Nadya's grandmother had tried to improve her chances in the next world by sending him to the Komissarov School in Moscow. A couple of years later he had moved on to the Fine Arts Institute, where he spent practically fifteen years before barely scraping through with a diploma in architecture. He hadn't practised architecture, though, but had taken a job with a Moscow lithographic firm. He would come and stay with Grandmother almost every summer—to rest and recuperate, for he was more or less an invalid.

At the moment he wore a buttoned-up frock-coat and shabby canvas trousers frayed at the bottoms. His shirt was unironed. He looked rather frowsty, by and large. Very lean, with big eyes and long, thin fingers, he was bearded and swarthy—yet handsome. He was practically one of the family, feeling completely at home with the Shumins. For years the room in which he stayed had been called Sasha's.

While standing in the porch he spotted Nadya and went up to her. 'Isn't it nice here?'

'Of course it is. You should stay on till autumn.'

'Yes, I expect it will come to that. I dare say I'll stay till September.' He laughed for no reason and sat down by her.

'I've been sitting looking at Mother,' said Nadya. 'She seems so young from here. Mother does have her foibles, of course,' she added after a pause. 'Still, she is rather special.'

'Yes, she's a good sort,' Sasha agreed. 'In her own way your mother's a very kind and charming woman, of course, but—how can I put it—I happened to go into the kitchen early this morning and four of your servants were asleep on the bare floor. They have no beds or bedding: only rags, stink, bugs, cockroaches. Nothing's changed in twenty years, nothing at all. Never mind your grandmother, now—she can't help it. But your mother does speak French, you know, doesn't she? She acts in private theatricals. You'd think she'd understand.'

While speaking Sasha would point two long, wasted fingers at whoever he was addressing.

'This place seems rather outlandish when you're not used to it,' he went on. 'Nobody ever does anything, damn it! Your mother spends all day gadding about like some duchess, your grandmother doesn't do anything either. Nor do you. Nor does your future husband, Andrew.'

Nadya had heard all this last year and also—she thought—the year before. That Sasha was incapable of thinking in any other way she knew. Once that had amused her, now it rather annoyed her.

'That stuff's all out of date and boring.' She stood up. 'Can't you think of something new?'

Laughing, he stood up too, and they went to the house together. Tall, good-looking, well-built, she looked so healthy and presentable compared with him—sensing which, she felt sorry for him and rather embarrassed.

'You're always putting your foot in it,' she told him. 'You just said something about my Andrew, for instance. But you don't know him, do you?'

'*My* Andrew! To hell with *your* Andrew! Your wasted youth . . . that's what I deplore.'

As they went into the dining-room everyone was just sitting down to supper. Grandmother—'Gran' to the family, a very stout, ugly, bushy-browed, bewhiskered old woman—spoke loudly, unmistakably the head of the household in her voice and manner. She owned rows of stalls in the market and this period house with its columns and garden, but every morning she prayed to be preserved from bank- ruptcy, weeping as she did so. Then there was her daughter-in-law Nina—Nadya's mother: a fair-haired, tightly corseted woman sporting a pince-nez and diamonds on every finger. There was old Father Andrew—thin, toothless, looking poised to tell a very funny story. And there was his son: Andrew Junior, Nadya's fiancé—stout, hand- some, curly-haired, looking like a musician or artist. All three were discussing hypnotism.

Gran addressed Sasha. 'One week in my house and you'll be well again. But you must eat more—just look at you!' She sighed. 'Dread- ful, you look. A regular Prodigal Son, I call you.'

'He wasted his substance with riotous living,' said Father Andrew slowly, with laughter in his eyes. 'He filled his belly with the husks that the swine did eat.'

'I'm so fond of my old man,' said Andrew, touching his father's shoulder. 'A wonderful old chap, he is—such a dear old boy.'

No one spoke. Then Sasha suddenly laughed and pressed a napkin to his mouth.

'So you believe in hypnotism, do you?' Father Andrew asked Nina.

'That I believe in it I naturally cannot asseverate,' Nina answered, assuming an earnest—not to say severe—expression. 'But that many things in nature are mysterious and incomprehensible I must own.'

'I quite agree—while adding, however, that religion materially curtails the realm of the Unknown.'

A large, exceedingly plump turkey was served. Father Andrew and Nina went on talking. Diamonds sparkled on Nina's fingers, after which tears sparkled in her eyes. She was excited.

'I don't dare argue with you,' she said. 'But there are plenty of insoluble puzzles in life, grant me that.'

'Not one, I venture to assure you.'

After supper Andrew played the violin, accompanied by Nina on the piano. Ten years ago he had taken an arts degree, but he had never done a job and had no fixed occupation apart from an occasional appearance at charity concerts. They called him a 'musician' in town.

Andrew played while everyone listened in silence. The samovar quietly bubbled on the table, but only Sasha drank tea. Then, after twelve o'clock had struck, a violin string suddenly snapped. They all laughed, bestirred themselves and began to say good night.

After seeing her fiancé out, Nadya went upstairs, where she and her mother had their rooms—Gran occupied the lower floor. Down in the dining-room they had started putting out the lights, but Sasha sat on drinking his tea. He always spent a long time over his tea, Moscow fashion, drinking seven glasses at a sitting. Long after Nadya had undressed and gone to bed she could hear the servants clearing away downstairs and Gran's angry voice. In the end all was quiet except for the occasional deep cough proceeding from Sasha's room.

II

It must have been about two o'clock when Nadya woke. Dawn was breaking, and a watchman was making his banging noises somewhere far away. She wasn't sleepy. It was uncomfortable lying there—too soft. As always on past May nights, she sat up in bed and reflected, her thoughts being the same as those of the night before. Monotonous, futile and obsessive thoughts they were: about Andrew paying his addresses and proposing, about her accepting him and then gradually growing to appreciate so kind, so intelligent a man. But now that the wedding was less than a month away she felt vaguely scared and troubled as if faced by some prospect imprecise but disagreeable.

A desultory clicking thud was heard: that watchman again.

Through the large old-fashioned window she could see the garden with burgeoning lilac beyond it—drowsy and lifeless in the cold. A thick white mist slowly bore down on that lilac, wanting to submerge it. On far-away trees tired rooks cawed.

'God, why am I so depressed?'

Perhaps—who knows?—every young girl felt like this before her wedding. Or was it Sasha's influence? But Sasha had been on and on about all this for several years now, hadn't he? He sounded like a copybook: so unsophisticated and strange. Why, why, why couldn't she get him out of her head, though?

The watchman had long stopped his din. Birds started singing beneath the window and in the garden, the mist vanished, everything was radiant in smiling spring sunlight. Soon the whole garden, warmed and caressed by the sun, came to life with dew-drops glittering on the leaves like diamonds. Though old and long neglected, the garden seemed young and brightly decked that morning.

Gran was awake already, Sasha was coughing his deep, rough cough. Nadya heard the servants putting on the samovar downstairs and moving chairs.

The hours passed slowly. Nadya had been up and about the garden long ago, but still the morning dragged on.

Out came Nina, tears in her eyes, carrying a glass of mineral water. She practised spiritualism and homoeopathy, she read a lot, and she liked discussing the doubts which assailed her—all of which, thought Nadya, had some deep, mysterious significance. She kissed her mother and fell in by her side.

'Why were you crying, Mother?'

'I was reading a story last night about this old man and his daughter. The old fellow has a job somewhere, you see, and the man he works for falls in love with the daughter. I haven't finished it, but there was one bit . . . you couldn't help crying.' Nina sipped from her glass. 'I remembered it this morning and cried again.'

'I've been so depressed these last few days,' said Nadya a bit later. 'Why can't I sleep?'

'I don't know, darling. When I can't sleep I close my eyes ever so tight, like this, and imagine Anna Karenin walking about and talking. Or I think of something historical, from the ancient world.'

Her mother neither did nor could understand her, Nadya felt, felt it for the first time in her life—which positively terrified her. Wanting to hide, she went to her room.

They lunched at two. As it was a Wednesday—a Church fast—Grandmother was served with beetroot soup followed by steamed bream and buckwheat.

To tease Grandmother, Sasha took two kinds of soup: the beetroot variety *and* some meat broth of his own. He joked all through lunch, but his jokes all had some laboured moral and fell flat. When he introduced a witticism by uplifting his long, wasted, corpse-like fingers, and when you noticed how ill he was—that he wasn't long for this world—the effect was anything but funny, and you felt so sorry for him that you could cry.

After lunch Grandmother went to lie down in her room. Nina played the piano for a while, and then she went out too.

Sasha started his usual after-lunch discourse. 'My dear, good Nadya —if you would only, only listen to me——'

She was ensconced in an antique arm-chair, eyes closed, while he slowly paced the room.

'If you would only go away and study,' said he. 'Educated, dedicated people . . . they're the interesting ones, we don't need any other kind. The more such people there are, the more quickly the Kingdom of Heaven will come on earth, won't it? Bit by bit, you'll find, there won't be one stone left on another in your town. The place will turn topsy-turvy, change as if by magic. There will be splendid great mansions, marvellous gardens, wonderful fountains, outstanding people. But that's not what matters. The great thing is that the rabble as we know it, as it exists today . . . that evil will be no more because each man will have faith. Each will know the purpose of his life, and none will seek support in public opinion. Do leave this place, Nadya darling. Do show them all how bored you are by this stagnant, drab, reprehensible existence—or at least show your own self!'

'I can't, Sasha, I'm getting married.'

'Oh, really! What nonsense!'

They went out in the garden and walked a little.

Sasha continued. 'Say what you like, my dear, but this idleness of yours is sordid and immoral. Don't you realize, can't you see? Look— isn't it obvious that if you, say, and your mother and the wretched Gran never do anything, it means you're living on others, you're ruining the lives of people you don't even know. Pretty sordid, that! Pretty squalid, eh?'

Nadya wanted to say that, yes, he was quite right—wanted to tell him that she understood. But tears came to her eyes, she suddenly grew quiet, hunched her shoulders and went off to her room.

Andrew arrived in the late afternoon and as usual played his violin for a long time. Never a talkative man, he perhaps liked fiddling because it gave him an excuse to say nothing.

He started leaving for home at about half past ten, and already had his overcoat on when he embraced Nadya, greedily kissing her face, shoulders, hands.

'My dear, my darling, my beautiful one!' he muttered. 'Oh, how happy I am, I'm in a sort of mad ecstasy.'

But it sounded like something she had heard long ago in the distant past, or had read about in some antiquated, dog-eared, long-abandoned novel.

Sasha sat at the dining-room table drinking tea and balancing the saucer on his five long fingers. Gran played patience, Nina read. The icon-lamp sputtered, all was quiet and—it seemed—well. Nadya said good night, went up to her room, lay in bed and fell asleep at once—but woke up, as on the previous night, with the first glimmer of dawn. She wasn't sleepy, she felt troubled and depressed, she sat with her head on her knees—thinking of her fiancé and her wedding.

She happened to recall that her mother had never loved her husband, now deceased, and that she now had nothing, being entirely dependent on Gran—her mother-in-law. Why had Nadya always regarded her mother as someone special and out of the ordinary? Why had she never noticed that this was a commonplace, average, unhappy woman? Why? However much Nadya racked her brains she just couldn't say.

Sasha couldn't sleep either—she heard him coughing down below. What an oddity, what an innocent he was, thought Nadya. His dreams, all those 'marvellous gardens' and 'wonderful fountains' . . . there was something rather absurd about them, she felt. But his innocence, his very absurdity even . . . they had something so fine about them that the very thought of going away and studying at once sent a cold thrill through her, body and soul, flooding her with joy and rapture.

'But it's far, far better not to think about it, I mustn't,' she whispered.

The watchman's clicking thuds echoed from somewhere far away.

III

In mid-June Sasha suddenly felt bored and prepared to leave for Moscow.

'I can't stand this town,' said he gloomily. 'No water supply! No drains! It's not a very nice place to eat your meals—that kitchen's filthy beyond description.'

'Not so fast, Prodigal Son,' Grandmother urged him, in a whisper for some reason. 'The wedding's on the seventh.'

'I don't care.'

'But weren't you going to stay till September?'

'Well, I don't want to now, I have work to do.'

The summer had turned out damp and cold, the trees were sodden, everything in the garden looked dejected and uninviting—it really did make you feel like working. All over the house, upstairs and downstairs, strange women's voices sounded, and the sewing-machine rattled away in Grandmother's room as Nadya's trousseau was hurriedly made up: there were no less than six fur coats—to mention nothing else—and the cheapest of them was costing three hundred roubles, Gran said. All this fuss irritated Sasha, who sat fuming in his own room. Still, they did persuade him to stay on—he promised not to leave before the first of July.

Time passed quickly. After lunch on St. Peter's Day Andrew took Nadya to Moscow Street for another look at the house which had been rented and made ready for the young couple some time ago. It was of two storeys, but so far only the upper floor had been decorated. The drawing-room had a gleaming floor painted to look like parquet, Viennese chairs, a grand piano and a violin-stand. There was a smell of paint. On the wall hung a large, gilt-framed painting of a naked lady with a broken-handled mauve vase by her side.

'Exquisite!' signed Andrew respectfully. 'A Shishmachevsky!'

Then came a parlour with a round table, a sofa and arm-chairs upholstered in bright blue. Above the sofa hung a large photograph of Father Andrew complete with purple hat and decorations. They entered a dining-room with a sideboard, and then the bedroom. Two beds stood side by side in the murk, looking as if that room had been furnished with the idea that nothing either would, or possibly could, ever go wrong in the place. Andrew led Nadya through the house, clutching her waist all the time. But she felt weak and guilty, she hated all these rooms, these beds, these arm-chairs. And that naked lady made her feel sick. She was no longer in love with Andrew, that was obvious—perhaps she never had loved him. But how she could say it, who she could say it to, what the point would be . . . that she neither did nor could understand, though she thought about it all day and night.

Andrew held her by the waist, he spoke so affectionately and modestly, he was so happy striding about these rooms of his, whereas she could see nothing in all this but sheer complacency—sheer stupid, mindless, intolerable smugness. That arm encircling her waist . . . it seemed hard and cold as an iron hoop. Every minute she was on the point of running away, sobbing, or throwing herself out of a window. Andrew took her to the bathroom, reached for a tap fixed in the wall —and suddenly water flowed.

'How about that!' he laughed. 'I had a two-hundred-gallon tank put in the loft, so we shall have water now, you and I.'

They walked round the yard, then into the street and took a cab. There were thick clouds of dust blowing. It looked like rain.

'Aren't you cold? asked Andrew, squinting in the dust.

She said nothing.

'Remember yesterday—Sasha criticizing me for never doing anything?' he asked after a brief pause. 'Well, he's right, absolutely right! I don't do anything, I can't. Now, why is that, my dear? The mere thought of ever sticking a cockade on my cap and going into government service . . . why does it so repel me? Why am I so put off when I see a lawyer, a Latin master, a county councillor? Oh Russia, Russia, Russia—what a lot of useless loafers you do support! My poor long-suffering motherland, fancy having to put up with so many people like me!'

He even built a theory round his own idleness, seeing it as a sign of the times.

Then he went on to say that 'when we're married, dear girl, we'll live in the country together. We're going to work! We'll buy a small plot of land by a river with a garden. We shall toil, we shall watch the world go by. Now, won't that be nice?'

He took off his hat and his hair streamed in the wind.

'God, God, I want to go home!' she thought as she listened.

They had nearly reached the house when they overtook Father Andrew.

'Ah, there's Father,' rejoiced Andrew Junior with a wave of the hat. 'I'm so fond of my old man, honestly,' he said, paying the cabby. 'A wonderful chap he is, such a dear old boy.'

As Nadya went into the house she felt cross and unwell. There would be guests to entertain all evening, she reflected. She must smile, listen to that fiddle and all sorts of rubbish, talk of nothing but her wedding. Grandmother, magnificently dignified in her silk dress, and haughty— as she always seemed with visitors—sat by the samovar. Father Andrew came in, smiling his crafty smile.

'I have the pleasure and blissful gratification of seeing you in good health,' he told Grandmother—seriously or in jest, it was hard to tell which.

IV

The wind beat on windows and roof, there was whistling, and a phantom in the chimney set up a grim, piteous drone. It was past midnight and everyone in the house had gone to bed, but no one could sleep, and Nadya had an impression of someone playing a violin downstairs. There was a sharp bang—a shutter must have been ripped off. A minute later in came Nina in her nightgown, with a candle, and asked Nadya what 'that bang' was.

With her hair in a single plait, with her nervous smile, Nadya's mother looked older, uglier, shorter, on this stormy night. Nadya remembered how recently she had thought of her mother as someone rather special. How proudly she had listened to her mother's words, whereas now she simply couldn't recall those words—all that came to mind was so feeble and futile.

Suddenly, it seemed, several bass voices seemed to start intoning in the stove—even the words could be distinguished: 'Oh good God, good God.' Nadya sat up in bed, suddenly clutched her hair.

'Darling Mother,' she sobbed. 'Oh, if only you knew what is happening to me! Please, I beseech you, let me leave this place.'

'What's that?' Nina asked, not understanding, and sat down on the bed. 'Where is it you want to go?'

Nadya cried for a long time, couldn't utter one word. 'Let me leave this town,' she said at last. 'There can't be any wedding—there shan't be, I tell you. I don't love that man, I can't even talk about him.'

'No, no, no, darling,' said Nina quickly. She was utterly horrified. 'Do calm yourself. You're just upset—it will pass. These things happen. I suppose you've been quarrelling with Andrew, but lovers' tiffs always end in kisses.'

'Oh, go away, Mother, do!' sobbed Nadya.

'Yes,' said Nina after a pause. 'You were a child, just a little girl not so long ago—and now you're engaged to be married. It's a law of Nature, this is: the transmutation of matter. You'll be a mother yourself before you know where you are—you'll be just another old lady with a naughty little daughter like mine.'

'My good, kind darling, you're so clever, really, and you're unhappy,' said Nadya. 'You're so unhappy—but why, for God's sake why, must you make these cheap remarks?'

Nina wanted to speak, but couldn't utter one word—just gulped and went to her room. Those bass voices seemed to be booming in the stove again and Nadya suddenly took fright, jumped out of bed and rushed to her mother's room. Nina, her eyes full of tears, lay in bed under a pale blue quilt with a book in her hand.

'Do listen, Mother,' said Nadya. 'Do please concentrate, do try and see—just try and see how petty and degrading our lives are. My eyes have been opened now, I see everything. Just what does the wretched Andrew add up to? He's not at all bright, you know, Mother. God, he's so stupid—can't you see that, Mother?'

Nina sat up abruptly.

'You and your grandmother are torturing me,' she sobbed. 'I want a bit of life—yes, life!' she repeated, twice striking her chest with her fist. 'So give me my freedom. I'm still young, I want a bit of fun—and you two have made an old woman out of me!'

She wept bitterly, lay down and curled up under the quilt, seeming oh so small, pathetic and foolish, while Nadya went to her room, dressed, sat by the window and settled down to wait for morning. She sat there all night musing, while someone seemed to be banging a shutter from outside and whistling.

In the morning Grandmother complained that the wind had blown all the apples off in the orchard during the night, and had broken an old plum-tree. It was so grey, so dim, so cheerless—dark enough for the lamps. Everyone complained of the cold, rain drummed on the windows. After breakfast Nadya went to see Sasha and knelt down in the corner by his arm-chair without a word, hiding her face in her hands.

Sasha asked what the matter was.

'It's too much!' she said. 'How I could ever stand this life . . . I don't, I simply don't understand. I despise the man I'm engaged to. I despise myself, I despise this idle, pointless existence.'

'Now, now,' said Sasha, not yet realizing what the trouble was. 'It's nothing, it'll be all right.'

'I'm sick of this life,' Nadya went on. 'I can't face another day of it, I shall leave this place tomorrow. For God's sake take me with you.'

Sasha looked at her for a minute in surprise. Then, at last, he understood and was childishly pleased, throwing up his hands and gleefully doing a sort of tap-dance in his slippers.

'Splendid!' He rubbed his hands. 'God, this is wonderful!'

She stared at him—her eyes unblinking and enormous, like a girl in love, like one spellbound—expecting him to come straight out with some saying of vital and transcendental significance. He hadn't told her anything yet, but she felt broad, new, hitherto unsuspected horizons opening out before her and gazed at him in rapt expectation, ready for anything: death, even.

'I'll leave tomorrow,' he said after reflection. 'You can pretend to see me off at the station. I'll put your things in my trunk and get you your ticket. Then, when the bell rings for the train to leave, you can jump on board and off we'll go. You can come with me as far as Moscow, and then go on to St. Petersburg on your own. Have you your identity documents?'

'Yes.'

'You'll have no regrets, I swear it, no second thoughts,' said Sasha eagerly. 'You go and do your studying—then let your destiny take over. Only transform your way of life and everything else will change too. The great thing is to revolutionize your whole life. Nothing else matters. Do we leave tomorrow then?'

'Yes, yes, for God's sake yes!'

Nadya was greatly agitated, she had never been so depressed in her life, she was faced with misery and agony of mind from now till the moment of her departure. Or so she felt. But no sooner had she gone up to her room and lain down than she immediately dropped off and slept soundly—with tears in her eyes and a smile on her face—right up to evening.

V

A cab had been sent for. Nadya went upstairs in hat and coat for one more look at her mother and everything that had been home. She stood in her own room near the still warm bed, looked about her, then went softly to her mother's room. Nina was asleep, it was quiet in there. Nadya kissed her mother, patted her hair, stood for a couple of minutes.

Then she walked slowly downstairs.

It was raining hard. The cabby had put the top up and stood by the porch, wet through.

'There's no room for you, Nadya,' said Grandmother as the servants began loading the luggage. 'Fancy seeing someone off in this weather! You should stay at home—goodness me, what rain!'

Nadya wanted to speak, but couldn't. Then Sasha helped her in, covered her legs with a rug and settled down by her side.

'Good luck and God bless you,' Grandmother shouted from the porch. 'Now, do write to us from Moscow, Sasha.'

'Certainly. Bye bye, Gran.'

'May heaven protect you.'

'Confound this weather,' said Sasha.

Only now did Nadya start weeping. She actually was leaving home, only now did she realize it—she still hadn't believed it when saying good-bye to Grandmother and looking at Mother. Farewell, old town! Everything suddenly came back to her: Andrew, his father, the new house, that naked lady with vase—but none of it scared or depressed her any longer, it was all so inoffensively trivial and seemed to be receding further and further into the past. They got into their carriage, the train started, and all her past life—which had once loomed so large and serious—now shrank into a small compass, and a vast, broad future unfurled before her . . . a future hitherto barely conceivable. The rain drummed on the carriage windows and nothing was seen but green fields with glimpses of telegraph-posts and birds sitting on the wires. She suddenly caught her breath out of sheer joy: remembered that she was on her way to freedom, that she was going to study—it was just like running away to join the Cossacks in the old days. She laughed, wept, prayed.

'Everything's all right, it really is,' Sasha grinned.

VI

Autumn passed, winter followed. Nadya was very homesick. She thought about Mother and Grandmother every day—about Sasha too. The letters which came from home were calm and friendly—all had been forgotten and forgiven, it seemed. Healthy and cheerful, she set off for home after her May examinations, stopping on the way to see Sasha in Moscow. He hadn't changed since last summer. He still had that same beard and dishevelled hair, still wore the same frock-coat and canvas trousers, still had those fine big eyes. Yet he looked ill and worn out—he had aged, he was thinner, he kept coughing. To Nadya he seemed rather grey and provincial.

'Good God, if it isn't Nadya!' He laughed merrily. 'My own dearest little darling!'

They sat for a while in the printing room with its smoke and overpowering, stifling smell of indian ink and paint. Then they went into his room—also smoke-impregnated, with traces of sputum. On the table near a cold samovar lay a broken bowl and a piece of dark paper. There were masses of dead flies on table and floor. All this showed how slovenly Sasha's way of life was. He lived any old how, utterly scorning all comforts. Had anyone raised the question of his personal happiness, of his private life—or of anyone loving him—it would have meant nothing. He'd just have laughed.

'Everything's fine, it's all been for the best,' Nadya said quickly. 'Mother came to see me in St. Petersburg in the autumn. She says Grandmother isn't angry, but keeps going into my room and making the sign of the cross over the walls.'

Sasha looked cheerful, but kept coughing and spoke in a cracked voice. Nadya kept watching him. Was he really seriously ill? Or was it just her fancy? She couldn't tell.

'You *are* ill really, aren't you, Sasha dear?' she asked.

'No, I'm all right. I am ill, but not very——'

This upset Nadya. 'Good God, why don't you see a doctor, why don't you look after your health? My dear, good, darling Sasha——'

Tears spurted from her eyes. And why did Andrew loom up in her imagination, together with that nude lady with vase and all that past life which seemed as distant from her, now, as her childhood? She cried because she found Sasha less modern, intellectual and attractive than last year.

'Sasha dear, you are very, very ill. I'd do anything to stop you being so pale and thin. I owe you so much. You've done such a lot for me, my good, kind Sasha—more than you can ever imagine. You're nearer and dearer to me than anyone, now, you really are.'

They sat and talked for a while. But Nadya found, after spending a winter in St. Petersburg, that Sasha—his words, his smile, his entire person—had the outmoded, antiquated, obsolete air of something long dead and buried.

'I'm off to the Volga the day after tomorrow,' said Sasha. 'And then, well, I'm taking a koumiss cure: going on a fermented mare's milk diet. A friend and his wife are coming with me. The wife's a wonderful person. I've been working on her, trying to persuade her to go away and study. I want her to turn her life upside down.'

After this chat they went to the station, where Sasha treated her to tea and apples. When the train started he smiled and waved his handkerchief, the very shape of his legs indicating that he was extremely ill and not long for this world.

Nadya reached her native town at noon. As she was driven home

from the station the streets seemed very wide, the houses small and
squat. There was no one about except for the German piano-tuner in
his brown overcoat. The houses all seemed covered with dust. Grandmother—a really old woman now, as stout and ugly as ever—flung
her arms round Nadya and cried for some time, pressing her face
against the girl's shoulder and unable to break away. Nina also looked
much older and worse for wear. She had a rather haggard air, but was as
tightly laced as ever, with those diamonds still flashing on her fingers.

'Darling, darling, darling!' She trembled all over.

They sat silently weeping. That the past was utterly lost and gone
for ever Grandmother and Mother both sensed, obviously. Their
social position, their former prestige, their right to entertain guests . . .
they were all gone. It was like living without a care in the world until,
suddenly, there is a police raid, the house is searched, and the head of the
family turns out to be an embezzler or forger . . . which puts paid to all
that living without a care in the world.

Nadya went upstairs and saw the same old bed, the same old
windows with their unpretentious white curtains, and through those
windows the same old garden: cheerful, noisy, drenched with sunlight.
She touched her table, she sat, she brooded. Then she had a good
lunch and drank tea with delicious thick cream. There was something
missing, though, the house felt empty inside and the ceilings seemed so
low. When she went to bed that night and pulled the blankets over her
it seemed rather funny to be back in that same snug, very soft bed.

Nina came in for a moment and sat down guiltily, looking nervously
about her.

'Well, how are things, Nadya?' she asked after a pause. 'Happy, are
you? Very happy?'

'Yes, Mother.'

Nina stood up and made the sign of the cross over Nadya and the
windows. 'I've taken up religion, you see. I study philosophy now,
you know, I do a lot of thinking. Many things are crystal clear to me
these days. The great thing, I think, is to filter your whole life through
a prism.'

'Tell me, Mother, how is Grandmother keeping?'

'She seems all right. When you went off with Sasha and we got your
telegram, Grandmother just collapsed when she read it. Three days she
lay—never moved. Then she kept praying and crying, but she's all
right now.'

Nadya's mother stood up and paced the room.

Clicking thuds were heard: that watchman again.

'The great thing is to filter your whole life through a prism,' said Nina. 'In other words, that is, one's apprehension of life must be split down into its simplest components like the seven colours of the rainbow, and each component must be studied in isolation.'

What else Nina said Nadya did not hear. Nor did she hear her mother leave because she soon fell asleep.

May passed, June began, Nadya had grown used to being at home. Grandmother fussed over the samovar, sighing deeply, and Nina spoke of her philosophy in the evenings. She was still very much the poor relation and had to ask Grandmother for every twenty-copeck piece. The house was full of flies and the ceilings seemed to get lower and lower. Gran and Nina never went out in the streets, fearing to meet one of the Andrews, father or son. Nadya walked in the garden, walked down the street, looked at the houses, looked at the grey fences. The whole town was so outmoded and antiquated, she felt. Was it awaiting its own end? Or expecting something fresh and original to begin? It was never quite clear which. Oh, if it would only hurry up and begin . . . that brave new world where you can face your own destiny boldly, where you can be cheerful and free, knowing you're in the right! Now, such a life *will* come about sooner or later. The time will surely come when Grandmother's house, so arranged, now, that four servants are forced to share a single filthy basement room . . . the time will come when that house will vanish without trace, be forgotten, pass from memory. Meanwhile Nadya's only diversion came from the little boys next door who would bang on the fence when she was walking in the garden, laughing and jeering at her.

'Who thought she was going to get married?'

A letter came from Sasha in Saratov. In his sprightly, dancing hand he wrote that his Volga trip had been a complete success, but that he had contracted some minor ailment in Saratov, had lost his voice and had been in hospital for a fortnight. Realizing what this meant, Nadya felt a foreboding akin to certainty. It was disagreeable, though, to find that neither this premonition nor her thoughts of Sasha distressed her so much as before. She craved excitement, she wanted to be back in St. Petersburg, while her friendship with Sasha—delightful as it was —now seemed a thing of the far, far distant past. After lying awake all night she sat by the window next morning, listening. Yes, there really were voices down there: the agitated Gran was firing off questions about something, and then someone burst into tears.

A MARRIAGEABLE GIRL 235

Going downstairs, Nadya found Grandmother praying in a corner, her face tear-stained. There was a telegram on the table.

After walking about the room listening to Grandmother crying for some time, Nadya took the telegram and read it. Its burden was that Alexander Timofeyevich or Sasha for short had perished of tuberculosis in Saratov.

Grandmother and Nina went to church to arrange a memorial service while Nadya went on pacing about the house, musing. That her life had been transformed to Sasha's recipe, that she was a lonely stranger—unwanted in a place from which *she* wanted nothing—that her entire past life had been ripped away, had disappeared as if burnt to ashes scattered in the breeze . . . all these things she keenly realized.

She went and stood in Sasha's room. 'Farewell, Sasha darling.'

Thus brooding, she pictured her new life opening before her, with its broad horizons. Still obscure, still mysterious, that life lured and beckoned her.

She went up to her room to pack. Next morning she said good-bye to the family. Vigorous, high-spirited, she left town: for ever, presumably.

NOTES

6 *Poltava*: town in the Ukraine, about 70 miles south-west of Kharkov.

15 *If you marry a Tolstoyan he'll make you mow*: the novelist and thinker L. N. Tolstoy (1828–1910) was a proselytizing simple-lifer.

    the Proudhons and the Buckles: reference is to the French Socialist thinker Pierre Joseph Proudhon (1809–65); and to Henry Thomas Buckle (1821–62), the English social historian and author of *History of Civilization* (1857–61), which enjoyed a great vogue in Russia.

16 *Schopenhauer*: the German philosopher Arthur Schopenhauer (1788–1860).

    Elijah's Day: 20 June.

18 *Butlerov hives*: the invention of A. M. Butlerov (1828–86), an eminent Russian chemist whose other interests included agriculture, tea-growing in the Caucasus and spiritualism.

LIGHTS

34 '*declined into the vale of years*': Shakespeare, *Othello*, III. iii.

35 *Baltic baronial ancestry*: in the Baltic lands, as incorporated in Russia by Peter the Great in the early eighteenth century, the social élite consisted of Germans, some of whom had the title baron. Such Baltic Germans, or 'Baltic barons'—russified except in respect of their surnames and a reputation for stern efficiency—were prominent in Imperial Russia's civil and military hierarchies.

37 *soon after the War*: reference is to the Russo-Turkish War of 1877–8.

38 *Chukhloma*: small town, about 275 miles north-east of Moscow.

Kashira: town, about 70 miles south of Moscow.

39 '*He stood on that deserted strand* . . .': the opening lines of Pushkin's poem *The Bronze Horseman,* written in 1833.

Sakhalin: the large island and penal colony (which Chekhov was to visit in 1890) in the Russian Far East between the Sea of Okhotsk and the Sea of Japan.

42 '*But these are tales of ancient times* . . .': the couplet comes from Canto One of Pushkin's poem *Ruslan and Lyudmila* (1820).

44 *Malinin and Burenin*: reference is to *Sobraniye arifmetiches-kich zadach dlya gimnazy* [*Collected Arithmetic Problems for High Schools*] by A. Malinin and K. Burenin (Moscow, 1866), p. 126.

47 *Santorin wine*: the Greek island of Santorin, also known as Thera, is the southernmost island in the Cyclades. 'Its excellent red and white grapes, the island's chief product, are made into strong wine exported principally to Odessa.' (Brokgauz and Efron, *Entsiklopedichesky slovar,* vol. 56, St. Petersburg, 1900), p. 366.

50 *Circassians*: inhabitants of an area in the northern Caucasus.

52 '*For the hour is coming* . . .': John 5: 28.

55 *Pyatigorsk:* town and health resort in the northern Caucasus.

58 *a Yakut's*: the Yakuts, a Turkic-speaking people living over a large area in eastern Siberia, have been subject to Russia since the seventeenth century.

60 *Mount Ararat*: the highest point (17,000 ft.) in Armenia.

THE PRINCESS

69 "*thirty-five thousand couriers*": the reference is to Act Three, Scene vi of the comedy *The Inspector General* (1836) by N. V. Gogol (1809–52), where the hero, Khlestakov, boasts that 'thirty-five thousand couriers' once had to be sent out

to find him and persuade him to take charge of a
government department.

70 *"The Glory of our Lord in Sion . . ."*: anthem of the Russian
Orthodox Church, often sung at funerals and on other
solemn occasions.

village elder: elected by the village assembly, consisting of
heads of households, the elder was responsible for tax
collection, and certain aspects of village discipline and
administration.

71 *What's Hecuba to you . . .?*: a paraphrase of Shakespeare's
Hamlet, II. ii: 'What's Hecuba to him, or he to Hecuba . . .?'

AFTER THE THEATRE

75 *Eugene Onegin*: Reference is to the opera *Eugene Onegin*
(1877–8) by P. I. Tchaikovsky (1840–93), based on Pushkin's verse novel with the same title. In it the heroine,
Tatyana, writes a letter declaring her love to the hero,
Eugene Onegin.

THREE YEARS

78 *Sokolniki*: district containing a large park, to the north-east
of Moscow; a favourite place for out-of-town excursions.

81 *Pyatnitsky Road*: long street in the merchant quarter south
of the Moscow River, running north towards the river
from Serpukhov Square.

Khimki: river port a few miles north-west of Moscow.

84 *picturesquely miserable bumpkins*: literally, 'an Anton
Goremyka'—reference being to the hero of the short story
Anton Goremyka (1847) by D. V. Grigorovich (1822–99).

86 *"it will sort itself out"*: the phrase occurs in the novel *Anna
Karenin* (1875–7) by L. N. Tolstoy.

95 *a comic figure from an operetta*: literally, 'a Gaspard from *Les
Cloches de Corneville*' (1877), the popular operetta by the
French composer Robert Planquette (1848–1903).

100 *Tambov*: town about 300 miles south-east of Moscow.

101 *bold and proud is woman's heart*: literally, 'for woman's heart is a Shamil.' The guerrilla leader Shamil (1797–1871) led the Caucasian tribesmen in their struggle against conquest by the Russians.

102 *Fley's*: a well-known *pâtisserie* on Neglinny Drive in the centre of Moscow.

103 *Vologda*: town about 300 miles north of Moscow.

Nikolsky Road: in central Moscow, leading north-east from the Red Square.

What sickening humbug!: literally, 'how like Shchedrin's Iudushka'—the sanctimonious hero of the novel *The Golovlyov Family* (1876–80) by M. Ye. Saltykov-Shchedrin.

105 *'The prophet Samuel ...'*: the relevant passage occurs in 1 Sam. 17:4–5.

106 *Anton Rubinstein*: the composer (1829–94).

the Conservatoire: in Great Nikitsky Road in the west of central Moscow; founded by Nicholas Rubinstein (1835–81), brother of Anton.

107 *Guerrier's courses*: V. I. Guerrier (1837–1919), professor of history at Moscow University, 1868–1904.

108 *the Gentry Club*: on Great Dmitrovka Street, leading north-west from central Moscow.

Ostozhenka: road running roughly south in south-west Moscow, beginning about half a mile from the Kremlin.

Savelovsky Street: a turning off Ostozhenka Road.

109 *Great Nikitsky Road*: west of the centre of Moscow.

Reinheit: German for 'purity'; often the subject of whimsical discussion in the unpublished letters between Chekhov and Lydia (Lika) Mizinov, this supposedly expressed one of the qualities which he required in his young female friends.

111 *Presnya*: district in the west of Moscow.

112 *the Second High School on Razgulyay Square*: an actual school in the north-east of central Moscow, a three- to four-mile walk from Pyatnitsky Road.

114 *Little Dmitrovka*: street in the north-west of Moscow.

Old St. Pimen's Church: a few hundred yards west of Little Dmitrovka Street.

116 *Strastnoy Boulevard*: in the north of central Moscow.

Tver Road: running north-west from the Red Square in central Moscow.

the Iverian Chapel: near the Red Square, site of the famous miracle-working Iverian Madonna.

Filippov's Café: on the corner of the Tver Road and Glinishchevsky Street.

117 *Volokolamsk*: town about 60 miles north-west of Moscow.

apply to be registered as gentlefolk: more literally, 'to seek the status of *dvoryanin*' (gentleman), the most privileged of the various classes or estates to one or other of which all Russian citizens were assigned in law.

The Maid of Orleans: opera (1881) by P. I. Tchaikovsky.

Mariya Yermolov: noted Russian actress (1853–1928).

118 *the Maly Theatre*: in central Moscow, near the Bolshoy Theatre.

Hotel Dresden: on the Tver Road in central Moscow.

120 "*In the sweat of thy face . . .*": Gen. 3:19.

121 *an under-secretary*: literally, 'a Privy Councillor'—Class Three in Peter the Great's Table of Ranks, which, introduced in 1722, provided grades for all officials of the government and the court, with equivalents in the armed forces.

122 *Merchants' Club*: on Little Dmitrovka Street.

123 *The Yar Restaurant . . . the Strelna*: both these establishments were located out of town in the Petrovsky Park to the north-west of Moscow. Both were, according to Baedeker, 'much frequented in the evening (not cheap)'.

128 *School of Art*: in north-west Moscow.

129 *Shishkin*: I. I. Shishkin (1832–98), Russian landscape painter.

130 *the Exaltation of the Cross*: Church festival, celebrated on 14 September.

Yaroslavl: town about 200 miles north-east of Moscow.

133 *Muscovy*: name commonly applied to the Moscow-ruled Russian state between the fourteenth and the early eighteenth century.

Krasny Prud ... at St. Alexis's Convent: reference is to the area of Krasny Prud ('Red Pond') in the north-west of Moscow, about 3 miles from the Red Square. The two friends were approaching the centre of the city, moving south-west past the convent and along Krasnoprudny (Red Pond) Road.

134 *Lyapunovs*: P. P. Lyapunov (d. 1611), hero of Russian national resistance against the Polish invader in the early seventeenth century; also his slightly less famous brother Z. P. Lyapunov.

Godunovs: Boris Godunov (1552–1605) was first Regent, and then—from 1598 until his death—Tsar of Muscovy.

Yaroslav: Yaroslav I, the Wise, prince of Kiev; ruled 1019–54.

Monomakh: Vladimir Monomakh, prince of Kiev; ruled 1113–25.

Pimen's soliloquy: a famous speech from Pushkin's *Boris Godunov*.

Dmitrovka Street: Great Dmitrovka Street, leading north-west from Teatralny Square in central Moscow.

Polovtsians: another name for the Cumans, a Turkic-speaking people engaged in sporadic struggle with Kievan Russia between 1054 and their defeat by the Mongol-Tatars in 1238.

135 *the St. Alexis Cemetery*: on the northern outskirts of Moscow.

136 *"A person well may stupid be ..."*: from Act Three of

the celebrated play *Woe from Wit* (1822–4) by A. S. Griboyedov (1795–1829).

139 *valley in the Caucasus*: literally, 'I feel as if I'm lying in a Daghestan valley.' Reference is to the first line of Lermontov's lyric *The Dream* (1841): 'In noontide's heat, in a valley of Daghestan, with a bullet in my breast, I lay motionless.' Daghestan is an area in the north-east Caucasus.

140 *a higher rank*: literally, 'Actual State Councillor'—Class Four in the Table of Ranks; see note to p. 121.

142 *policemen of all kinds*: literally, 'constables and gendarmes', the former representing the ordinary and the latter the political police.

148 *Bubnov's Inn*: untraced.

'*Old Nero*': literally, 'Malyuta Skuratov'. Reference is to Malyuta ('Babe') Skuratov, died 1573: the dreaded leader of the Oprichnina, Ivan the Terrible's private Mafia.

149 *south-bank Moscow*: in the original 'Zamoskvorechye'— literally 'the place beyond the River Moscow'. The merchant quarter south of the river.

150 *Butovo*: village about twelve miles south of Moscow.

151 *the Exhibition*: reference is to the World's Columbian Exposition at Chicago, Illinois (1893).

THE ARTIST'S STORY

152 *T—— Province*: *The Artist's Story* owes some of its inspiration to Chekhov's stay at Bogimovo (in Tula Province, south of Moscow Province) in 1891. 'T——'therefore presumably stands for 'Tula' here.

a peasant jerkin: the *poddyovka,* a sleeveless, long-skirted coat, fastened at the side, was mainly worn by peasants or merchants. Some landowners like Belokurov adopted it as a form of national dress.

pneumatic stoves: literally, 'Amosov stoves'. These were a kind of stove invented in about 1835 by Major-General Nicholas Amosov (1787–1868).

155 *Lake Baikal*: the largest lake in Siberia.

156 *a Buryat girl*: the Buryats are an indigenous Siberian tribe of Mongol race. The reference might be autobiographical since Chekhov crossed Lake Baikal on his journey through Siberia to Sakhalin in 1890.

159 *embroidered smock*: another item of national dress affected by Belokurov.

in traditional Russian dress: 'This [for women] usually consisted of a white, puff-sleeved embroidered blouse, worn with a full gathered skirt on a yoke ... and a white pinafore. With it went several rows of multicoloured beribboned beads and a red, or other bright-coloured, kerchief.' G. A. Birkett and Gleb Struve (eds.), *Anton Chekhov: Selected Short Stories*, Oxford, 1951, p. 136.

163 *Gogol's Petrushka*: Petrushka, Chichikov's servant in the novel *Dead Souls* by N. V. Gogol (1809–52), was fond of reading things which he did not understand.

since the time of the Vikings: reference is to the Varangians (Normans or Vikings) whose prince, Ryurik, was traditionally the founder of the Russian state.

166 *"A crow picked up a piece of cheese"*: the first line of a well-known fable, an adaptation of La Fontaine's *Le Corbeau et le Renard*, by I. A. Krylov (c. 1769–1844).

Penza Province: Penza—town about 500 miles south-east of Moscow.

HOME

173 *the Tomb of Saur*: Saur is the hero of certain legends of Tartar origin prevalent in the south Russian steppe (one feature being the fight between a father and a son whom he does not recognize, as in *Sohrab and Rustum*). Tomb of Saur is the name given, in various places, to certain of the *kurgany* (characteristic burial mounds) in the steppe.

176 *Berdyansk*: port on the Sea of Azov in south Russia, founded in 1827.

Oryol Province: Oryol—provincial capital about 200 miles south of Moscow.

A CASE HISTORY

182 *a baggy uniform*: uniforms being very much in vogue in Imperial Russia, even non-governmental organizations such as the merchants' guilds tended to devise their own.

a medal and Red Cross badge: an indication that Lyalikov may have been decorated for doing charitable work.

certain noises: Russian night-watchmen were detailed to improvise banging noises to warn thieves, to prove that they had not fallen asleep, or—in the present case—to strike the hours.

183 *Polyanka Street*: in the merchant quarter in the south of Moscow.

187 *Lermontov's Tamara*: reference is to the long poem *The Demon* (1839) by M. Yu. Lermontov (1814–41), in which the devil's kiss destroys Tamara, the girl whom he loves.

ALL FRIENDS TOGETHER

189 *Tula*: provincial capital about 120 miles south of Moscow, an old centre of the metal-working industry.

190 *Brest Station*: on the western side of Moscow, for trains to Smolensk, Brest-Litovsk, Warsaw, etc.

the Hermitage: a restaurant on Trubny Square in Moscow.

Little Bronny Road: in north-west Moscow.

193 *Ufa*: town near the Urals, now capital of the Bashkir Autonomous Republic.

Perm: town about 800 miles east of Moscow.

194 '*Through narrow cuttings . . .*': this and the quotations which follow come from the poem *The Railway* (1864) by N. A. Nekrasov (1821–78).

196 *'Before he'd time to turn a hair ...'*: the lines come from the
fable *The Peasant and the Workman* by I. A. Krylov
(1769–1844).

199 *'Thou sha-alt be quee-een of all the world'*: the line is from
Lermontov's poem *The Demon* (1839).

202 *in the days of serfdom*: dating from before 1861, the year in
which the serfs were emancipated.

THE BISHOP

213 *bridegroom who cometh at midnight*: Matthew 25:1–6.

216 *'Now is the Son of Man glorified'*: John 13:31.

since Christianity had first come to Russia: in about AD 988
with the conversion of Vladimir, Grand Prince of Kiev.

A MARRIAGEABLE GIRL

221 *'He wasted his substance ... filled his belly ...'*: Luke
15:13–16.

223 *Anna Karenin*: reference is to the heroine of the novel *Anna
Karenin* (1875–7) by L. N. Tolstoy.

226 *St. Peter's Day*: 29 June.

'A Shishmachevsky': the name appears to be an invention
of Chekhov's.

230 *identity documents*: a Russian citizen was required to possess
a 'passport' for purposes of internal as well as external
travel.

231 *to join the Cossacks*: a reference to the custom of escaping
from the centralized Muscovite state to lead a wild, free
life among the Cossacks of the periphery, especially before
they were brought under tighter control by Catherine the
Great in the eighteenth century.

232 *koumiss*: a fermented liquor prepared from mare's milk. A
koumiss diet was prescribed as a cure for tuberculosis, and
Chekhov himself went on such a diet in 1901.

234 *Saratov*: town on the Volga, about 500 miles south-east of
Moscow.

LUDOVICO ARIOSTO	**Orlando Furioso**
GIOVANNI BOCCACCIO	**The Decameron**
MATTEO MARIA BOIARDO	**Orlando Innamorato**
LUÍS VAZ DE CAMÕES	**The Lusíads**
MIGUEL DE CERVANTES	**Don Quixote de la Mancha** **Exemplary Stories**
DANTE ALIGHIERI	**The Divine Comedy** **Vita Nuova**
BENITO PÉREZ GALDÓS	**Nazarín**
LEONARDO DA VINCI	**Selections from the Notebooks**
NICCOLÒ MACHIAVELLI	**Discourses on Livy** **The Prince**
MICHELANGELO	**Life, Letters, and Poetry**
PETRARCH	**Selections from the *Canzoniere* and Other Works**
GIORGIO VASARI	**The Lives of the Artists**

The Oxford World's Classics Website

www.worldsclassics.co.uk

- Information about new titles
- Explore the full range of Oxford World's Classics
- Links to other literary sites and the main OUP webpage
- Imaginative competitions, with bookish prizes
- Peruse *Compass*, the Oxford World's Classics magazine
- Articles by editors
- Extracts from Introductions
- A forum for discussion and feedback on the series
- Special information for teachers and lecturers

www.worldsclassics.co.uk

American Literature

British and Irish Literature

Children's Literature

Classics and Ancient Literature

Colonial Literature

Eastern Literature

European Literature

History

Medieval Literature

Oxford English Drama

Poetry

Philosophy

Politics

Religion

The Oxford Shakespeare

A complete list of Oxford Paperbacks, including Oxford World's Classics, OPUS, Past Masters, Oxford Authors, Oxford Shakespeare, Oxford Drama, and Oxford Paperback Reference, is available in the UK from the Academic Division Publicity Department, Oxford University Press, Great Clarendon Street, Oxford OX2 6DP.

In the USA, complete lists are available from the Paperbacks Marketing Manager, Oxford University Press, 198 Madison Avenue, New York, NY 10016.

Oxford Paperbacks are available from all good bookshops. In case of difficulty, customers in the UK can order direct from Oxford University Press Bookshop, Freepost, 116 High Street, Oxford OX1 4BR, enclosing full payment. Please add 10 per cent of published price for postage and packing.